COLLINGRIDGE
STANDARD
GUIDES
ROSES

The popularity of roses needs no underlining–almost every garden in the country has its quota, whether these are elegant hybrid teas, free-flowering floribundas, showy climbers or modern shrub roses. With this enormous interest, it is not surprising that there are many gardeners who wish to know more about these magnificent, adaptable and versatile flowers than can be culled from the pages of less comprehensive guides. *Roses,* by the distinguished rosarian Leonard Hollis, is designed to meet this need–a book on all aspects of roses and their cultivation which is based on hard-won knowledge gained over almost half a century of personal experience. This is the first of the new series of *Collingridge Standard Guides.*

The author has cast his net wide to make this a book of great value to the enthusiast at all stages of experience, his subject matter ranging from the evolution of the rose and its uses in the garden to the selection, planting, pruning, feeding and general aftercare of the various categories of roses, their propagation, hybridisation and exhibition. Other subjects which receive detailed attention are labour saving in the rose garden, growing roses in pots under glass, the cultivation of standard, half-standard and weeping standard roses, roses for fragrance, autumn in the rose garden, and renovating a neglected rose garden.

An invaluable guide for those building up a collection of roses or adding to existing plantings are the detailed descriptive lists of hybrid tea, floribunda, rambling, climbing and pillar roses, shrub, hedging and miniature roses. The author, a leading member of the Royal National Rose Society (he is a Vice-President and Editor of the Society's publications), is a practising rosarian who has a collection of nearly 2,000 rose trees in his own garden. He is also a judge, lecturer and successful exhibitor, and is, for all these reasons, in a unique position to appraise individual varieties critically.

A distinctive feature of the book is the 'At-a-Glance' Colour Charts which appear at the end of each descriptive list of varieties, these charts incorporating all the varieties described. They are certain to be time-saving and in other ways helpful to readers. Selections of roses are also given for various purposes.

Other features of special interest are chapters on rose awards in Britain and other countries and notable rose display gardens. There is also a Glossary of terms used by rosarians.

This book is superbly illustrated with 47 colour pictures, 89 black and white illustrations and 30 line-drawings.

COLLINGRIDGE
STANDARD
GUIDES

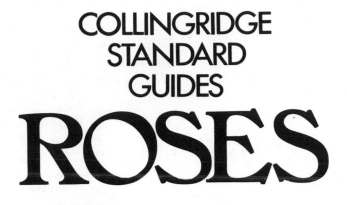

ROSES

LEONARD HOLLIS

COLLINGRIDGE BOOKS
LONDON · NEW YORK · SYDNEY
TORONTO

*To my wife, a rose-widow
indeed, but for whose forbearance
this book would never have
been written*

First published in 1970 for
Collingridge Books by
THE HAMLYN PUBLISHING
GROUP LIMITED
LONDON · NEW YORK · SYDNEY · TORONTO
Feltham, Middlesex, England

Printed in Hong Kong
by Lee Fung Printing Co. Ltd

SBN 600 44248 9

Contents

Foreword   9

Introduction   11

PART ONE

1 The Evolution of Modern Roses   15
2 Adaptability and Versatility   19
3 The Uses of Roses   26
4 Selecting and Ordering Roses   36
5 Choosing and Preparing the Site   44
6 Planting and Display   52
7 Pruning and Training   69
8 Feeding and Mulching   83
9 Aftercare   90
10 Pests and Diseases   102
11 Propagation   115
12 Hybridisation   124
13 Exhibiting Roses   129
14 Roses in Pots under Glass   140
15 Labour Saving in the Rose Garden   146
16 Roses for Fragrance   151
17 Standards, Half-standards and Weeping Standards   156
18 Autumn in the Rose Garden   164
19 Renovating the Neglected Rose Garden   170

PART TWO

20 Descriptive List of Hybrid Tea Roses   179
21 Descriptive List of Floribunda Roses   210
22 Descriptive List of Rambling, Climbing and Pillar Roses 235
23 Descriptive List of Shrub and Hedging Roses   249
24 Descriptive List of Miniature Roses   262

PART THREE

25 Rose Awards in Britain and Other Countries   267
26 Notable Rose Display Gardens   272
Selections of Roses for Various Purposes   277
Some Recommended Suppliers of Roses and Rootstocks 283
Glossary   285
Appendix   289
Acknowledgements   291
Index   292

5

Illustrations

COLOUR PLATES

Piccadilly (H.T.) — *Frontispiece, facing page* 3
King's Ransom (H.T.) — 14
Papa Meilland (H.T.) — 32
Belle Blonde (H.T.) — 32
Lady Seton (H.T.) — 49
Super Star (H.T.) — *between pages* 56 *and* 57
Elida (H.T.) — 56 *and* 57
Silva (H.T.) — *facing page* 64
Kronenbourg (H.T.) — 81
Bettina (H.T.) — 81
Blessings (H.T.) — *between pages* 88 *and* 89
Tradition (H.T.) — 88 *and* 89
Grandpa Dickson (H.T.) — 88 *and* 89
Duke of Windsor (H.T.) — *facing page* 96
Mischief (H.T.) — 113
Percy Thrower (H.T.) — 113
Roses used as a screen — *between pages* 120 *and* 121
Elizabeth of Glamis (Flori.) — 120 *and* 121
Joyfulness (Flori. H.T. type) — *facing page* 128
Circus (Flori.) — 128
Manx Queen (Flori.) — 145
Orange Sensation (Flori.) — 145
Evelyn Fison (Flori.) — *between pages* 152 *and* 153
Shepherdess (Flori. H.T. type) — 152 *and* 153
Golden Slippers (Flori.) — 152 *and* 153
Sir Lancelot (Flori.) — *facing page* 160
Molly McGredy (Flori. H.T. type) — 177
Orange Silk (Flori.) — 184
Bashful (Flori. dwarf) — 185
Dopey (Flori. dwarf) — 185
A standard specimen of Peace — 192
Conifer and floribunda roses — 192
Bantry Bay (Cl.) — 209
Handel (Cl.) — *between pages* 216 *and* 217
Pink Perpetue (Cl.) — 216 *and* 217
Golden Showers (Cl.) — 216 *and* 217
Nevada (Shrub) — *facing page* 224
Lavender Lassie (Shrub) — 224

6

Fred Loads (Flori. shrub) 241
Chinatown (Flori. shrub) *between pages* 248 *and* 249
Penelope (Hybrid Musk shrub) 248 *and* 249
Three miniature roses, Baby Masquerade,
 Little Flirt and New Penny 248 *and* 249
Canary Bird (Shrub) *facing page* 256
Rose suckers compared with a cultivated rose 273

MONOCHROME PLATES

Rose borders in The Royal National Rose
 Society's display garden *facing page* 15
Queen Mary's Garden in Regent's Park 15
Rambler rose New Dawn 33
A bank of roses 33
The Kordesii climber Leverkusen 48
The formal rose gardens at Luton Hoo, Bedfordshire 48
Mme Gregoire Staechelin 56
The tall-growing floribunda Queen Elizabeth 56
Preparing roses for planting 57
Planting a rose 65
Good and bad pruning cuts 80
Lightly pruned hybrid tea roses 80
Pruning a bush rose 88
Pruning a hybrid musk rose 89
A weeping standard after pruning 97
Pegging down and training 97
Pruning a rambler rose 112
Cutting back stems to outward-pointing eye 120
Disbudding for exhibition and garden display 120
Removing suckers and faded flowers 121
Flower 'balling' 121
Rose pests 129, 144 *and* 152
Rose diseases 153 *and* 161
The budding sequence 176
Budding standard roses *between pages* 184 *and* 185
Preparing and inserting cuttings 184 *and* 185
Layering a rose shoot *facing page* 193
Exhibiting roses 208
Faults in exhibition roses 216
Choosing a site for a special feature 217
Planting and staking a standard rose 225
The recurrent climber, Schoolgirl 240
The Wichuraiana rambler, Albertine 240
The Kordesii climber, Parkdirektor Riggers 248
The Bourbon climber, Zéphirine Drouhin 248
Dorothy Wheatcroft (Flori. shrub) 249
The Rugosa shrub, Pink Grootendorst 249

7

Young red wood of *Rosa sericea pteracantha*   *facing page* 249
Decorative rose heps   257
Miniature roses   272

LINE-DRAWINGS

Figures
1 Double digging the site for a rose bed   *page* 48
2 The correct planting depth for roses   57
3 to 8 Some modern treatments of rose beds in
   present-day garden design   65, 66, 67 *and* 68
9 Position of dormant eyes on rose shoots
   showing the 'staggered' effect   70
10 Modern forms of secateurs   71
11 Pruning a climbing rose on a wall   78
12 A standard hybrid tea before and after pruning   80
13 A standard floribunda before and after pruning   81
14 De-shooting in spring and summer   91
15 Disbudding for exhibition   92
16 Types of continuous-action sprayer   94
17 Training a single-pillar rose   101
18 A cross-section of a rose bloom   125
19 Rose hybridisation   126
20 Using a bloom protector to shield an exhibition bloom   131
21 Tying rose blooms for exhibition   132
22 Two methods of wiring roses   134
23 An exhibition box for six rose blooms   135
24 Pruning roses in pots   142
25 Applying paraquat weedkiller around rose bushes with a
   dribble bar fixed to a watering-can   150
26 Comparative budding heights of standards and half-standards   157
27 Standard roses used to screen the top of a fence   158
28 An umbrella trainer for a weeping standard rose   161
29 Protecting the head of a standard rose with straw   167
30 A tripod and a single pillar for displaying pillar roses   238

Foreword

MAJ.-GEN. R. F. B. NAYLOR

Past President of The Royal National Rose Society

Millions of people grow roses, but how many of them *know* how to grow them? As with anything else in life, if one wants to get the best results one must do something to achieve them.

In the case of the rose you can, if you wish, buy one, stick it in a hole in the ground, and, with luck, you may get some blooms from it. But they will not last long, nor compare in any way with those you would have had if you had taken more trouble.

Apart from providing a nice show of blooms in the garden and cut flowers for the house, growing roses is a fascinating hobby. The first step in achieving success is to buy a book which will give you the knowledge you need, written by an author who knows his subject and who can convey it clearly.

Having worked with Leonard Hollis as a fellow member of the Council of The Royal National Rose Society for many years I know that in him you have such an author. He is a dedicated rosarian with many years' experience and he knows the essential points an amateur must pay heed to if he is to grow roses successfully.

Joining The National Rose Society, as it was then called, in 1926, he has been a member of its Council for 35 years. For some years he edited *The Rose,* a magazine devoted solely to this flower, and has been a regular and much sought-after contributor of articles on roses to the horticultural press. In 1963 he became Hon. Editor of The Royal National Rose Society, since when he has been responsible for its publications, which include *The Rose Annual,* of world-wide repute, the handbook *Roses: A Selected List of Varieties,* published every three years, and *The Cultivation of the Rose,* which is revised and re-published as necessary to keep abreast of the times.

For many years Leonard Hollis was a successful exhibitor at rose shows, including those of The Royal National Rose Society, and he grows some 2,000 rose trees in his own garden in Surrey, which he tends himself in such time as he can spare from a full-time job in London. I know well that he always demands a high standard and in his search for perfection does not hesitate to speak his mind when the occasion demands.

Many good books about roses have been written in the past and there will be many more in the future, as there is always a demand for an up-to-date, authoritative work written by an expert. This book will, I feel confident, not only meet the needs of amateurs wishing to learn how to get satisfaction from growing roses, but it will also make a notable addition to the literature of the rose.

Anybody who reads this book can hardly fail to realise what an absorbing pastime growing roses can be. Readers may gain added interest by becoming members of The Royal National Rose Society and enjoying the many benefits available.

Introduction

For more than 44 years I have been contributing rose articles to the horticultural press as a form of safety valve. But in recent years the urge to produce a comprehensive work of practical value has become well-nigh irresistible, with this as the outcome. At least I cannot be accused of rushing into print. One cannot be a rose-growing fanatic (my wife puts it more strongly than this!) over some 48 years without acquiring a deal of practical knowledge, and this I have attempted to pass on to the reader in the following pages.

No work on roses can be literally complete—it would have been quite easy to have extended this volume by many thousands of words without having to introduce any padding. But a reasonable balance is looked for between what is ample for the requirements of the vast majority of amateur rose growers, and the highly specialised needs of the professional and a handful of advanced amateurs. I am convinced that the more experience one acquires of growing roses on different soils and under varying climatic conditions the more open-minded one tends to become, and therefore the less dogmatic. It would be dull, indeed, if there were complete unanimity on such controversial matters as planting, pruning and propagation, to mention only three facets of the subject.

I am greatly indebted to The Royal National Rose Society and to Mr E. F. Allen, M.A., Dip.Agric (Cantab.), A.I.C.T.A., its Honorary Scientific Adviser, for information contained in the Society's publications which I have drawn on, particularly in relation to pests and diseases. Apart from these publications, of which I am also Honorary Editor, I have tried not to be influenced by existing rose books, although insofar as many of them have been read and some of them reviewed by me in the past, it is difficult, if not impossible, to remain entirely free from their influence.

I acknowledge with gratitude the colour transparencies and black and white photographs which have been supplied by various organisations, firms and individuals. Detailed acknowledgement for these illustrations is given on page 291. I would also like to thank

Mr Norman H. J. Clarke, F.I.L.A., for his designs of garden features incorporating roses, and Miss Lambert for her line-drawings of cultural operations and other aspects of rose growing.

It is sometimes said that a new book on roses becomes partially out of date between the completion of the manuscript and its date of publication. In this instance I have tried to forestall any such tendency by taking advantage of my advance knowledge of some novelties which are only now just coming on the market, acquired through the kindness of the raisers or distributors in allowing me to try these out in advance in my own garden. 'One swallow does not make a summer', though, and one season's experience of otherwise untried novelties can be misleading when making an assessment. Ideally, one needs to study patterns of behaviour under varying climatic conditions before making up one's mind, in fairness to the raiser no less than to the rose-growing public. The constant spate of novelties does at least indicate a healthy striving after improvement at a time when, perhaps, the rose has never been more popular throughout its long history. Nevertheless, it is perhaps salutary to remind the beginner that there is no merit in novelty merely for its own sake; and that until such time as a new rose has been *proved* an advance on a well-tried favourite, it is as well to regard it with some measure of reserve.

If, after reading this book, the reader is induced to grow better roses than he – or she – did before, my purpose in writing it will have been accomplished.

East Horsley,   LEONARD HOLLIS
Surrey

Part One

The Rose–Its Evolution, Adaptability and Versatility

Its Uses and Cultivation

Propagation and Hybridisation

Exhibiting

Labour Saving in the Rose Garden

King's Ransom (H.T.)

Top: Rose borders in The Royal National Rose Society's noted display garden at Bone Hill, St. Albans, Herts. *Bottom:* Part of Queen Mary's Garden in Regent's Park, London where one of the finest collections of roses in the world is grown

1

The Evolution of Modern Roses

The history of modern roses – Originally wild forms – The influence of the Red rose, the Dog rose, the Musk rose and the Phoenician rose – Chance seedlings and sports, with doubling or trebling of petals – The Gallicas, Damascenas and Centifolias – The Autumn Damask rose – The Bourbon roses – Portland roses – The Hybrid Perpetuals – Tea roses – The Hybrid Teas – The first yellow garden hybrid and the Pernetianas – The Polyantha Pompons – The Hybrid Polyanthus, later to be re-named Floribundas – The recent development of the Floribunda-Hybrid Tea type

A good deal of conjecture has entered into much of what has been written concerning the early history of the rose. But it can be said without fear of contradiction that originally all roses grew wild – the idea of planting them in gardens is comparatively new, bearing in mind that fossils of roses which geologists believe to be upwards of 35,000,000 years old have been discovered in Europe, Asia and America.

It has been estimated that something like 200 species have been discovered growing in various countries in the Northern Hemisphere, with colours ranging from white, through pink, red and yellow. The species bear single flowers, that is, having one row of five petals only (in one case, *Rosa sericea*, four petals only). With few exceptions their period of flowering is short, usually in May or June, but in certain instances (e.g. *R. wichuraiana*) in July and August.

Paucity of Early Records

Records concerning the early roses are remarkably scanty and unreliable, partly because of the absence of any standard terminology among early botanists. It is fair to assume, though, that some of the species were hybridised, no doubt being pollinated by insects, and improved forms evolved over hundreds or even thousands of years.

Probably the Red rose (*R. gallica*), the Dog rose (*R. canina* of the English hedgerows), the Musk rose (*R. moschata*) and the Phoenician rose (*R. phoenicia*) were the sources of most of the garden roses cultivated before 1800, especially *R. gallica*. Chance seedlings or mutations (sports) would occur in which the petals of the original single roses would be doubled or trebled by the replacement of some of the stamens and styles with petals.

Rosa gallica, the French rose, is the ancestor of the Gallicas, the Damascenas and the Centifolias, which were so popular before modern roses were evolved, and still have their devotees. The Damask rose, *R. damascena*, in course of time produced a variant with a tendency to bloom in the autumn as well as in the summer. This was popularly known as the Autumn Damask, *R. damascena bifera*, also known as Rose des Quatre Saisons and *R. damascena semperflorens*. It is supposed to be the rose grown by the Romans at Paestum in great quantities for decorations at feasts at the time of Nero.

The first Bourbon roses were believed to be natural crosses between the China rose, *R. chinensis*, and the Autumn Damask rose, about 1817. It is thought too, that the Autumn Damask rose and the Old Crimson China rose (*R. chinensis semperflorens*) hybridised by chance pollination about this period to produce improved types which became known as Portland roses, after the first of this type, named Duchess of Portland. These in turn were chance pollinated with the Bourbons, Gallicas and Hybrid China roses, largely in France, where the warmer climate made it possible for the seeds to ripen out of doors. After careful selection improved forms were developed which became known as the Hybrid Perpetuals, although they were a long way from being repeat flowering as we understand the term today, let alone perpetual. These were nearly all in shades of pink, red and a few whites.

Ancestors of the Tea Roses

Also early in the nineteenth century, one or two hybrids from *R. odorata* × *R. gigantea* were imported from China into Europe, these being closely allied to *R. chinensis*, which has the valuable quality of recurrent flowering. From these developed the race of Tea roses so popular in the last century, with their delicate colours, dainty form and distinctive fragrance, said to resemble that of a freshly-opened tea chest. Unfortunately the tea roses were not very hardy – I recollect trying to grow them in South Lancashire, where the long wet winters would kill the wood back to soil level. The tea roses were crossed, either naturally or deliberately, with the hybrid perpetuals, and the seedlings from these crosses were the first Hybrid Tea roses. La France, introduced in 1867, is generally acknowledged to be the first of this class, but it is significant that the raiser himself, M. Guillot of France, did not know its parentage, as it was one of a batch raised from chance pollination. The early hybrid teas were improved by back-crossing with the hybrid perpetuals and with those of their own class.

Colour Breakthrough

But the dramatic improvement in colour range developed when M. Pernet-Ducher, of France, succeeded in crossing the Persian yellow rose, *R. foetida persiana*, with Antoine Ducher, a violet-red hybrid perpetual, which yielded Soleil d'Or, orange-yellow shaded red, in 1900. This variety, when crossed with a hybrid tea, Mme Mélanie Soupert, produced in 1910 the first pure yellow garden hybrid, which was named Rayon d'Or. Once this breakthrough had been achieved, numerous new shades of orange, copper, flame, terracotta and salmon were obtained by crossing this variety with hybrid teas. The bicolor roses, too, with scarlet on the inside of the petal and golden-yellow on the reverse, began to appear. At first these early crosses were known as Pernetiana roses and sometimes as Hybrid Austrian Briars. At a later stage, though, these were inter crossed with the hybrid teas to such an extent that no line of demarcation was possible and they were merged with the hybrid teas.

More recently, Wilhelm Kordes of Germany succeeded in breeding the blue out of the crimson colouring when he crossed Baby Château, a polyantha rose, with Crimson Glory to yield Independence (Kordes' Sondermeldung), a pure scarlet or 'red-lead' shade, and the parent of many modern roses of vivid colouring.

While the early hybrid teas were becoming known in competition with the hybrid perpetuals and the teas, the first Polyantha Pompon was introduced in 1875. This was an almost pure white variety, Pâquerette, thought to have been obtained from *R. multiflora* × *R. chinensis*. It seems reasonably certain that its recurrent-flowering habit was derived from the pollen parent. Probably the cross between these two species was made both ways and some of the first generation seedlings crossed back with *R. chinensis* and its hybrids at this stage. Such early polyantha pompons as Mignonette (1880), Anna

Maria de Montravel (1880) and Marie Pavic (1888) no doubt were crossed with some early ramblers and tea roses, such as Mme Falcot, in obtaining further polyanthas. Indeed, Mme Falcot is the pollen parent of Perle d'Or, a polyantha very much on the same lines as Cécile Brunner, which is said to be derived from a polyantha × Mme de Tartas, a tea rose which was an ancestor of many hybrid teas, including the famous Mme Caroline Testout. A feature of many of the polyantha pompons was the frequency with which they produced sports of a different colour.

The First Hybrid Polyanthas

It was as recently as 1924 that Svend Poulsen of Denmark raised the first Hybrid Polyanthas by crossing the polyantha pompons with the hybrid teas. The first two varieties were the well-known Else Poulsen and Kirsten Poulsen, both derived from crossing the polyantha pompon Orléans rose with the hybrid tea Red Star. But it was some years thereafter before the hybrid polyanthas were officially recognised as a separate group. The first yellow hybrid polyantha (Poulsen's Yellow) was introduced in 1938, just before the Second World War. Soon after hostilities ceased development went ahead at a tremendous pace, with some raisers crossing back with other species, such as *R. microphylla* and *R. rubiginosa*. The form of flower became more like a small hybrid tea with the typical pointed centre, as compared with the unsophisticated single and semi-double form of the pre-war hybrid polyanthas. As the parentage of the post-war varieties contained less and less true polyantha strain it became evident that the name hybrid polyantha was an anachronism, and the description 'Floribunda' was officially adopted instead.

The Latest Development

Already the modern floribundas have been crossed with the hybrid teas to such an extent that some varieties have been placed in a sub-group termed floribunda-hybrid tea type. These varieties have the typical hybrid tea shape, although the individual blooms are smaller. They are carried in clusters or trusses, sometimes with footstalks so long that the individual blooms may be cut for house decoration without removing the truss. The dividing line between the hybrid teas and the floribunda-hybrid tea type has now disappeared for all practical purposes, and it is no longer possible to say, just by looking at a variety, whether it is a hybrid tea or a floribunda.

18

2

Adaptability and Versatility

The adaptability of the rose – Its tolerance of a wide range of soils and growing conditions – Town gardens, industrial areas and country gardens – Roses in full sun and partial shade – Drought and wet weather – Conditions which roses should not be expected to tolerate – Rose growing fallacies

Perhaps most amateurs only develop a keen interest in gardening in middle life, when they tend to be physically less fitted for the more strenuous sports and pastimes. It is only natural that the houseowner with a plot of land to cultivate will normally take a greater interest than, say, a top-floor tenant in a tall block of flats in a built-up area, whose scope for practical gardening may be confined to some window boxes and a few pot plants and bowls of bulbs.

Even so, what may start with the young married man as the wearisome chore of tidying up the garden, will sometimes burgeon, given suitable encouragement in the shape of one or two early successes, until the owner becomes really garden conscious – one might even say garden proud, in the same sense as the housewife who cherishes her modern kitchen. I am not for a moment suggesting that it is necessarily a good thing to be a fanatic. It is possible to make the garden too much of a show-piece, instead of treating it as a source of healthy recreation and relaxation, and particularly as a means of restoring the jaded senses of the industrial or office worker when he gets home at the end of the day.

All the joys claimed for gardening, such as the creation and preservation of something beautiful from what may have been little more than a rubbish dump in the first place, may be found in the growing of roses. There are, indeed, so many groups and widely diversified types of roses that the amateur might well specialise in them. There would be no danger of him exhausting the subject in a lifetime, having regard to the many thousands of varieties listed and described in

19

Modern Roses 6* and the hundreds of novelties that are swelling the ranks every year. I have been specialising in roses myself, as an amateur, for more than 45 years, and over this period I must have tried well over 1,000 new seedlings, as I aim to try 40 or 50 novelties every year. It is really fascinating to study the growth of these end-products of the breeder's skill and infinite patience, exercised, maybe, over many generations of seedlings, in endeavouring to achieve his goal. While many of these seedlings may disappoint, some few will prove winners and become household words among rose lovers throughout the world.

Proven Adaptability

When I was a small boy I was familiar with quite a number of the old hybrid perpetual roses, which were then featured in a separate section in the popular rose catalogues – stalwarts like Captain Hayward, Margaret Dickson, Ulrich Brunner, Mrs John Laing and Hugh Dickson. These and some hundreds of varieties of hybrid teas, apart from the ramblers and climbers, polyantha pompons and a few of the shrub roses, flourished in my father's garden, located in an industrial area and developed mostly with pick and shovel on the site of what had been the greenhouses and stables of a large house, the foundations of which were unfortunately largely intact. The 'soil' comprised mainly ashes from the greenhouse boilers, cobbled courtyards (over which the lawns were laid) and the brick foundations of the greenhouses, which had to be prised out one brick at a time. There was a wonderful crop of that tenacious weed coltsfoot over a substantial area, flourishing among large stones and mortar rubble from the demolition of the old buildings. Practically all the soil had to be barrowed in from outside, but there was no shortage of ballast for path making. The fact that the roses flourished as they did says much for their adaptability, hardiness and tenacity.

Indeed, the adaptability of the rose to a wide range of soils, climates and environmental conditions is one of its outstanding characteristics. I have myself grown roses in the heart of industrial Lancashire, in the London metropolitan area, on a barren hillside on the North Wales coast overlooking a limestone quarry, with solid rock from the grass roots downwards in the higher part of the

* A check-list of rose names, prepared in co-operation with the International Registration Authority for Roses and compiled by The McFarland Company in association with The American Rose Society.

garden, and, more recently, in rural Surrey, on a very flinty soil deficient in humus, on which the spade is of little use because of the multitudes of large flints which were much favoured for building the brick and flint houses and walls of the district.

Roses in Towns

It never ceases to surprise me that such good roses are grown in town gardens and industrial areas, where the ubiquitous privet hedge often seems to eke out a precarious existence. In the comparatively few cases where some enlightened householder has planted a hedge of floribunda roses or one of the other vigorous groups well adapted for hedging, the effect is most refreshing and often delightful. There seems to be some law of compensating returns operating between town and country gardens, so far as roses are concerned. Whereas growth is adversely affected by the polluted air and the smoke pall in industrial areas, this very pollution acts as a fungicide, and the serious diseases of roses – rust and black spot – are seldom seen in such areas, whereas they are a constant menace in rural gardens where roses otherwise grow lustily in the pure air.

Roses for Varying Climatic Conditions

While roses succeed best in a sunny position, which provides some shade from the hottest sun for part of the day, they will also give satisfactory results in far from ideal surroundings. In small gardens hemmed in with out-buildings or tall hedges, it is sometimes worth considering planting standard roses on 3 ft. stems, to obtain the benefits of maximum sunlight. Alternatively, long pruning of the more vigorous varieties will achieve the same result, and a sturdy specimen bush 5 ft. high is not difficult to build up over a few years if the right varieties are selected.

There are types of roses to suit all climatic conditions, too. In a rainy season or a notoriously wet area, the single and semi-double varieties will delight the eye when the very full-petalled specimen blooms are unhappy. At the other extreme, in hot and dry conditions, such as were experienced in the exceptional summer of 1959, hybrid teas like Karl Herbst, Memoriam, Tiffany and Montezuma are really superb and hardly recognisable as the same varieties that can prove so disappointing in the rain. The sensible amateur will therefore be prepared for all contingencies by planting a proportion of each type of flower – single, semi-double, thinly and fully double.

Sites to Avoid

Despite their extreme adaptability and hardiness, roses should not be expected to thrive in draughty passages between two houses, under the overhanging branches of large trees, in beds bordered by privet hedges, with their dense growth and voracious root system, or near flowering cherries or other larger flowering trees whose roots will quickly invade the rose bed. Nor should they be planted in positions shaded from the sun for more than half the day, or in soil so poor that it dries out completely in hot weather and consists largely of sand. Another type of soil not favoured by roses is one with a distinctly alkaline reaction, such as is found in shallow soils overlying chalk. Every effort should be made to reduce the alkalinity by removing at least an extra foot or so of the solid chalk below the natural soil when preparing a rose bed, and adding any vegetable matter available in its place. Even old clothes, newspapers, sacking, old carpets and rugs, matting, flock mattresses and the like do not come amiss, as well as old hay and straw, old turf and potting compost, dead leaves from deciduous trees (not from roses), garden compost, spent hops, shoddy, sewage compost, tea leaves, kitchen vegetable waste and the fibrous matter from the bags of vacuum cleaners. Anything of vegetable origin capable of rotting should be used to increase the depth of soil above the chalk.

A COOL LOOK AT OLD BELIEFS

Gardeners 50 years ago seemed to base their methods of cultivation and rules of conduct on numerous old saws, maxims or gardening lore. I am not saying that there was not some element of truth in many of these, but like all 'rules of thumb', they could not possibly be right under all the varying conditions under which gardens are made and maintained. Roses were no exceptions – indeed, rose growing was perhaps richer in these old beliefs than most branches of horticulture. When I was a boy it was an article of faith that roses *must* have a clay soil to thrive. It is, of course, common knowledge that a clay soil is more fertile than, say, a sandy soil, but with the particles being so much smaller than those of a sandy soil, they easily clog together and present a lumpy, sticky appearance in wet weather and become baked to a brick-like hardness in a drought, unless much labour is spent in working the clay to achieve a reasonably good tilth.

Even today a few die-hards assert that clay is the only soil for roses, conveniently forgetting the glorious displays often seen on gravel soils, including those at The Royal National Rose Society's display gardens at St Albans.

This whole question of soils for roses cannot be dealt with as simply and dogmatically as our grandparents seemed to think. Most people know that roses propagated commercially in this country, with the exception of some of the old garden roses and miniatures, are budded on to rootstocks of various species, or 'wild' roses. The root system of the maiden or first-year plant bought from a nurseryman is that of the 'wild' rose or rootstock, and the top growth belongs to the cultivated rose. These rootstocks are natives of different countries and prefer different types of soil accordingly. Thus, the Dog rose (*R. canina*) is the native English Briar, and succeeds best on a rather heavy soil. On the other hand, the Rugosa rootstock (*R. rugosa rugosa*) also known as the Japanese rose, as it is a native of Japan, succeeds best on light sandy soils, but not on chalk. The Multiflora rootstock (*R. multiflora japonica, R. polyantha multiflora, polyantha* Simplex or just Simplex is also a native of Japan and succeeds on sandy, shallow soils on which *R. canina* would be a failure. Each of these, in turn, may be propagated from either cuttings or from seeds, and the root system will vary according to the method of propagation as well as the type of rootstock. A seedling normally will have a deeper root system than a cutting, and this difference may be exploited by the rose grower in certain circumstances. For example, the shallow root system of a cutting stock enables quicker results to be obtained from liquid feeding, and sometimes this may be an advantage, from the rose exhibitor's standpoint, if his plants are a little backward.

'Going Back to Briar'

Another old belief is that sometimes garden roses 'go back to briar'. What really happens is that suckers, which are growths from the rootstock, are allowed to grow unchecked, and these divert the sap flow from the cultivated rose and take the ascendancy. Eventually the cultivated rose, or scion, dies of starvation, leaving only suckers or top growth of the rootstock, which eventually bear the single flowers typical of the particular species to which it belongs. In very neglected gardens one sometimes sees large bushes of Rugosa roses, bearing large, single flowers in a magenta or carmine-pink shade.

23

These probably started out as the standard stems for cultivated varieties of hybrid teas, but suckers starved out the standard head which died, and the more vigorous rootstock took over.

So-called Tea Roses

Many people – not keen rose growers, of course – cherish the belief that all creamy-yellow and buff or pale apricot varieties are 'tea roses'. They have perhaps heard them so described by their parents or grandparents in their childhood. While it is true that most of the pure tea-scented roses were in delicate tints of ivory and cream, sulphur yellow, buff, pale apricot and subtle combinations of pearly pink, cream and primrose, the bush forms of these varieties are now seldom grown in this country except by the specialist firms supplying old garden roses, as they have a rather tender constitution. However, the climbing forms of some of these old roses are still to be found, especially Climbing Lady Hillingdon, Climbing Mrs Herbert Stevens and the old warrior Gloire de Dijon. Actually the early hybrid teas, which as a class provide the large-flowered and shapely bedding roses of today, were obtained from crosses made between the tea-scented roses and the hybrid perpetuals, a rather coarse-flowered but hardy group which was very popular during the second half of the nineteenth century. The vigour and hardiness of the latter group were thus eventually combined with the dainty shape, refined colours and repeat flowering of the pure tea group.

Sucker Recognition

Another dogma quoted to me on countless occasions is the so-called rule for distinguishing a sucker from the cultivated rose. 'If it has five leaflets it is a garden rose, but if it has seven or more it is a sucker' must have been responsible for the destruction of more lovely new basal shoots, under the mistaken impression that they are suckers, than I would care to estimate. The truth of the matter is that many varieties will produce leaves comprising seven leaflets with good cultivation – and quite often without it. Other varieties will tend to produce leaves with only five or sometimes three leaflets. Some ramblers, notably the hybrid Wichuraiana ramblers, normally produce leaves with more than seven narrow leaflets, and these are certainly not suckers. There are so many more reliable methods of recognising sucker growths that it is a little surprising to find these naïve beliefs surviving in this era of sophistication. The colour of the leaves and wood of the sucker is normally a much paler green compared with the red, bronze or crimson-tinted young leaves of the garden roses. The sucker leaflets are very narrow as compared with the rounded, broad leaflets of nearly all garden roses, and the prickles or thorns of the sucker are narrow or needle-like, more numerous and usually pale in the early stages as against the much broader and reddish or bronze thorns of garden roses. The infallible test is to trace the suspect growth to its point of origin with the aid of a small trowel. A sucker will develop from either the root system direct or from the main stem *below* the budding point, which is the swollen part from which the top growth emerges. If the doubtful shoot starts from this point it belongs to the cultivated variety and should be cherished; if it starts from lower down, it should be pulled off carefully at the point from which it starts as soon as possible, to avoid any weakening of the cultivated variety.

Recognition of sucker growths from the various rootstocks used by rose nurserymen in this country is essential, and never more so than when standard or half-standard roses are grown, budded on Rugosa stems. These are always liable to produce suckers from any point on the stem below the head, or from the root system, and the latter may often appear a yard or more away from the standard stem itself. The beginner may not connect them with the standard rose at first. Rugosa suckers have very numerous, needle-like prickles all round the stem and carry light green, wrinkled (rugose) leaves, which are rounded at their extremities rather than pointed. This rootstock unfortunately is very prone to suckering, and inadequate staking will often aggravate the trouble. Shallow planting and adequate staking and tying should be the rule for all standard roses.

If some of the points touched on very briefly in this introduction seem a little complicated to the beginner, there is no need for him to shy away from the subject. He may take comfort in the reflection that if he can produce quality vegetables or hardy annuals in his garden then he can grow excellent roses by following the simple procedures explained in the succeeding chapters.

3

The Uses of Roses

The role of roses in modern gardens – Varying requirements of the amateur rose grower – Exhibiting – Garden decoration – Cut flowers for the house and floral arrangements – The main groups and the purposes for which they are best suited – Rose classification

The uses of roses in modern gardens are almost unlimited. It is not merely for permanent bedding schemes that they serve the amateur well, although this is an important role of the hybrid teas and the floribundas. They are also invaluable for screening ugly sheds and outhouses, or the compost heap; for clothing trellis or pergolas, or for training on upright pillars or tripods. Old fruit trees or large tree stumps may be converted into really attractive garden features by planting some of the more rampant climbers and ramblers near the base and allowing them to scramble up the trunks. Alternatively, where there are steep banks, due to the garden being constructed on a slope, some of the flexible-caned rambler roses are ideal for covering the slope, either by planting them at the top and allowing the long canes to ramble downwards, using a few pegs to anchor them discreetly, or by planting them at the bottom and training them up the slope. Ugly out-buildings can also be effectively disguised with rambler roses.

One of the earliest uses of the climbing roses was for planting against the walls of the house and some of the choicest and tenderest varieties will thrive with the warmth and protection afforded by a south or west wall. Many of the climbing hybrid teas do well on such walls and may be trained to reach a height of 30 ft. or more over the years. On walls with such aspects they will usually provide some of the earliest flowers of the season – I have had blooms from Climbing Shot Silk in a sheltered angle between a south wall and a close-boarded fence as early as April 20. In the same garden I had

26

three specimens of Climbing Mrs Sam McGredy planted against the gable end of a detached brick garage, and these made a wonderful display in the first half of June every year, and covered a large area of the roof as well.

Hedges are another role for the adaptable modern rose, and whether these are boundary or internal hedges, it is not a difficult matter to find types of roses which are admirable for the purpose. For boundary hedges it is often advisable to make use of some of the group of shrub roses, such as the hybrid Rugosas or the hybrid sweet briars, which are well armed with prickles and may be relied upon to discourage marauding animals and other intruders.

Shrub roses are a special study in themselves. They embrace not only the various species and their hybrids, but all groups of old garden roses dating back to the nineteenth century at least and in many instances centuries earlier, with their origins often lost in antiquity. I have in mind the many varieties variously classified as Albas, Bourbons, Centifolias, Chinas, Damascenas, Gallicas, Spinosissimas, Muscosas and others too numerous to mention here. Many of them, especially some of the species, such as *R. hugonis* and *R. xanthina spontanea*, will make a beautiful display in May before the more conventional bedding roses have started to flower.

Nor does this exhaust the manifold uses of the rose in modern gardens. The miniature roses, which are mainly descended from *R. chinensis minima*, are delightful little plants, often not more than 6 in. high and covered with tiny roses for much of the summer. These are dainty replicas of the hybrid teas, with the same elegant shape, and the leaves are scaled down in proportion. They are sometimes used in rock gardens, but are also planted in stone troughs, window boxes and in miniature gardens of their own, with miniature standard roses often included in the planting scheme. While they may also be grown in pots, it is inadvisable to keep them in the dry atmosphere of a living room for any great length of time if they are to thrive.

Objectives

The use the amateur makes of the various groups of roses at his disposal will depend to some extent on his main object in growing them. Thus, the ardent exhibitor will tend to concentrate on those hybrid teas which are capable of producing a high proportion of large, perfectly formed, full-petalled blooms which will last well in water after cutting. He will also grow some of the floribundas, probably preferring those which will normally carry a large, well-spaced truss of flowers of bright colouring on a long stout stem, with healthy foliage support. As his main hobby is exhibiting, he will probably not be interested to any great extent in the many other groups with single or semi-double flowers, or in the climbers and ramblers and the pillar roses, although he may grow a proportion of his hybrid teas and floribundas as standards or half-standards as well as in bush form. He may not grow any of the modern shrub roses or the old garden roses and the rose species, and I cannot help thinking that by specialising to this extent he is missing a lot of the pleasure and interest of rose growing.

On the other hand, the vast majority of amateur growers are only interested in roses for garden decoration and for cutting for the house, and may have no ambition at all to exhibit them, even at their local horticultural show, let alone at The Royal National Rose Society's shows. It has been estimated that less than 1 per cent of the members of the R.N.R.S. are exhibitors, so the proportion of all amateur rose growers who exhibit their roses will probably be no greater.

There is also a small but growing band of rose growers – mainly ladies – who are keenly interested in floral arrangements and use their roses for this specialised purpose. For this, and for cutting for indoor decoration generally, varieties with long stems, reasonably free from thorns, are desirable. The buds should be slender, developing slowly, with elegant petals forming a flower of medium size, carried erect on a stiff neck. Varieties of particular merit from the floral artist's viewpoint are not always the best for garden display – some of them, indeed, may be quite drab, such as the lavender, lilac and mauve shades.

Roses under Glass

These few examples are given to indicate that the purpose for which one grows roses will often influence the choice of types and varieties. I have yet to mention another specialised side of rose growing – growing plants in heated greenhouses, either in pots or in permanent beds, to obtain early flowers, usually in April and early May. A couple of dozen pots containing full-petalled hybrid tea varieties will be a source of interest and pleasure at a time when work out of doors may be held up by bad weather.

THE MAIN GROUPS OF ROSES

A broad outline of the main groups of roses, their characteristics and their uses, may be helpful to the beginner who has still to experience the joy of growing perfect blooms. This outline is necessarily incomplete at this stage; the reader is referred for greater detail to some of the later chapters which are devoted to these individual groups.

Hybrid Teas

The hybrid tea group embraces nearly all the large-flowered, shapely and often highly fragrant bedding roses which have been so popular throughout the present century. They were first obtained late in the nineteenth century by crossing the hybrid perpetuals with the tea-scented roses, and were so successful in combining the best qualities of both groups – the vigour and hardiness of the former and the shape, elegance and repeat flowering of the latter, but with a much wider colour range – that they have superseded both groups almost completely. They are the aristocrats of the rose world, and provide the large specimen blooms of immaculate form so dear to the heart of the exhibitor. They flower intermittently from early June in the south until severe frost puts an end to their activities, with main flushes of bloom in June, August and mid-September to early October in the south, but several weeks later in the north. The autumn display of flowers is often exceptionally fine, and in good weather may sometimes be more highly coloured and of better substance than the earlier blooms. They cover every known colour and combination of colours in roses, and include many varieties of dainty form and medium size, ideal for cutting to provide decorative bowls for house decoration.

Floribundas

These are the other extremely popular group of bedding roses. Of quite recent origin, the first varieties date back to 1924, when Poulsen of Denmark introduced Kirsten Poulsen and Else Poulsen, two seedlings from a cross between the polyantha pompon Orléans rose and the hybrid tea Red Star. They were known as hybrid polyanthas when they were numerous enough to justify a separate group, and resembled the polyantha pompons in their freedom and continuity of flowering, their single or semi-double flowers and

29

their habit of flowering in trusses. The foliage and growth, though, was not unlike that of the hybrid teas. Their colour range was limited before the war and it was not until 1938 that the first yellow variety in the group, Poulsen's Yellow, was introduced.

Following the war they were crossed with so many other varieties outside the group, and with certain species, that the term 'hybrid polyantha' ceased to be appropriate, and the more comprehensive term 'floribunda' was substituted in the late 1940s. Today, the colour range is as wide almost as that of the hybrid teas, not excluding the tangerine, apricot, orange, flame, salmon, lavender and lilac shades, as well as striking bicolors. Some growers feel that they may eventually supersede the hybrid teas for general garden display, but even today, with a vastly improved shape of flower and in some instances a pleasing fragrance, they cannot really compare with the hybrid teas for individual quality and refinement. Where they do score is with their spectacular massed display of colour when planted in beds or groups of the same variety, and with their extreme ease of cultivation and hardiness.

Floribunda – Hybrid Tea Type

In fairly recent years – since about 1950 – varieties have appeared which are just on the border line between the floribundas and the hybrid teas. They may produce their early summer crop in the same way as hybrid teas, with individual flowers of good form or in small clusters of three or four blooms. Later in the season, though, they tend to produce basal shoots which branch out in candelabra fashion and bear large trusses of flowers in the tradition of floribundas. These varieties have been saddled with the rather cumbersome designation 'floribunda – hybrid tea type', often shortened to 'floribunda – H.T. type'. They are usually bred from a floribunda × hybrid tea, or *vice versa,* and when they have large flowers some inconsistencies in classification may well arise. For example, I have seen the variety Miss France described as a hybrid tea, floribunda and floribunda – H.T. type respectively in three different rose catalogues. Clearly this could happen only in the comparatively few cases where the flowers are large and of fairly high quality, but the border line between the hybrid teas and the floribunda – H.T. types on the one hand, and between the latter and the floribundas, on the other hand, has now virtually disappeared. He is a bold man who will take it upon himself to classify a new variety on one inspection.

As previously mentioned, some varieties display quite different characteristics between the early summer and the later crops, just as some hybrid teas will often in the autumn throw up huge trusses of buds in the manner of the floribundas. Spek's Yellow has this propensity and is a good example of the tendency towards some overlapping between the groups.

Polyantha Pompons (*Poly. Poms.*)

These bushy bedding roses have been largely displaced by some of the shorter-growing modern floribundas, but are still to be found in some catalogues. They are descended from *R. multiflora* crossed with a dwarf China rose, and the small rosette-type flowers, carried freely in clusters or trusses, are very similar to those of the early Wichuraiana ramblers of the Dorothy Perkins and Excelsa type. In fact, they resemble nothing more than the flowers of these ramblers, borne on a bushy plant; even the narrow leaflets comprising the foliage are similar. Compared with the modern floribundas they are less impressive for massed display, and many of them may suffer from mildew. They did make a notable contribution to the development of the colour range in modern roses by introducing vivid shades of orange-scarlet and orange-salmon into the group in the late 1920s, with such varieties as Golden Salmon, Paul Crampel and Gloria Mundi.

Today, they are mainly considered for small beds for which something intermediate between the miniatures and the floribundas in habit of growth is required. Even then, perhaps the very low-growing Eblouissant or one of the polyantha compactas (dwarf polyanthas) named after the Seven Dwarfs, and which are closely related to the polyantha pompons, would be preferred. Many of the polyantha pompons were distinct coloured sports from earlier and maybe less pleasing varieties, such as Orléans rose, which was one of the most sportive of all roses. Unfortunately, it frequently happened that the colour of the sport was not fixed, and reversion to the original colour would occur – perhaps most of a truss, or only the odd flower or parts of a flower – striking sometimes a discordant note of, say, carmine-pink in a bed of orange-scarlet or orange-salmon roses.

Miniatures

These delightful little plants, descended from the dwarf China rose, *R. chinensis minima,* seldom exceed a foot in height when established.

Indeed, many of them keep below 6 in., and this is one of their attractions. Normally they are best planted together away from the stronger-growing types of roses. Their Chinese ancestry is revealed in their freedom and continuity of flowering. If they are raised from cuttings they are more likely to keep their characteristic dwarf habit, whereas if they are budded on small rootstocks and planted in a rich soil they tend to grow taller. Several breeders have concentrated a great deal of attention on these miniature roses since the war, and they are now available in a wide range of colours and even multicolours. They are becoming increasingly popular in this country, as they take up very little space and may also be grown successfully in window boxes, deep stone troughs and large tubs if good drainage is provided and the roots are not allowed to become dry at any time.

Wichuraiana Ramblers

These are hybrids of *R. wichuraiana,* a late-flowering species of trailing habit found growing wild in Japan, which was crossed with various garden roses to produce a group of rosette-flowered ramblers. The main characteristic of the early members of this group (e.g. Dorothy Perkins) is that they are summer flowering only, and then concentrate their energy on producing new canes from the base for flowering during the following summer. Thus it is usually possible to cut out all the canes which have flowered and to cover the allotted space with new flexible canes from the base of the plant.

This group was extremely popular for about the first 40 years of the present century and was planted extensively for covering arches, fences, pergolas and pillars, and for growing in weeping standard form as isolated specimens on lawns. Although the flowering season is short it is exceptionally colourful and impressive at its peak.

Wichuraiana Climbers

These are similar in many respects to the above group, but usually have a rather larger flower and do not renew themselves from the base every year. A proportion of the new wood is produced from part way up the older wood, so that it is not possible to cut out all this older wood. The growth tends to be stiffer than that of the earlier Wichuraiana ramblers and therefore the varieties in the group (e.g. Paul's Scarlet Climber and Chaplin's Pink Climber)

Top: Papa Meilland (H.T.)
Bottom: Belle Blonde (H.T.)

Left: The delightful flesh pink recurrent rambler rose New Dawn in The Royal Botanic Gardens, Kew
Below: A bank clothed with roses can be extremely attractive, given the right setting

will not make graceful weeping standards. The foliage is closer to that of the hybrid teas than that of the Wichuraiana ramblers, which is narrower, with more leaflets. The flower trusses also tend to be smaller than those of the earlier group, although the buds are shapelier and often of finer quality.

Climbing Sports of Hybrid Teas

These are vigorous sports from the bush hybrid tea varieties of the same name. They originate as an extra-strong shoot on the bush hybrid tea; the eyes on this shoot are budded on to rootstocks in the hope that the extra-strong growth will be perpetuated or 'fixed'. When the climbing habit has been fixed, the prefix 'Climbing' is added to the name of the bush hybrid tea (e.g. Climbing Etoile de Hollande) and if the climbing sport proves reasonably free flowering, it may be placed on the market. The flower and foliage are identical in every respect with that of the parent variety – only the habit of growth and repeat flowering are different. If these sports would only flower as freely and over as long a period as their parents they would be much more popular. As it is, some of them give a fine display in June and then produce only a few blooms for the remainder of the season. A few are reasonably reliable, especially in June and in the autumn, but certain varieties are too shy at all times.

Climbing Sports of Floribundas

These are sports from the bush floribunda varieties of the same name. They originated in precisely the same way as the climbing sports of the hybrid teas. Unfortunately, like a number of the latter, they seem to have acquired their extra vigour at the expense of their freedom and continuity of flowering.

Climbing Hybrid Teas

Apart from the sports of bush hybrid teas, there are a number which originated as seedlings from deliberate crosses and have no bush counterpart. These include such excellent climbers as Guinée, Meg, Allen Chandler, Chastity and Paul's Lemon Pillar. With the exception of the last named, which is early summer flowering only, these bear a few flowers after the June flush.

Repeat-flowering Climbers

In the main these are large-flowering modern climbers which bear more than one flush of flowers each season, and which in most cases are of less rampant growth than the once-flowering climbers. This makes them particularly valuable in the small garden for training on single pillars and tripods, to provide colour and interest for much of the season. The flowers of nearly all the modern members of this group are of hybrid tea type, although there are a few exceptions, such as Danse du Feu.

Kordesii Climbers

These are a new group of exceptionally hardy climbers, bred by Kordes of Germany to withstand very cold winters. The type of flower is not as large, full and shapely as that of the hybrid teas, and the colour range is mostly confined to shades of red and pink, with one pale yellow and a white variety so far available. Their main virtues are the exceptionally glossy and healthy foliage of most varieties, recurrent flowering and absolute hardiness.

Shrub Roses

Broadly speaking, roses which fall outside the previously mentioned groups, but are not climbers or ramblers, are usually referred to as shrub roses. They form an extremely heterogeneous group, embracing the species and their hybrids, the old garden roses, the modern shrub roses and such groups as the Pemberton hybrid musks, the hybrid Rugosas, the hybrid Spinosissimas and many others which are not covered elsewhere. Roses belonging to these groups are considered in Chapter 23, its references to old garden roses, however, being devoted mainly to those which bloom more than once in each season. Roses falling within this loose definition provide ample scope for a book in themselves, and it is certainly not possible to do them justice in a general rose book.

Rose Classification

It will be evident from the foregoing remarks that the present system of rose classification mainly by reference to parentage has caused some confusion in recent years. This is because there has been so much hybridising between what used to be distinct groups having well-defined characteristics, that there is no longer any distinct line of demarcation. The hybrid tea type floribundas have bridged the gap between the hybrid teas and the floribundas. At the other end, very vigorous floribundas are now merging with the shrub roses – modern varieties such as Chinatown, Dorothy Wheatcroft and

Fred Loads are normally too vigorous for formal bedding and are becoming known as floribunda shrub roses. Even the modern miniature roses are tending to merge with the floribunda dwarfs, with varieties such as Baby Masquerade sometimes classified as miniatures and sometimes as floribunda dwarfs. Similarly the various groups of climbers, ramblers and pillar roses have been tending to merge, while some of them of more restrained growth are being grown successfully as shrub and hedging roses.

This trend has been receiving a lot of attention in recent years, and proposals for revised schemes of classification, submitted by The Royal National Rose Society and by The American Rose Society respectively, were discussed in some detail at the Fourth International Rose Conference, held in London in 1968. Broadly, both schemes are based mainly upon the flower type and inflorescence, the frequency of flowering, habit of growth and other physical characteristics instead of on parentage; there are differences of detail between the two schemes as at present formulated.

It goes without saying that there would have to be international agreement before any new classification system could be introduced, and it would have to be reduced to the simplest possible form to become universally acceptable. At this stage it would be premature to go into details, but it seems unlikely that the familiar group names will be discarded in the near future, although this might come ultimately.

4

Selecting and Ordering Roses

Making a start – Ordering roses – What to avoid – Making a suitable selection – Visiting nurseries and rose shows – Local horticultural societies – The Royal National Rose Society and its literature

The first step towards growing good roses, assuming that you already have a garden under cultivation which is producing other crops successfully, is to place your order with a reliable rose specialist early in the season. In this context, 'early' would imply ordering in June or the first half of July, not leaving it over until September or October, by which time many of the varieties in greatest demand will almost certainly be sold out.

I have stipulated a reliable rose *specialist* deliberately. This is not intended as a reflection on some of the large mixed nurseries which have a rose department, and are jealous of their reputation for quality and fair dealing. But it never ceases to surprise me that many amateurs of intelligence are nevertheless quite content to buy their roses from a departmental store. It is not just a matter of buying a first-quality maiden plant, with well-ripened wood and of the variety required. The plant must be in healthy condition, free from disease spores, budded on a suitable rootstock with an adequate root system which will transplant readily. It must also be true to name, with a guarantee to this effect.

The state of affairs today is not as bad as it was before the Second World War, when bare-root roses were exposed for sale on the counters of departmental stores, in an overheated atmosphere for plants, and often with the wood and roots dehydrated and shrivelled. But it is still bad enough. The custom today is for these same stores to offer the plants pre-packed in individual polythene bags, bearing a lurid and very misleading colour picture of what the variety is supposed to look like. Unfortunately, each of these individual bags, in the warmth of the store, soon becomes a miniature greenhouse and forces the plant into tender premature growth, which receives short shrift when it is planted in the garden and exposed to the elements and insect pests.

I am not saying that it is not possible to obtain satisfactory results from roses obtained from these stores – people have from time to time gone out of their way to boast to me how well they have done, although they tend to keep quiet about the failures. What I am suggesting is that, for the sake of an extra 18 pence or so per plant, for something that will give pleasure for a dozen years or more, it is just not worth risking the success of the operation. From personal observations I have made over a long period, many of the varieties offered in the departmental stores are waning in popularity and, in some instances, are already superseded by improved varieties. Does one, therefore, wish to go to the same trouble of preparing the site thoroughly and planting and pruning, for something which may already be second rate?

The advice I invariably give to the beginner is to order his plants from a rose specialist *who actually does his own budding*, as distinct from the middle-man, such as the departmental store. The aim should be to obtain delivery of the plants soon after they have been lifted at the nursery. This usually starts in mid-October under suitable weather conditions and delivery of orders takes place in rotation. Hence the importance of placing the order as early as possible in the season so that early delivery may be obtained while the ground, one hopes, is in suitable condition for planting.

Placing an Order

Should one place the order with the small local rose specialist or with one of the larger national firms? I think this is a matter for each amateur to decide for himself against the background of perhaps personal recommendations and the availability of the varieties he particularly fancies. In theory, the small local rose nurseryman, perhaps budding his 20–40,000 stocks each year, should be producing a similar maiden plant to the large national firm with its 500,000 or more per annum. Differences do arise in practice, based on the soil, manuring, the rootstock used and the scope for resting the land from roses under a crop rotation system. While a small local rose nursery is more convenient for visiting, and the varieties may be seen actually growing under local conditions, besides enabling the plants to be collected by arrangement, with no risk of drying out in transit, there are one or two disadvantages. The range of varieties offered may be less comprehensive than that of some of the large growers, and first and even second-year novelties may not be available at all. On balance I would say that if you are not particularly wanting the latest novelties, and are satisfied from personal recommendations that a local grower supplies plants of top quality, then he is the obvious source of supply in the first instance. It may also be that he is able to supply the same quality maiden plants slightly cheaper than the large national rose specialist, as he does not normally spend much on advertising, nor does he issue an elaborate catalogue with expensive coloured illustrations.

Container-grown Plants

The beginner who has prepared the site thoroughly and is impatient to make a start might well take advantage of the modern trend towards container-grown roses. These are offered at the nursery in light-weight pots which can be collected and the roses planted at any time during the growing season, even when they are in flower. Some of the smaller local rose specialists have developed this scheme with enthusiasm. While the price is naturally slightly higher than for bare-root roses of the same variety, it is very convenient to use these container-grown plants for filling occasional gaps in rose beds where a plant has died and it would otherwise be too late to replace it. Fresh soil must be used around the pot.

Cautionary Advice

The beginner would be well advised not to succumb to end-of-season cheap offers. These plants are normally those that have not been taken up by the rose public through the usual channels, although after a particularly bad season for planting, such as 1968/69, even leading rose specialists may be left with many fine plants on their hands. Surplus plants may be varieties which have not proved popular for sufficiently good reasons – liability to disease or inability to open in the rain, for instance – or they may be little-known foreign introductions which have made no impact in this country, and are therefore something of an unknown quantity. Except those offered by the reputable specialists, they are not suitable for the beginner, as they are unlikely to be as good as plants ordered early in summer and despatched in the autumn. This is because they may have been handled and heeled in more than once between first lifting in

October or November and being offered at a cheaper rate in March, and every handling may involve some damage to the plant. Damaged wood is made less obvious by offering these roses pruned ready for planting, but if there has been shrivelling of the wood because of drying out, special precautions are necessary to plump up the wood before they are planted in their permanent beds. It should be remembered that since the end of the Second World War until recently there has been a seller's market for roses and price reductions are not made without a very good reason.

These references to end-of-season cheap offers do not apply to collections of roses offered throughout the season at a saving in price compared with ordering the individual varieties separately. Such collections are normally a convenient way for the beginner to start growing roses, provided they are obtained from a reputable rose specialist; they are also economical, and there is no reason to think that the plants supplied are not as good as those ordered separately from the same source. Collections do represent some economy in labour and administration from the nurseryman's point of view, and this is reflected in the lower inclusive price charged.

The beginner is warned against ordering roses at seemingly bargain prices at any time, whether the reason given is that they have lost their labels or that the land has to be cleared. Perhaps in horticulture more than in most walks of life one gets what one pays for, and this is certainly true when buying roses. Until recently it has not been considered feasible to lay down definite standards to which a first-quality rose plant should conform. There was merely the broad grouping used by the trade as between first and second quality plants, and this was on the whole left to the discretion of each nursery. Some of the best-known rose specialists would not risk their reputation by offering second-quality plants to the public under their own name at reduced prices, but others might not be so scrupulous.

As a general guide, and based on my own experience of ordering roses over something like 48 years, I would feel suspicious of the quality of any roses offered for sale, customer's choice, at more than one shilling below the current general price for varieties which have been available for years – i.e. those that do not command a 'novelty' premium. Some of the smaller growers, who may do most of the actual budding themselves, instead of employing expert budders under contract or otherwise, and who probably do not spend as much, in proportion, on advertising as the large firms, are able to cut their price to this extent without the quality suffering. But to order roses at about half the normal price and expect first-quality plants is unreasonable and certain to lead to disappointment.

As recently as 1966 the British Standards Institution laid down minimum dimensions for first-quality roses and these are summarised in the Appendix on p. 289.

A pitfall for the novice to avoid is the offer of 'rose-like' hedging plants, advertised at apparently ridiculously cheap prices equivalent to a few pence each. These are nothing more than various types of rootstocks which are used to provide the root system of cultivated roses. Their flowers are single, usually insignificant in both size and colour and last a very short time, and they bear only the one crop. In layman's language they are 'wild' roses and will prove extremely disappointing in a small garden, as they do not even have a neat habit of growth as hedging plants.

Making a Personal Assessment

Having indicated some of the snags in ordering roses, what is the best procedure likely to ensure gratifying results? If it is at all possible, I think it is highly desirable not only to see blooms of the actual varieties before ordering them (as types and shapes vary so widely) but also to see them growing. Cut blooms can be seen at the leading rose shows in quantity, but these do not give a reliable indication of habit of growth, colour stability, freedom of flowering, resistance to rain or disease and many other points of interest to the potential grower. Seeing the plants in their nursery rows is a help, but even this does not give the full story. The best guide is to see an established bed of a variety, as only this can give a reasonably accurate idea of its character. Sometimes, particularly in the case of the larger rose nurseries, display gardens are planted, in which may be seen many of the varieties offered growing as 'cut-backs', i.e. established plants at least two years old. In the nursery proper, all the plants in the rows will be maidens, i.e. the first season's growth from the budding eye, and this may not always be typical of subsequent years.

When looking round the rose nurseries, however, it is a good plan to keep an eye open for disease as, if a variety shows itself to be susceptible in the open field, the likelihood is that it will be even more prone to the disease in the average small enclosed garden, which may be hemmed in with outhouses and hedges. It is also useful to look round the nursery on at least one occasion after a period of rain, and to note which varieties are then making a bold display, as against others showing obvious dislike of wet weather. If it is intended to plant roses in beds cut in a lawn it is as well to avoid varieties having a sprawling habit of growth, as this will be bound to interfere with mowing. Any with this type of growth, if otherwise desirable, should be noted for planting elsewhere.

Unfortunately, it will not be possible to assess the potentialities of the many ramblers, climbers and shrub roses from nurseries which do not have a display garden, since these groups, particularly the ramblers and climbers, give very little indication of their freedom of flowering in the first season. Sometimes useful information may be gleaned by visiting public parks and gardens, many of which make a feature of roses. London is fortunate in having Queen Mary's Garden in Regent's Park, which features many thousands of plants with each bed comprising between 100 and 200 plants of a variety. It is well worth while paying a special visit to this garden in about the third week of June, as many of the shrub roses and pillar roses are featured here as well.

Another useful plan is to join your local horticultural society. Quite apart from visiting the shows, attending lectures and at a later stage perhaps doing some exhibiting, it does put you in touch with others in your area who may be keen rose growers, and who may be able to show you varieties established in their own gardens. This may even be a better guide than seeing them in the nursery, as the chances are that they will be growing in soil and under conditions similar to those in your own garden. Certainly a local horticultural society which maintains a fairly high standard in its rose classes is a valuable training ground for the amateur aspiring to win prizes at The Royal National Rose Society's shows in due course. I must say that I have happy memories of a number of these local societies' shows at which I used to compete; the officials and members are nearly always friendly and helpful. It is also usual for these societies to offer facilities for ordering roses and other plants, fertilisers and garden sundries on advantageous terms.

The reader may feel that I am labouring this point about making a suitable selection, but its importance justifies even more elaboration. Probably the least reliable method of making a selection is to order merely from catalogue descriptions or coloured plates in such catalogues. While the standard of colour printing is now infinitely

41

better than it was, it is still not easy to obtain a really faithful representation, and the quality of paper used is not always a help. If the beginner is unable to attend any leading rose shows, to visit any rose display gardens or nurseries or to join a local horticultural society with some keen rose growers among its members, then he will be obliged to rely more on the recommendations of friends and on rose literature.

Apart from consulting up-to-date rose books, the beginner is strongly advised to become a member of The Royal National Rose Society, which offers impartial advice on all aspects of rose growing. Indeed, the handbooks alone, which are issued free to members, will provide him with expert guidance on the varieties to choose for any particular purpose, and all that he need know about preparation of the site, planting, pruning and general cultivation. The Rose Analysis, included each year in the *Rose Annual*, is an up-to-date tabulation of the most popular varieties in each main group for various purposes, as voted on by leading nurserymen and amateur growers. If, therefore, the novice chooses the top few varieties in each table in which he is interested, he cannot go far wrong. The Royal National Rose Society is one of those extremely rare bodies whose minimum subscription has remained virtually unchanged over more than 90 years – 10s. in 1876 and 10s. 6d. today, although an increase is now imminent. When one reflects on the respective price levels then and now, it is little wonder that the membership is so much larger (116,000 at the time of writing) than that of any other horticultural society of any type. Members may visit the very fine display gardens at the Society's headquarters at St Albans, or see the varieties which have received awards at its trial grounds; they may also see then and now, it is little wonder that the membership is so much Southport and Taunton, and further centres are to be provided. The scheme makes it possible for many thousands of members, who could not manage to make the journey to the St Albans' headquarters, to see the newer varieties being grown.

A word of caution is timely to the beginner who decides to make his own selection from rose catalogues only. Choose only those varieties which appear in the catalogues of several well-known rose specialists. It is reasonable to conclude that if a variety is widely catalogued it is in general demand and more likely to give general satisfaction. On the other hand, if it can be found in only the one catalogue, the chances are that it is of the grower's own raising, and is either too new or not considered of sufficient merit to be taken up by other trade growers. In either event, it is largely a gamble which may not succeed, and not to be recommended to the beginner.

To give a little background advice, when it comes to selecting varieties in the various colour groups, as a broad generalisation it may be said that those in shades of red and rose-pink tend to be less susceptible to black spot and to frost damage than those in shades of yellow, orange, flame, apricot and the scarlet and gold bicolors. Dark velvety crimson varieties and white roses show more than an average tendency towards mildew, while the white and other very delicate shades tend to be more liable to damage from rain than the strong shades. Do not take this advice too literally, though, as there are exceptions to every generalisation.

5

Choosing and Preparing
the Site

*Choosing the site – Frost pockets – Soil preparation – Drainage – Soil improve-
ment – Bed levels – Problems of chalk and light soils*

It has already been indicated in Chapter 2 that roses prefer as open
a site as possible, either in full sun or so placed that they receive the
benefit of the sun for the greater part of the day. In a particularly
exposed garden, such as may be found sometimes at the sea coast,
where salt-laden gales may prove detrimental to growth, it is sometimes necessary to erect wattle hurdles or other windbreaks, but
generally the problem in small gardens in built-up areas is to find
a sufficiently open position to avoid growth becoming drawn
towards the light. This may happen where the bed is made beneath
large overhanging trees, or near outbuildings or large dense
hedges. By all means plant the climbers against outbuildings, but
try to make the site for bedding roses as much in the open as possible.
This will usually mean cutting beds in the lawn in a small garden,
and although this will cause more complications in mowing and
trimming, it will offer the best prospects of success, especially
where a wall, thick hedge or close-boarded fence encloses the garden.
Where, however, chain link fencing forms the boundary, and
there are no large trees overhanging, there will be no loss of light,
and therefore no objection to rose borders being prepared adjacent
to the lawn. These may be made serpentine in outline to avoid the
rigid formality of straight lines as far as possible.

Open Sites

An open position must not be confused with a draughty one, which
roses definitely dislike. For this reason they do not usually do very
well in the narrow piece of garden between two houses where
draughts are the rule, and where little sun will reach the plants. In

emphasising the importance of an open position, it is as well to point out that disease is always a greater problem in hemmed-in gardens or those which are badly overcrowded. The average small garden in industrial areas or in the suburbs of large cities will not be afflicted with the two most serious rose diseases, black spot and rust, which flourish in pure air, but mildew can be troublesome in most seasons. This disease seems to thrive exceedingly in small enclosed gardens, especially where the free circulation of air is impeded by tall hedges or outbuildings. It is also not without significance that these are the very sites where dryness at the roots is frequently found, either because they are deprived of most of the benefit of any rain by the dense hedge or the outbuilding, or because the roots of the hedge or the porous brickwork of the wall absorb much of the natural moisture in the soil. Dryness at the roots and lack of free air circulation being two of the factors conducive to trouble with mildew, they should both receive full consideration before the site of a new rose bed is finally chosen.

Frost Pockets

Some low-lying gardens form natural frost pockets, and where there is a choice of site available, it is better to plant the roses in the higher part of a garden constructed on a slope. Otherwise, in many seasons, late frosts may play havoc with the new growth made after pruning, resulting in malformed flowers or even a much reduced early summer crop. There is the danger, too, on heavy land, that the beds in the lower-lying part of the garden will be more subject to flooding and waterlogging after heavy rain – and roses definitely do not like standing in stagnant water.

Where Roses have been Grown Before

Before making a start, it is wise to ascertain whether roses have been grown on the site before, or at any rate within the last few years (this is necessary when taking over a house and garden from a previous owner). If they have, and there is an alternative site which has not grown roses previously, then the latter is to be preferred. On the other hand, if other crops have been grown successfully for several years since the roses were last grown on a site, and the land is generally in good heart, there is no compelling reason for not growing them there again, subject to suitable preparations being made to give them a flying start.

Drainage

I can remember the time when, in the preparation of a rose bed, it was considered necessary to dig as deeply as 3 ft. 6 in. or even 4 ft. But it was not pointed out that, unless the remainder of the site was also loosened to this depth, this meant that on heavy land the bed inevitably would act as a sump for the draining of the surrounding land and be waterlogged for long periods. There is probably no other single factor certain to affect roses so adversely as bad drainage. On heavy land it may be essential to lay field drains leading to a ditch or a sump specially dug out and filled with clinker, gravel, builders' rubble or other porous material. Clearly the field drains must fall gradually to the ditch or sump at the lowest point if trouble from flooding on a heavy clay is to be avoided.

If conditions are not bad enough to warrant the laying of field drains, it may be feasible to drain the site adequately by digging out a deep Y-shaped trench and filling it with gravel, stones, broken tiles, broken bricks and clinker; there are generally plenty of these materials to be disposed of on the site of a new house before digging can proceed. The extra soil removed from the trench may be used to build up the level of the bed slightly above that of the path or adjacent lawn, and this is always advisable on heavy land. Where the garden is to be laid out on a natural slope falling away from the house, drainage will be less of a problem than where the site is level or almost level.

*Soil Testing and p*H *Value*

Having made sure that the drainage arrangements on a heavy soil are above reproach, i.e. that there will be no stagnant water accumulating in the rose beds, it is advisable to have a soil test made. Presumably the general nature of the soil will be known already, namely whether it is heavy or light, the nature of the subsoil, and whether it is full of flints or large stones, or mainly free from such obstructions to cultivation. It will also usually be evident from cultivation whether it is deficient in humus, and the success or failure of certain plants or shrubs may also indicate other characteristics. For example, if rhododendrons and azaleas flourish without the importation of lime-free soil it would suggest that the soil is acid, with a high peat content and a low pH value. On the other hand, road excavations in the laying of sewers or underground cables nearby may show solid chalk to be at no great depth below the surface, in which case the problem will be to correct excess alkalinity. Unless this is done there will be the danger of the iron in the soil combining with calcium to form an insoluble compound, leading to iron deficiency, as evidenced by lime-induced chlorosis. It is well known that roses prefer a slightly acid soil, expressed as a pH value of 6·0 to 6·5. The neutral point is 7·0; above this the value is increasingly alkaline, and below it is increasingly acid, and it may be advisable to seek the advice of your County Horticultural Adviser, who may be contacted through your Local Authority, or via the Ministry of Agriculture, Fisheries and Food.

Treatment of Heavy Soil
It is easy enough to indicate the ideal, but an entirely different matter trying to achieve something approaching it on a limited budget. Happy is the man who has at his command an open site comprising a medium fibrous loam for at least a full spit in depth, with a workable subsoil and perfect drainage, yet reasonably retentive of moisture during periods of drought. We lesser mortals have to do the best we can with whatever natural resources we have at our command.

If our soil is heavy, apart from improving drainage, we must improve its texture or crumb structure, so that in time it will become more friable i.e. less of a glutinous mass during rain, and not as liable to bake and crack in dry weather. This is not something that can be achieved in a single season – it must evolve gradually as the result of years of cultivation, with the addition of organic matter, preferably stable manure if obtainable, to the top spit. Ridging of the site after rough digging in autumn, to expose as much of the clay as possible to the action of severe frosts will also help to obtain a reasonable tilth on such soils, but this, of course, cannot be done once the roses have been planted. Gypsum (sulphate of lime) may also be used with the same object of improving the tilth.

If stable manure is out of the question, there is no need to lose heart. Granulated peat, garden compost, spent hops, leafmould, old rotted turf and old hay and straw will all be of value, forked in and thoroughly incorporated with the top spit. So far as the subsoil is concerned it is a good plan to loosen this by forking *in situ*. To do this effectively the site will require to be double dug, and this involves making sure that the relatively fertile top spit remains at the top and the subsoil stays below.

47

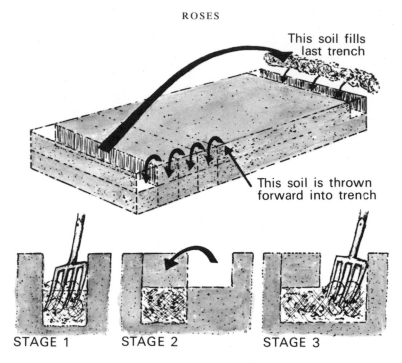

This soil fills last trench

This soil is thrown forward into trench

STAGE 1 STAGE 2 STAGE 3

Figure 1. Double digging the site for a rose bed in strips 18 in. wide

To avoid any danger of the layers of soil becoming transposed, it is usually found convenient, in practice, to dig the site in strips about 18 in. wide. The topsoil from the first strip is barrowed to the other end of the bed, eventually to be used for filling in the final strip. The subsoil of the first strip is then forked over *in situ* and if it is very heavy clay, a dressing of hydrated lime may be applied at up to 2 lb. per sq. yd., depending on how heavy the subsoil really is. This should help to break it up, making it much more suitable for the root systems of the roses, but the lime should not be applied on light soils. The top spit from the second strip is then thrown forward on top of the subsoil of the first strip and the garden compost, leafmould, old turf, hay and straw mixed in, together with a generous dressing of meat and bone meal – say, 6 oz. per sq. yd. – and coarse-grade hoof and horn meal – say 3 oz. per sq. yd. All these additions to the top spit should be really thoroughly mixed in and not simply left in a layer. The preparation of the entire site will proceed in the same manner strip by strip, using the top spit of the

Left: The Kordesii climber Leverkusen, with pale yellow flowers, is a pleasing pillar rose. It is resistant to disease

Below: The formal rose garden at Luton Hoo, Bedfordshire. Formal rose gardens on a smaller scale can also be very attractive

Lady Seton (H.T.)

later strip to throw forward on top of the subsoil of the previous one. As already indicated, the final strip will be filled to the proper level by adding the top spit from the first strip which was transported to the end of the bed for this express purpose.

There may be a temptation on a heavy clay to improve its texture quickly by applying heavy dressings of hydrated lime to the top spit as well as the subsoil. While this will improve the crumb structure it will also increase the pH value of the soil, making it less acid or more alkaline. It is a practice which cannot be recommended unless the soil is very acid in the first place and will still be on the acid side after the lime has done its work. On balance there are more troubles encountered in trying to grow good roses on an alkaline soil than on a heavy one.

After the bed has been double dug in strips as outlined, the level will be several inches higher than before, partly because of the extra humus-forming materials added and partly because of air pockets, and it will take several weeks of settling before the soil is again consolidated. This is one of the reasons for the oft-repeated advice to prepare a bed several weeks before the plants are due to be delivered.

Sandy Soil

On a light soil deep digging is inadvisable, as the subsoil may often be almost pure sand, with drainage too fierce for normal requirements. The main problem here is to build up the humus content of the soil, to make it more retentive of moisture and to improve its fertility. I know of keen exhibitors on a sandy soil replacing the original top spit with fibrous loam at considerable expense, with the object of producing first-quality specimen blooms. It is not necessary to go to these lengths to obtain a satisfactory garden display, but steps will have to be taken to avoid drying out of such soils during the summer.

It is an excellent plan to add farmyard, cow or pig manure, if procurable, to the subsoil. It should be well rotted for preference, and forked into the subsoil along with a heavy dressing of bonemeal at the rate of 8 oz. per sq. yd. Immediately above this it is useful to have a layer of old broken fibrous turf, grass side downwards. This will also provide a reserve of moisture for the roots, but if neither this nor the animal manure is available, old carpets or rugs, old sacking and doormats, cast-off clothing, old newspapers, lawn mowings, old hay and straw and dead leaves from deciduous trees may all be added to retain precious moisture. All of these should be thoroughly moistened before being added, especially the newspapers and old carpets, rugs and clothing. The top spit should be enriched as recommended for heavy soils, being, if anything, more generous in the addition of granulated peat and garden compost.

Chalk Soil

On a shallow soil over chalk, it will be necessary to remove the solid chalk so as to ensure a depth of at least 18 in. of reasonable soil above the chalk. Quite apart from the importance of building up the humus content of the soil there is the vital need to reduce the alkalinity. A dressing of flowers of sulphur at the rate of 2 oz. per sq. yd. will help to do this and so will most of the bulky animal manures and peat, which have an acid reaction, but mushroom compost should never be used on such soils because of the chalk pieces which it contains. On all shallow, hungry soils it is helpful to apply a generous mulch of peat or compost, preferably at least 2 in. thick, to the surface of the bed immediately after planting, to conserve the moisture. It is also recommended that on such light soils the final level of the bed should be several inches *below* the level of the adjacent path or lawn, to ensure that the full benefit of any rain or artificial watering undertaken during drought conditions will be retained. The bed will then tend to attract moisture from the higher surface.

Flinty and Gravelly Soils

Where the soil is full of flints, as in my present garden, it will be found that a spade is of little use in the initial preparation of the site. There may be a layer of flints or stones of varying sizes a few inches below the surface, arranged in the manner of stones in a river bed, and these will have to be removed to enable the necessary depth of soil to be prepared. Otherwise, it is neither necessary nor practicable to try to remove all the flints or stones, and any left lying on the surface of the bed will help to keep the soil cool in hot weather. It is particularly important that the level of the beds on such soils be kept several inches *below* that of the lawn. Otherwise, the birds will cause a great deal of trouble by scratching any surface mulch on to the grass, and with it there is sure to be a number of small flints. These play havoc with the motor mower, and I have more than once had to have the cylinder re-welded because of flint damage. I sometimes feel that, because of this, mulches are more of a liability than an asset on rose beds or borders cut in or adjacent to a lawn on a flinty soil. Unfortunately, such soils tend to dry out quickly and are just the ones that should benefit most from a mulch of peat, animal manure or compost. Similar arguments will apply on a gravelly soil, although perhaps to a lesser extent.

6

Planting and Display

*Planting and allied matters – The best time to plant -- When the plants arrive –
Treatment of shrivelled wood – Heeling in – Soaking the roots before planting –
Trimming the roots, soft top growth and leaves – Sucker inspection – Preparing
the planting mixture – Planting distances – Cautionary advice on treading in –
Special precautions when making late plantings – Mulching newly-planted
beds – Growing bedding plants with roses: the pros and cons – Colour grouping –
Associating slow-growing conifers with roses – Roses and clematis – Planning and
laying out rose beds*

The nurseryman likes to wait until the wood on his maiden plants
is well ripened before starting lifting operations and this means that
one or two moderate frosts will be needed to check their growth and
possibly to assist the shedding of the foliage. This is in the customer's
interest, as sappy plants full of lush growth will not transplant as
well as smaller but well-ripened specimens. Many of the larger rose
specialists now lift their plants by mechanical methods, and some
of them also trim the top growth mechanically. This doubtless
saves labour, but sometimes causes considerable mutilation of the
wood. In cases where the plants show evidence of rough treatment,
such as shoots split down their length or almost severed at the
union, or with most of the eyes damaged, or the secondary growth
blackened by frost or badly diseased, the buyer should report this
fact to the supplier within a few days of receipt of the consignment.
Provided the vital few inches of wood just above the union are undamaged and the root system is strong and healthy, the plants should
be able to survive the damage. But I feel strongly that if the top price
has been paid the customer is entitled to receive healthy, top-size
plants, free from damage, whether this has occurred during lifting
and packing or in transit.

Nowadays, the almost general practice of the large rose specialists is to despatch the plants in large paper sacks, of several ply thickness, which are machine-stitched to close them. I cannot help feeling regret at the passing of the familiar but exciting pyramidal straw bundles in which the roses used to be despatched. In my view these were a better protection against severe frost and rough handling in transit than the modern paper sacks, and the straw could always be composted or used during planting. No doubt man-power problems and steadily mounting costs have necessitated this change of practice. As in the past, the usual procedure is to notify the customer by card a few days before the plants are due, saying that it is intended to despatch during the next few days and quoting the order number, which should be referred to in any correspondence. For orders placed during the summer, the advice of despatch should arrive some time during November in a normal lifting season, but a spell of very wet weather or severe frosts could delay matters for a week or two.

The Best Time to Plant

The best time of year to plant will depend to some extent on the weather, the soil and the district. In a very wet autumn, spring planting may have advantages and will certainly be preferable to planting in the autumn if the ground is then unfit. In areas of high rainfall, such as the north-west, with its cold and wet winters, my experience has been that spring planting will give at least as good results in most seasons.

The arrival of the advice of despatch should be a warning to the customer to prepare a trench in a sheltered part of the garden for the reception of the roses until such time as he can plant them in their permanent quarters. Whereas roses would keep for a fortnight in perfect condition in the straw bundles of a dozen years ago, it is inadvisable to leave the plants in their paper sack, as received, for more than a day or so and even then they should be stored in an unheated but frost-proof shed. They should be examined at the very earliest opportunity, and if the roots are at all dry they should be soaked in water for 12 hours before the plants are placed individually in the trench at an angle of 45 degrees, with the paper label of the variety well clear of the soil. The roots and the lower part of the top growth should then be covered with fine soil which is made firm, to avoid any risk of drying out in east winds. Plants so heeled in may be left without harm until planting conditions are suitable, even though in a bad winter this may not be until March.

It may occasionally happen that there is delay in transit, and that when the consignment eventually arrives the wood is found to be shrivelled. It is quite useless to plant them as they are, in the hope that they will recover of their own accord. The plants should be placed horizontally in a trench and then completely covered with soil, so that the stems are all covered to a depth of at least several inches. The soil should be firmed to ensure full contact with the stems and if it is at all dry it should be watered. After about a week or 10 days, if the plants are then carefully uncovered it should be found that the wood is quite plump and firm, and planting may then be undertaken in the normal way.

Preparing the Plants

Before outlining the planting procedure, though, I feel it is important to indicate the steps which should be taken to prepare the plant itself. The roots should be soaked for several hours in either water or a mixture of clay and water, the object of the latter being to coat the root fibres to reduce the risk of drying out. Each plant should then be inspected individually. If a snag has been left beyond the union from which the top growth emerges, it should be cut back flush with the rootstock and pared smooth with a sharp knife. Any broken roots should be cut back just beyond the damaged part, and the main or anchoring roots trimmed slightly, using sharp secateurs. It is also useful to look for any sign of suckers developing from the root system; if any are seen they should be pulled off cleanly where they join the stock or one of the roots. Never again will there be such an opportunity to examine the roots so thoroughly, so make the most of it.

If the plants are received early – say in November – they may still have most of their foliage intact and perhaps some flower buds as well. All buds and foliage must be cut off, to avoid transpiration losses and possible shrivelling of the wood in consequence. In addition, any obviously unripe and sappy wood should be cut away, as this will not survive the winter frosts. This can easily be recognised, as it usually consists of new secondary growth from the union, produced late in the season and without having had time to flower. The leaves and the stems may still be highly coloured in reddish or bronze tints, and if the wood is pressed between the thumb and forefinger, it will be found to yield to such pressure. Any broken or otherwise damaged wood should also be shortened. By this time the plant will look much less impressive than when it arrived but, provided the remaining wood is hard and therefore well ripened, all should be well. If you live in a pure-air district where rose diseases are likely to be troublesome, it is worth while immersing the top growth in a weak solution of Jeyes Fluid, in case there are spores of the diseases on the wood. Any extra-long growth should be shortened before planting, but this is usually done before the plants are despatched from the nursery.

PLANTING, STEP BY STEP

Let us assume that the plants have been prepared as indicated above and that the roots have been placed in buckets of water awaiting planting. The soil should be in a suitable condition, i.e. friable, by which is meant that it is not too wet to crumble after being pressed in the hand. This last point is important, as it is difficult to plant satisfactorily when the soil is sticky. Air pockets will be left, because it is not possible to firm the soil adequately; apart from the plant not having a flying start, there is little pleasure or satisfaction to be derived from handling soil when it is too wet.

The prepared bed can easily be tested for condition before the final preparations are made, and in this context it is worth remembering that soil which has been recently disturbed will retain more moisture than a bed which has not been recently dug. On a very heavy clay soil it may be advisable to keep a supply of lighter friable soil under cover to be used in the holes immediately round the roots – otherwise planting will be very difficult, if not impossible, in a wet winter.

If the soil is in suitable condition, the next step is to prepare the planting mixture. This consists of moist granulated peat which is mixed with meat and bone meal in the proportion of a double handful of meat and bone to one large bucketful of peat. I also like to add a little hoof and horn meal for good measure. Make quite sure that the peat is moist but not sodden as, if dry peat is used around the roots, it may absorb water from the plant, and thus damage it.

Spacing

Use small sticks to mark the positions of the plants in the bed. The distance apart at which the plants are set depends on the vigour of the variety and its habit of growth – whether it is upright, branching, or even sprawling; it also depends on the requirements of the grower. If the plants are too far apart, the effect is not as pleasing, as too much soil and not enough flowers will be visible. On the other hand, close planting makes routine cultivation, especially weeding, more difficult, and also encourages disease, which tends to spread more rapidly. Probably 18 in. apart each way will be satisfactory for an average grower on most soils, but some of the exceptionally strong varieties like Peace and Rose Gaujard would probably be better spaced 2 ft. apart each way.

The Planting Operation

Take out the soil to form a shallow hole in the area of the first marker stick at one end of the bed. A depth of 6 in. will normally be sufficient if the site has been thoroughly prepared in advance. Mix two or three handfuls of the planting mixture with the soil forming the base of the hole, and stand the plant in it to test for the correct planting depth. This is usually stated to be when the union or budding point from which the top growth emerges is covered with 1 in. of soil when the hole is filled to the normal level. I think this is correct on a medium or light soil, but I would prefer to finish with the union flush with the level of the bed on heavy soil. If it is the intention to cover the bed with a mulch of peat or compost when planting is completed, this will need to be borne in mind, as it is a mistake to plant too deeply, especially in the case of standard roses.

After adjusting to the correct depth and, if necessary, extending the hole to accommodate the roots when spread out to their maximum extent – they should not be coiled around the circumference of the hole – throw several large handfuls of the planting mixture over the roots, then add a couple of inches of fine soil and move the plant up and down gently to eliminate any air pockets. Then make firm by treading, not too heavily, round the circumference of the hole and working towards the centre. This will avoid upsetting the level of the plant in the hole. Before completing the filling-in operation I like to add a layer of chopped turf, grass side downwards, on which I sprinkle a little meat and bone meal. I then fill in the hole, tread moderately – repeat moderately – to consolidate the soil and add a further inch or so of loose soil to finish off. In recent years I have made a practice of heaping some granulated peat over the base of the stems and over the budding point as well, but this is probably an unnecessary refinement.

56

Left: The fragrant, large-flowered pink climber Mme Gregoire Staechelin will bring colour to a wall in early summer

Below: The tall-growing floribunda variety Queen Elizabeth—one of the best roses of its kind for hedge making

Super Star (H.T.)

Elida (H.T.)

Top left: New plants which are dry at the roots should be soaked for 12 hours
Top right: If immediate planting is impossible heel in the plants in a trench
Bottom left: Cover roots and lower parts of top growth with fine soil, firm and water. *Bottom right:* Before planting, remove any snag beyond original budding union, cut back broken roots and shorten top growth

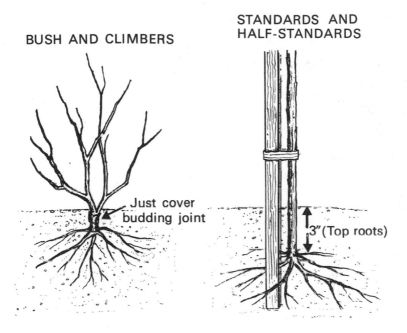

BUSH AND CLIMBERS

STANDARDS AND HALF-STANDARDS

Just cover budding joint

3"(Top roots)

Figure 2. The correct planting depths for roses

Some growers are now advocating planting in short furrows or V-shaped trenches instead of in the orthodox round holes, but frankly I cannot see that it can make any difference at all if the soil has been well prepared some time before the plants arrive. There is a natural tendency to modify the shape of hole and its size according to the root system of the rose tree next to be planted, and the important point is to ensure that the roots are not contorted to fit a preconceived idea of where they ought to be. Some plants will have the roots arranged in the shape of a fan, whereas others will have them pointing in all directions. In the former case it will be more convenient to place the main stem at the far side of the hole and have the roots facing across the hole towards you; with the latter the central position will be required. This is simply a matter of convenience and common sense.

Treading in or otherwise firming newly-planted roses is a matter which beginners sometimes find perplexing. The advice frequently given when I was a boy was for you to wear the heaviest boots you could find and then tread the soil really hard, on the basis that there was only one cardinal mistake you could possibly make in planting roses – not planting firmly enough. On a heavy clay soil, of course, especially during a wet winter, it would be foolish to attempt to follow this advice. It would drive the air out of the soil and consolidate it into a putty-like mass which would act as a most unhelpful medium for the encouragement of new root growth. I think today there is less bigotry and a better appreciation of the fact that modifications of practice are necessary to suit one's own particular soil and conditions. While it is important that there should be firm contact between the roots and the soil, the crumb structure of the soil must not be destroyed in the process. The lighter the soil, the more it may be firmed during planting without risk of ill effects. On a fairly heavy soil it will usually be safer to tread only moderately when planting, but do make a point of going round the plants in late spring when the surface is dry to make sure that they are firm in the ground. Wind and frost often loosen even those trees which were trodden well in when planted.

Supporting Standards, Half-standards, Climbers and Ramblers

When planting standard and half-standard roses it is most important to drive the stake in really firmly while the roots are still exposed, to avoid the possibility of damage. Moreover, standards and half-standards must not be planted deeply – it is sufficient if the top roots are covered with 2 or 3 in. of soil, as the stake should prevent injury to the roots from swaying in high winds. If these forms are planted too deeply they will give a lot of trouble by producing numerous suckers at the expense of the development of a large-sized head.

Climbing and rambling types should always be tied loosely to some form of support – if only a temporary stake – after planting, to avoid possible damage to the roots. There is normally more top growth left on them than on bedding roses, so the risk of damaging the delicate new root fibres is a real one in the absence of tying. Loose tying is advised because there may be a certain amount of consolidation of the soil and settling in the following few weeks, so permanent ties should be left until later.

Special Precautions When Making Late Plantings

Planting in late spring, by which is meant March planting in the south, and up to mid-April or even later in the north, requires certain modifications in procedure compared with autumn planting.

It has to be recognised that the roots have comparatively little time in which to establish themselves before they will be required to support new growth and also face the hazards of drying east winds, frosts and possible late spring drought. The plants should be pruned immediately before planting, and it should be rather more severe than for autumn-planted roses for two reasons: first, because the more top growth there is left on the plants, the more serious is the risk of dehydration of the stems until such time as there is active root growth; second, the fewer eyes there are left to break into growth, the less strain is likely to be imposed on the root system. As a general guide, the main stems of late-planted roses should be left not more than 3 or 4 in. long, and all weak stems should be cut away at the base. Another wise precaution is to 'puddle' the roots in a thick mixture of clay and water just before planting. This could be done in a large bucket or a small bath, the object being to coat the root fibres with the mixture, especially on light soils, where there is a greater risk of the plants suffering from dryness at the roots. After spring planting it should be regarded as part of the routine procedure to apply a surface mulch of moist peat or compost to a uniform depth of 2 in. and this should be watered in dry weather to avoid any check to growth. Finally, the plants should be firmed in the ground by treading round the base on several occasions during spring and early summer, to ensure that there is full contact between roots and soil. These last three points are desirable for all newly-planted roses, especially the mulching of the new rose beds and the firming of the plants in the soil periodically and also after gale-force winds.

COLOUR GROUPING

Colour grouping is a subject which might well be touched on briefly in a chapter dealing with planting. It depends to some extent on the tastes of the grower; some prefer bright contrasts such as are obtained by planting orange-scarlet and deep golden-yellow varieties adjacent to each other, whereas others may consider the effect crude and would prefer soft blends and harmonies. In whatever direction your inclinations may lead you, there are certain rules which should be observed. The main object of careful colour grouping is to plant in such a way that the general effect is enhanced. Thus, by planting the white floribunda Iceberg next to the orange-scarlet Korona the purity of the white and the brilliance of the orange scarlet will be intensified by contrast. Other pleasing contrasts may be arranged with lavender-mauve and soft yellow varieties, or with those in dark velvety red and orange or orange-flame. Colour harmonies may also be planned, using soft pink, pink-shaded cream and gold, buff, apricot and coppery-pink varieties. Normally, it is a mistake to plant varieties in shades of red, cerise, carmine or deep pink close to each other. Carmine is a particularly difficult colour in roses and is safest toned down with white, cream or a very pale yellow. The pillar-box red shades need to be kept well away from the crimson varieties.

SIMPLIFIED COLOUR COMBINATIONS

The following information is given as a guide to intending planters:

COLOUR OR BLEND	ASSOCIATES WELL WITH
White Off-white Cream Cream, tinted with peach, flesh, lemon or apricot	1. Any strong shade, such as bright red, deep pink or carmine 2. 'Difficult' shades, such as lilac, lavender, mauve or magenta
Forms a useful 'buffer' between blocks of strong colours	
Rich yellow shades	1. Scarlet or crimson selfs 2. Scarlet and gold bicolors 3. Soft pink or pink and gold blends, but not hard blue-pink or carmine-pink
Orange, apricot, flame and terracotta shades	1. Dark crimson or scarlet-crimson 2. Pale yellow 3. Pink and soft yellow blends and buff-pink, but not blue-pink
Orange-carmine, orange-cerise, cerise, carmine and magenta shades	1. White, off-white or cream 2. Pale yellow 3. Buff, pale apricot and orange-yellow 4. Flesh pink, but not deep pink or scarlet
Salmon-pink, coral-salmon and orange-salmon	1. Light yellow or pale gold shades 2. Pale pink or pale pink and cream blends
Medium pink	1. Apricot or gold shades 2. Soft pink and yellow blends

COLOUR OR BLEND	ASSOCIATES WELL WITH
Deep pink, including madder and carmine pink	1. White, off-white or cream 2. Pale yellow 3. Flesh pink, but not scarlet, vermilion or crimson shades.
Scarlet, vermilion, geranium-red and orange-scarlet shades	1. White, off-white or cream 2. Pale yellow 3. Deeper yellow to taste, but not crimson, carmine or cerise and magenta shades
Crimson and maroon shades	1. White, off-white or cream 2. Yellow, apricot or orange, but not scarlet, vermilion, geranium-red, carmine or deep pink shades.
Lavender, lilac, mauve and lilac-pink shades	1. White, off-white or cream 2. Yellow shades, according to taste. A bright yellow will give life to a colour group which may seem rather drab in the garden
Bicolors	Either of the self colours comprising the inner face or the reverse of the petals
Blends	Selfs of any of the individual shades found in the blend

The Use of Bedding Plants

Colour schemes sometimes incorporate shallow-rooted bedding plants, such as violas, which may be used to carpet the rose beds. Where the roses are planted a fair distance apart, it may be a good plan to use non-invasive plants which flower well before the roses, to add colour and interest to the beds in the late spring, and of these violas are easily the best to use for underplanting. The old favourite in a soft mauve, Maggie Mott, is still worth growing. Hybrids of *Viola cornuta* are also first class and will make quite large clumps over the years in areas comparatively free from cold, damp winters. Apart from the purple, blue, white and pink forms, the hybrid Jersey Gem has flowers much larger than the type in a rich violet-blue shade. The objections to carpet bedding with violas will come mainly from exhibitors, and it must be admitted that cultivation is made more difficult when anything is planted among the roses. A compromise might be possible by leaving an extra-wide margin between the first row of roses and the lawn or path, and planting an edging of violas or some other shallow-rooted plant, to provide colour early in the season. Rampant-growing perennials, such as catmint (*Nepeta faassenii*) are not recommended, as although they make a very effective border with their grey leaves and mauve flower spikes, these plants quickly exhaust the soil and will make a border nearly a yard across after being battered down by heavy rain. Spring-flowering rock plants, such as aubrieta, arabis and some of the mossy saxifrages may be used, but they will require shearing back ruthlessly after flowering to induce them to form neat cushions of green in the summer and to avoid encroachment.

Ornamental Conifers and Roses

Slow-growing conifers may be used very effectively as isolated specimens at the back of long rose borders to relieve any flatness. As evergreens they provide some interest during the winter months when a rose garden tends to look forlorn, and roses may be planted quite close to them without any obvious ill effects. I am particularly fond of the Irish Juniper (*Juniperus communis hibernica*), an upright slender column in silvery green which looks particularly attractive early in the summer. Another handsome specimen, forming an upright column, but much broader and taller than the Irish Juniper, is *Chamaecyparis lawsoniana columnaris*, with bluish-grey foliage. Many other hybrids of *Chamaecyparis lawsoniana* are excellent in the rose garden. I can strongly recommend the varieties *ellwoodii* and *fletcheri* as being compact, upright growers, the former in a rich green and the latter with more feathery greyish-brown foliage; both are broad in proportion to their height and will stay below 5 ft. for many years. Of the somewhat taller growers, *C. l. pottenii*, *C. l. erecta viridis*, and *C. l. wisselii* are recommended, all three in shades of green, while two very fine golden forms are *lutea* and *stewartii*. *C. l. lutea* is easily the taller of the two and it has more open growth. *Cupressocyparis leylandii* is also effective in a large garden, with graceful feathery foliage in a pleasing light green, but it grows too large to be suitable for small gardens. The Irish Yew (*Taxus baccata fastigiata*) and the golden form *aurea* make excellent specimens for adding character to the rose garden if time is not an important factor, having regard to their comparatively slow rate of growth.

Clematis and Roses

Clematis may also be introduced successfully into the rose borders, where they will make a striking display if grown up pillars, either on their own or mingled with a climbing rose. *Clematis jackmanii superba* looks glorious planted with a pink climbing rose, such as New Dawn or Aloha, and the intense violet-purple introduces a different colour among the roses.

PLANNING AND LAY-OUT

The planning and lay-out of the rose beds is a subject in itself. While there will be some comments in the chapter dealing with labour saving in the rose garden (see p. 146), it is not intended to give more than the barest outline in this book, because this is so obviously a personal matter. From the utilitarian angle, which nearly all of us have to consider, the width of the beds should assist, rather than hamper cultivation. This will normally restrict them to three rows of plants, which at 18 in. apart with 1 ft. at each side between the outside rows and the edge of the bed will mean a bed 5 ft. wide. If very vigorous varieties are planted, 2 ft. between the rows is needed, making a bed 6 ft. wide. The bed will look better furnished if the rows of plants are staggered in relation to each other. Simplicity in planning is desirable rather than intricate geometrical patterns. It should be remembered that numerous small beds cut in a large lawn will require a great deal of time spent on the trimming of the grass edges, if they are to look neat and tidy. Generally it is wiser to avoid a number of small beds, as these give an overall impression of fussiness, and are less effective, when it comes to colour grouping, than a lesser number of beds of medium size.

Beds of mixed varieties are not as effective as those devoted to one variety only, unless two or three in colours which blend harmoniously are chosen with care, taking particular trouble to ensure that they are compatible in habit and height of growth. Hybrid teas and floribundas look much better planted apart from each other in separate beds, as the flower form, size and flowering habit in most cases are so different. When planting mixed beds of one or other of these groups it is much better to have three or, preferably, six plants of each variety forming a distinguishable patch of colour, rather than single plants of a large number of varieties, as these can only give a 'spotty' effect, with no semblance of uniformity of growth.

Roses in a Lawn Setting

The most attractive setting for rose beds is undoubtedly grass, but this needs frequent mowing, weeding and trimming. Where grass is decided on, common sense dictates that at least one dry path should provide access for use in wet weather and for barrowing when alterations are being made, to avoid churning up the turf. It is an excellent plan when designing rose beds cut in turf to have the grass paths the exact width of the beds. This will enable the beds and the paths to be changed over when the roses show signs of having exhausted the soil in the original beds or there is evidence of this soil becoming 'rose sick'.

Silva (H.T.)

Top left: A fork or spade placed across the planting hole gives an accurate indication of the planting depth. *Top right:* The hole must be large enough to accommodate the roots at their full spread. *Bottom left:* Fine soil and moist granulated peat is filtered amongst the roots to aid early establishment, and the soil is well firmed as planting proceeds. *Bottom right:* Planting completed

Figure 3. Modern treatments of rose beds in present-day garden designs.
In contrast to the static patterned beds of traditional rose gardens, these play a
part in the general design of the garden and create rhythmic or progressive
lines which lead the eye on

Figure 4. The relative merits of straight, curved and zigzag borders in gardens –
alternative designs for the same site. Straight – static and dull; curved – flowing
movement; and zigzag – dynamic movement

Figure 5. A small rose garden for a level site, adaptable for gardens of any size.
The small, irregular beds in paving allow easy access to the roses
Figure 6. A design for a terraced rose garden in which the terracing corrects
the falling ground across the horizontal lines of the house

Figure 7. A small, enclosed rose garden with a white-painted rose arbour
Figure 8. A modern conception of the rose arbour, utilising a mound with a
background of evergreen shrubs and pegged-down roses covering the banks

7

Pruning and Training

The reasons for pruning – The first spring pruning and subsequent pruning – The influence of soil and feeding on pruning – Long and short pruning – Pruning tools – When to prune – Frost damage and pruning – Differential pruning of main rose groups – When light pruning or no pruning is advisable – Groups to train rather than prune – Pegging down as an alternative

One of the first questions the intelligent beginner will ask is: 'Why is it necessary to prune roses?' It is a fact that the formal pruning methods of today probably date back no earlier than the time when the exhibiting of roses in boxes first became popular about the middle of the last century, when the hybrid perpetuals were at their peak. In earlier times roses were not rated very highly as formal bedding plants, as those then available tended to make large bushes which required only some thinning out by cutting away the twiggy, dead or overcrowded wood. Today, the rose is used extensively for planting in ornamental beds, usually set in lawns, and this in itself is a reason for pruning. How otherwise would it be possible to keep the roses in the bed from overhanging the lawn, or from attaining such a height as to look grotesque?

Pruning has as its object the removal of all wood which is non-essential to the needs of the plant. This enables its energy to be concentrated on a lesser number of shoots at the peak of their vigour; these also are shortened, so that the rising sap has to feed comparatively few but strong eyes, or dormant shoot buds, instead of a multitude of weaker ones. This concentration means that fewer, but much finer blooms will be produced from a pruned plant, proportional to the severity of the pruning system adopted.

Another object of pruning is to rejuvenate the plant. Roses are hard-wooded shrubs which have a natural tendency to throw up new shoots from the base every season. These basal shoots are essential to the continued well-being of the plant – if they are not produced, then the older wood hardens, the bark thickens and it becomes even more difficult to induce the dormant buds at the base to break into growth through this thick bark. Unlike a forest tree, a rose has no permanent framework of trunk and main branches which increase in height and girth with the passing of the years. With a rose even the strongest basal shoot remains in full vigour for only a few years and then it begins to deteriorate as the sap supply is diverted to younger basal shoots. Thus, there is a cycle of growth in three phases – new young wood, strong growth in full vigour and older growth in decline.

Once it is understood that this is the natural habit of roses – that they must renew themselves regularly from the base – then much of the confusion and misunderstanding associated with pruning will vanish. The same phenomenon will be noticed with our native species. *R. canina,* the English Briar of the hedgerows and commons, which yields such excellent stems for budding our own standard roses, throws up vigorous new stems from the base and gradually kills off the old stems by a system of slow starvation. This is a long and wasteful process which the pruning of garden roses seeks to speed up by cutting away all decadent wood.

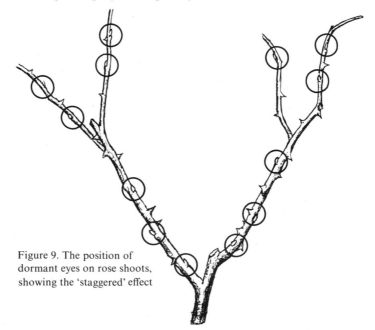

Figure 9. The position of dormant eyes on rose shoots, showing the 'staggered' effect

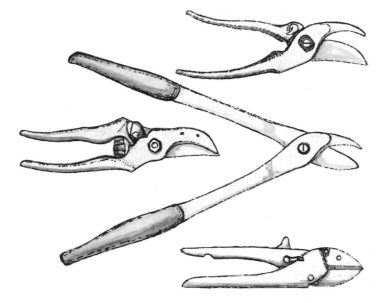

Figure 10. Modern forms of secateurs (with the anvil type shown on the right) and long-handled pruners, which can be extremely useful for cutting old stems

There is the further point, too, that the modern small garden does not have the space to allow roses to be featured as free-growing shrubs. They must be pruned to fit the garden, so that each shoot shall have room to develop without overcrowding. Pruning must also be undertaken to encourage the dormant eyes near the budding point to break into growth and furnish the base of the plant which, otherwise, would soon become leggy and bare. The observant novice will have noticed that rose shoots always taper towards the growing tip, which means that the eyes or dormant shoot buds will similarly vary in strength according to their distance from the base. This illustrates the main principle of pruning, which is to decide, once the superfluous wood has been removed, how far back to cut strong, healthy wood. The lower it is cut back, the stronger should be the new growth, assuming adequate feeding, and the finer, but fewer, the resultant blooms. Cutting back more moderately should produce rather smaller but more numerous flowers.

Tools for Pruning

The tools required for pruning include a really sharp and properly adjusted pair of secateurs, specially designed for rose pruning; a small saw, of the hacksaw type, for removing thick dead stems which would take the edge off the best pair of secateurs, and such accessories as a stout pair of gloves and a kneeling pad, which will often be a boon when removing old thick wood from the base of the plant. Some gardeners are still faithful to the pruning knife, and while there is nothing quite as good in the hands of a skilled worker, most amateurs will find a good pair of secateurs easier and quicker to use. A long-handled pair of rose pruners will also be found helpful in the larger garden, both for removing thick woody stems and also for heading back dormant budded stocks.

PRUNING AFTER PLANTING

Pruning in the first spring after planting is an emergency measure following transplanting and is no guide to the pruning methods to which the rose will respond best in subsequent years, when it is fully established and growing freely. Almost without exception, newly-planted roses should be pruned severely. This means that all weak and twiggy wood should be cut away entirely, and the two, three or four strong stems remaining should be cut back to an outward-pointing eye about 6 in. from the base. Floribundas and floribunda shrubs may be left rather longer – say up to 8 or 9 in. from the base. The reason for being severe with newly-planted roses is, first, that part of the root system necessary to support the existing top growth has been left behind in the nursery; second, there is insufficient time for the roots to establish themselves in what is probably quite a different type of soil, while supporting a lot of top growth. These factors may all assist in causing loss of moisture by transpiration during the cold, drying winds which are so often a feature of the spring months. If the top growth is cut back fairly hard, it will give the roots a chance by reducing transpiration losses; this is vital if the roses have been planted as late as March.

The only exceptions to severe pruning of newly-planted roses occur when the soil is light, hungry and deficient in humus, and when planting climbing sports of bush hybrid tea varieties and other repeat-flowering climbers. When planting on very light soils – those which are sandy, with fierce drainage, for example – it is wiser to prune all types of roses very little in the first spring. Merely tip the shoots, and try to encourage new basal growths by watering copiously in dry weather and by mulching the surface of the bed with well-rotted manure, garden compost or granulated peat.

The climbing sports of bush hybrid teas may not have as fixed a climbing habit as might sometimes be desired – the individual varieties show a remarkable variation in vigour as compared with each other, which is not in any direct ratio to the vigour of the respective parents in bush form. Experience has shown the advisability of merely removing any pithy tips to the growths and then carefully bending over the remaining growth by tying the ends to canes or horizontal wires, so that the long shoot forms an arc. This treatment forces the lowest dormant eyes near the base into activity and therefore has the same effect as pruning other groups severely after planting. Unless the main stems are trained horizontally, the rising sap will force only the topmost eyes on each of them into growth, and a very ungainly specimen will be produced.

PRUNING ESTABLISHED ROSES

Established roses, i.e., those which have made at least a complete season's growth after planting, should not be pruned strictly by rule of thumb, but should be dealt with in accordance with certain broad principles which will be modified in detail to suit the requirements of the grower, the feeding programme, the distance apart and the type of soil on which the plants are growing. Thus, if exhibition in the specimen bloom classes is the aim of the grower, he will prune more severely and feed the plants more intensively than if they are intended for garden display and occasional cutting for the house. The more severely the plants are pruned, the more important it becomes to feed them liberally to replace the nutrients normally stored in the wood which has been removed. The richer and heavier the soil, the more liberties may be taken with pruning as a general rule.

It is on the shallow, hungry soils which dry out rapidly and from which the soluble nutrients are leached by heavy rains that pruning should be circumspect. On such soils a system of moderate or light pruning will normally give the best results. These terms refer to the extent to which the strong, healthy growths should be cut back after all weak, twiggy, unripe, dead, damaged, diseased and decadent shoots have been cut away, as well as any which are badly placed.

This preliminary cleaning up of the plant applies under all systems of pruning, and no latitude is permissible here for variation. Under a system of light pruning, the remaining healthy growths of the previous season will merely be shortened to either the first or the second outward-pointing eye below the footstalk of the old flowers.

Moderate pruning requires these strong, healthy growths of the previous season to be cut back about half way, according to their strength – rather lower down if they are somewhat slender, but left rather more than half length if they are very strong and sturdy. There is a certain amount of judgment required here, but it will be evident, on reflection, that there is no point in leaving a slender growth very long, as any laterals or side shoots produced would soon bend it over, resulting in twisted stems and damage during high winds.

It is an excellent rule only to cut into wood which was produced in the previous season except when removing or cutting back old wood to near the base. The bark of the young wood heals over more quickly, it breaks into growth more readily and it usually carries the finest blooms. Always cut back into wood with sound white pith. If the pith is discoloured, this is indicative of frost damage, and it will be necessary to cut back still further into wood that is undamaged.

Time for Pruning

The best time to prune roses is a topic which has been debated at great length, to my knowledge, over the past 45 years, and probably much longer. My considered opinion is that it is not possible to earmark a best time according to the calendar, as this will vary each year. Undoubtedly the best time to prune is when the plants are dormant, or as near dormant as makes no difference. The severity of the winter will vary this period of dormancy – in the winter of 1962–63 the roses were dormant from December until the end of March, whereas in a mild winter in a sheltered garden in the south-west, some new growth may be found almost throughout the year. The very worst time to prune is late in the spring when the sap is rising strongly and new young growth clothes the upper half of the shoots, with perhaps even some flower buds to be seen. Pruning so late must result in considerable 'bleeding' from the pruning cuts and a corresponding loss of vigour. It is also a mistake when pruning so late in the spring – perhaps the end of March in the south or in mid-April in the north – to compromise by cutting back to one of the new shoots on the upper half of the stems. This will normally lead to a leggy plant, and the problem will have to be faced at a later stage by cutting further back.

In many years the first half of February may be a good time to tackle the pruning. At that time the plants should not have made much new growth except possibly in the mildest of winters in the south. It is important when pruning then to cut back each shoot to just above a dormant eye or shoot bud, facing away from the centre of the plant. Do not be tempted to prune to an eye that has already started into growth – otherwise this may suffer frost damage later.

Length of Pruning Period

Where there are many roses to be pruned there is no reason why this work should not be spread over 10 weeks or so, between December and February. This could be arranged either by pruning in stages, e.g. by cutting out all dead wood in December, all twiggy and weak wood and that which is pithy and unripe in January and leaving the shortening of the strong and healthy wood remaining until February. Alternatively, pruning could be tackled by dealing with groups of roses, starting with the hardy shrub roses, the Wichuraiana ramblers and the floribundas, and leaving the less hardy groups, including the hybrid teas and the climbing sports of hybrid teas, until later. In pruning such a large group as the hybrid teas, it is advisable to prune the bush forms before the standards, and to prune those varieties in red and pink colouring before those in yellow, orange, flame and bicolors, as the latter tend to be less hardy.

A question sometimes raised is whether it is possible to minimise frost damage by late pruning. Unfortunately, nothing can protect the growing shoots against frosts late in May if these are at all severe, so the short answer is 'no'. Anybody unwise enough to defer pruning until the middle of May would find that his plants would suffer more of a check from pruning so late, with the inevitable copious bleeding, than if they had been pruned early and allowed to grow with the weather.

PRUNING OF PARTICULAR GROUPS

It has already been explained that the preliminary work of cleaning up the plants by removing all dead, damaged, decadent, diseased, badly placed, twiggy and unripe wood, is common to all groups of roses. The difference in treatment between the respective groups arises in dealing with the strong, ripe wood remaining. The purposes for which the various groups are grown differ so much that it is not surprising to find variations in pruning requirements. These are summarised in the following paragraphs and refer to established plants throughout.

Hybrid Teas

Ideally a knowledge of the habit of growth of each variety is useful in deciding on the most suitable treatment individually. Otherwise, pruning may be hard, moderate or light according to circumstances.

(a) Hard: This is considered to be somewhat drastic by present-day standards, and not even all exhibitors of specimen blooms feel it is necessary. In many parks and public gardens where the roses are closely planted in beds of one variety set in grass, it is still practised and consists of cutting back all the strong shoots to within 6 or 8 in. of the ground immediately above an outward-pointing eye, as with all pruning cuts. Such hard pruning must be followed by generous feeding. It is standard practice for pruning pot roses under glass.

(b) Moderate: Here the strong shoots of the previous season, whether from the base, or lateral growths from older wood, are cut back about half way. This is a useful mid-way course to steer for the amateur growing his roses on an average sort of soil, who is not ambitious to win championship cups and grows only for garden display and house decoration. After a few years of moderate pruning the plants will tend to become tall and leggy, and the occasional severe winter may have to be followed by more drastic treatment to cut out the dead and frosted wood.

(c) Light: The strongest shoots of the previous season's growth are merely cut back to the second outward-pointing eye below the footstalks of the old flowers. This method of pruning is recommended only for use on light, hungry soils which dry out quickly; on richer land it would produce an exceptionally leggy and ungainly plant. As part of this system the older wood is cut out whenever it can be spared. Hybrid tea varieties in shades of yellow often respond to light pruning such as this, and they certainly resent hard pruning. Where moderate pruning has not produced very satisfactory results light pruning should be tried with roses in this colour group.

Floribundas

This modern group is second only to the hybrid teas in popularity and seems to be overtaking them rapidly. These roses are essentially grown for garden display and lay no great claim to size and perfection of form, although the hybrid tea form of some of the modern varieties is delightful. As masses of flowers over the longest possible period are the objective, pruning must vary in severity between the different types of wood on the same plant, to ensure a succession of colour. The new basal growths of the previous season are merely tipped, and these will provide the earliest flowers. Laterals of last season's growth are cut back half way, while older wood, including that which has not borne a flowering lateral in the previous season, is cut back hard to within two or three eyes from the base. Thus, the rule to follow with established floribundas is to spare the young wood almost entirely and to be progressively more severe with older wood.

Polyantha Pompons

This old group has been largely superseded by the modern floribundas, which are of better form and have a wider colour range. A few of them are still grown, and the most convenient way of pruning them for bedding is to cut them down to within a few inches of the base each year. If lightly pruned they can be grown as small specimen shrubs. Examples are Paul Crampel, Coral Cluster and Eblouissant.

Wichuraiana Ramblers

These are the old ramblers with very long, pliable canes which were so popular before the Second World War, such as Dorothy Perkins and Excelsa. They provide one lavish display in summer for about three weeks and then concentrate on producing numerous new canes from the base for flowering in the following season. The best and simplest treatment is to cut away all the canes which have flowered as soon as possible after flowering and to tie in as many of the new canes as are needed to fill the available space. If it should happen on a dry soil that insufficient new canes are produced, one or two of the canes that have flowered may be retained for one more season, but all the laterals must be cut back to 2 or 3 in. from the main stem.

Wichuraiana Climbers

These are hybrid Wichuraianas of stiffer growth than the true ramblers, which do not renew themselves completely from the base each year. Instead, new wood is often produced from part way up the older wood, so it is not practicable to cut out all the older wood. The new growths are all retained and any older wood which can be spared is cut out. Paul's Scarlet Climber, Albéric Barbier and Chaplin's Pink Climber are typical varieties.

Repeat-flowering Climbers

These bear flowers, both on the laterals and on new wood, in the same season. Little pruning is necessary except to avoid over-crowding, to remove dead and twiggy wood and to cut back old laterals to within two or three eyes from the main stem. They are mostly grown as pillar roses and it is advisable to train the main growths spirally in one direction only round the pillar or tripod, to induce the lower eyes to break into growth and to avoid any tendency towards bareness at the base. Examples are Golden Showers, Parade, Casino and the Kordesii climbers.

Climbing Sports of Bush Hybrid Teas and Floribundas

It has already been explained why these should not be pruned in the first spring after planting. Pruning should be as sparing as

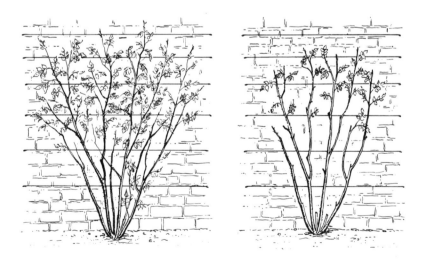

Figure 11. A stiff-stemmed climbing rose on a wall; before and after pruning

possible in subsequent years, being confined to the removal of dead or decadent wood and the shortening of lateral growths on the older canes to within two or three eyes from the main stem, according to their strength. Flowers are borne on laterals or sub-laterals (which are side shoots from the laterals), and free use of the knife or secateurs will only encourage rank new growth at the expense of flowers.

Horizontal training is recommended as quite the best method of inducing flowering laterals, either by tying down the growths to horizontal wires or tying down the tips of the growths to bamboo canes. This is directed towards checking the upward flow of sap which, otherwise, would merely force the few eyes at the extremities of the main stems into growth.

Varieties in this group give better results if they are fan-trained on a wall or a close-boarded fence rather than planted as single upright pillars. Examples are Cl. Shot Silk, Cl. Mrs Sam McGredy and Cl. Etoile de Hollande.

Shrub and Hedging Roses

These form a heterogeneous group, embracing such distinct types as the hybrid Rugosas, so-called hybrid musks, floribunda shrubs, many of the old garden roses, together with some semi-climbers and the strongest of the modern hybrid teas and floribundas. Grown as specimen shrubs or hedges they do not require much pruning beyond keeping them shapely, removing any exhausted or overcrowded wood and perhaps occasionally cutting back a main growth to within 12–18 in. from the ground to produce some colour lower down. Many varieties, including the famous Peace, pruned with discretion, will make a hedge of great beauty which may grow to some 5 or 6 ft in height.

Miniature Roses

These tiny hybrids, mainly descended from *R. chinensis minima,* need little pruning beyond trimming them into shape to avoid them becoming straggly, and cutting out some of the thinnest shoots to prevent overcrowding. It is usually more convenient to use a sharp pair of scissors rather than rose pruners for this work. They should not be allowed to grow out of character, as sometimes happens when they are budded on rootstocks instead of being grown on their own roots.

Figure 12. A standard hybrid tea before and after pruning

Upright Standards of Hybrid Teas and Floribundas

Standard roses, i.e. those grown on a standard stem, are normally pruned somewhat less severely than the same variety in bush form. The most important point is to build up a well-balanced head, which is not always as easy as it may sound. With double-budded standard roses, one bud may grow less vigorously than the other, resulting in a rather lop-sided head. The aim then will be to induce more vigorous growth on the weaker side by pruning back to stouter wood. The head should be thinned by removing weaker shoots entirely, as overcrowding must be avoided. With spreading varieties such as Josephine Bruce, it may be necessary to prune to an upward-facing eye to keep the head within bounds.

Weeping Standards

These will be treated in the same way as the same varieties grown as Wichuraiana ramblers. The canes which have flowered will be cut out if they can be spared, to allow space for the new canes developing from the unions. If, on a poor soil, or in a dry season,

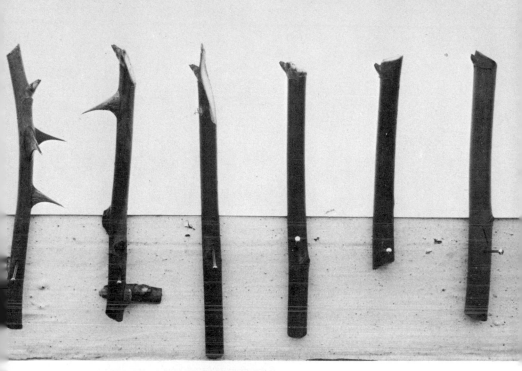

Above: Examples of good and bad pruning cuts. Left to right: Too far above bud; undercutting and damaging bud; jagged cut, again undercutting bud; cut too flat and too near bud; cut sloping wrong way; correct cut, sloping away from bud

Left: Lightly pruned hybrid tea roses. Generally speaking, the stronger growing roses are pruned less severely than those of moderate growth

Top: Kronenbourg (H.T.)
Bottom: Bettina (H.T.)

insufficient new canes are produced, one or two of the flowered canes may be retained, and the laterals all cut back to two or three eyes. These will produce flowers in the following season, but should then be discarded.

It will be observed from the foregoing details that light pruning or even little or no pruning is advised in certain circumstances and for certain groups. In the main this applies to growing on light, hungry soils or to groups which resent hard pruning, such as many yellow hybrid teas, the climbing sports of hybrid teas and floribundas and the repeat-flowering climbers generally. Climbers of this type should be trained rather than pruned.

Practical Tips

Finally, here are a few practical tips. If possible, choose a fairly cold day for pruning, to reduce sap loss by bleeding, but do not prune during severe frosts, otherwise there is a risk of the pith of the exposed surface being damaged. Always make a clean cut on the slant, just above an eye pointing outwards, and avoid leaving a snag above the eye, as this will die back. Keep the centre of the plant open, to allow a free circulation of air between the shoots, growth being outward and upwards. Gather up the prunings and burn them as soon as possible, as some of them may be diseased.

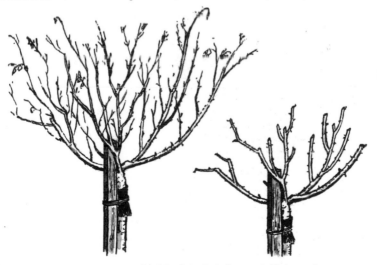

Figure 13. A standard floribunda before and after pruning

Most important, do not be afraid to vary your pruning to take account of the weather of the previous season. Thus, following a very wet season it is advisable to prune more severely than usual, as the wood will tend to be softer and unripe.

TRAINING AS OPPOSED TO PRUNING

An alternative to pruning for very vigorous varieties which produce strong canes 4 or 5 ft. long is pegging down.

Each of these strong canes is carefully bent over to form an arc and the tip is tied to a peg driven firmly into the soil. These arcs extend in several directions like the spokes of a wheel with the plant as the hub. The result of bending over is to force the eyes all along the length of these canes into growth, rewarding the grower with a wonderful flowering display. At the end of the season the pegged-down canes are cut out and the new canes of the current season's growth are pegged down to provide next season's display. This method can be adopted with varieties such as Hugh Dickson, Frau Karl Druschki, Uncle Walter, the Pemberton so-called hybrid musks such as Penelope, Cornelia and Prosperity, and many other strong-growing semi-climbers, such as Zéphirine Drouhin and its paler pink sport Kathleen Harrop.

8

Feeding and Mulching

Feeding your roses – Getting the best-out of them – The importance of watering – Feeding by mulches and topdressings – Liquid feeding – Foliar feeding – Feeding problem soils – Neutralising effects of intensive feeding – Sewage composts – Animal manures – Hop manure and leafmould

Roses are sometimes referred to as 'gross feeders', whatever this term may signify. Like other garden subjects, they will amply repay generous treatment with stronger growth, larger flowers of richer colouring and extra petallage, and abundant foliage. If the beds have been thoroughly prepared before planting, and liberal quantities of the peat and bonemeal planting mixture thrown between and over the roots during planting, it is not necessary to feed during the first season, although care should be taken to ensure that the roots never suffer from dryness. Provided that the soil is perfectly drained, roses can hardly have too much water on the roots, but it should be kept off the foliage and flowers in areas troubled with black spot.

Those who are keen on hosing their rose beds should remember that the more water is applied to the surface, the more danger there is of soluble nutrients being leached out of the soil or out of reach of the roots.

Time to Apply Fertilisers

Most keen amateur growers follow a definite pattern of feeding, which usually combines the use of organic and inorganic fertilisers in both solid and liquid form. The slow-acting fertilisers are usually applied before growth starts early in the year, and a dressing of meat and bone meal (3 oz. per sq. yd.)* and coarse-grade hoof and horn meal (1 oz. per sq. yd.) applied to the beds in early February

* This is not always readily available in small quantities and sterilised bonemeal may be used instead.

will release their nutrients slowly during the growing season. Immediately after pruning is a popular time for applying a reliable compound rose fertiliser such as Tonks', which is prepared to a standard formula based originally on the analysis of the ashes of an entire rose plant after burning it in a crucible.

Method of Application

A dressing applied then, usually at the rate of 2 oz. per sq. yd., may be pricked into the surface with a border fork and thus combines two operations – pricking over the beds after pruning and transferring some of the fertiliser below the surface. This pricking over should not disturb the soil other than superficially, i.e. not penetrating more than the top inch or two. Any deeper cultivation involves the risk of tearing the fine feeding roots which often lie just below the surface, especially in beds which are regularly mulched with animal manures, compost or peat. It is folly to dig deeply between the roses with a spade, as this must cut through large numbers of the fibrous roots, and probably one or two of the anchoring roots as well.

Mulching

It is an excellent plan to apply a mulch of well-rotted animal manure, compost or peat to the rose beds in spring. This should be at least 2 in. thick. It is a mistake to leave its application over until the new rose shoots are well developed, as it is then almost an impossible task to spread it without breaking a lot of brittle new shoots. On the other hand, if it is applied too early it tends to slow down the warming up of the soil. Probably the best compromise is to apply it about the middle or the third week of April. If garden compost or granulated peat is used, in the absence of animal manure, it is advisable to apply a dressing of compound rose fertiliser to the beds first, as neither of these materials contain the nutrients of animal manures.

Inorganic Fertilisers

Some amateurs like to mix their own compound rose fertiliser and it is usually cheaper to do this than to buy a proprietary brand. One which I have used for many years and have found satisfactory is as set out below. All parts are by weight:

16 parts superphosphate of lime
10 parts sulphate of potash

5 parts sulphate of ammonia
2 parts sulphate of iron
2 parts sulphate of magnesium

The ingredients should be mixed very thoroughly and any lumps crushed. It is better to store the various ingredients separately and not to mix them until immediately before application. Sprinkle about a tablespoonful round each plant, taking care not to drop any on the leaves or stems. Further dressings may be applied at intervals of three or four weeks, but not later than the end of July. If the soil is dry, water it in well. In applying inorganic fertilisers it is important to sprinkle them evenly over the soil where the feeding roots are likely to be. Normally this will be not less than 6 in. from the base of established plants.

Weathered soot, if obtainable in a dry state, is useful for applying to the surface of the rose beds in the spring. Its value lies not only in the ammonia content, but also in darkening the colour of the soil and thereby hastening the warming-up process, as dark soil absorbs the sun's heat better than light soil.

Liquid Fertilisers

Weak soot water, prepared by suspending a bag of soot in a barrel of rain water and diluting the liquid well before application, is a useful nitrogenous liquid feed applied every fortnight from the stage when the flower buds become visible. So also is soluble blood, diluted according to instructions: and nitrate of potash, applied at a strength not exceeding 1 oz. in 1 gal. of soft water. This is better balanced, as it provides both nitrogen and potash. The keen exhibitor will also use manure water, diluted so that it is no deeper than a pale straw colour, when the buds are swelling.

One of the most important rules to remember when applying such fertilisers is to use them very weak. It may be tempting to assume that something twice as strong will do twice as much good, but things do not work out this way. At the first sign of yellowing of the foliage, liquid feeding should be discontinued and the beds should be soaked with pure water, to dilute the too-high concentration of nutrients in the soil.

Always make sure that the soil is moist before applying liquid fertilisers – it is a great mistake to apply them to a dry soil. More harm is probably done by over-feeding than by under-feeding; provided that a mulch of organic material has been applied to the beds in the spring, with two or three light dressings of a reliable rose fertiliser later, there is really no need for the intensive liquid feeding which the keen exhibitor sometimes seems to consider essential.

Nutrients Required

Whatever method of feeding is selected, it will be realised that basically these are all variants on the standard theme of adding nitrogen, phosphorus and potash to the soil, plus a number of trace elements. Normally, proprietary compound fertilisers indicate the percentages of these elements by analysis, and it is wise to avoid those which are high in nitrogen, as this stimulates soft growth which falls an early victim to mildew and other rose diseases. Phosphate salts encourage root growth while potash is valuable for improving the colour and substance of the petals and for ripening the growth.

Bearing in mind that next season's blooms depend on hard, ripe wood being produced this season, it is a useful rule never to apply fertilisers which stimulate growth after the end of July. On the other hand, a dressing of sulphate of potash at the rate of 2 oz. per sq. yd. towards the end of August, or earlier in an abnormally wet season, will assist the ripening of the wood. It should be noted particularly that applications of potash are safest in the form of sulphate of potash – muriate of potash contains impurities which can be harmful to roses.

Organic Manures and Fertilisers

It is a sound rule to use organic manures whenever possible, as these will improve the structure of the soil in addition to containing valuable nutrients. If animal manures are not obtainable, bulk must still be added in the form of garden compost, granulated peat, spent hops, leafmould or old mushroom compost. As the last named contains granulated chalk, it should not be applied to calcareous soils nor to those which are neutral, or nearly so.

This does not mean that inorganic fertilisers should be avoided – as already outlined they play a very valuable part in the feeding of roses, and have the advantage over most organic manures of being quick acting and thus useful for application during the growing season as extra stimulants. Organic manures, on the other hand, are relatively slow acting and release their food value gradually over the season. For this reason, apart from the spring mulch which serves the dual purpose of keeping the roots cool and conserving moisture, as well as providing a weak stimulant during heavy rain, most organic manures are normally applied before growth starts for the season. There are exceptions, such as dried blood, which is applied during the growing season, as it is relatively quick acting.

Organic and Inorganic Fertilisers

Some minerals may be applied in either organic or inorganic form, and the following table may be of some assistance to the novice:

MINERAL	ORGANIC	INORGANIC
Nitrogen	Dried blood Meat and bone Hoof and horn Fish meal	Nitro-chalk Nitrate of potash
Phosphorus	Bonemeal Meat and bone	Superphosphate of lime Basic slag
Potassium	Fish meal	Sulphate of potash Nitrate of potash
Calcium	Meat and bone Fish meal	Ground chalk Gypsum Nitro-chalk Magnesium limestone Basic slag

Foliar Feeding

In recent years there has been quite a fuss made about foliar feeding. Some rose growers are enthusiastic about it and claim wonderful results, but on normal soils it seems to me that it involves a great deal of labour in spraying the nutrient solution on to the foliage, with much of it falling on the soil, when substantially the same results can be obtained far more easily by applying the liquid feed to the soil in the first place. Admittedly there may be instances of trace element deficiencies – say magnesium – when quicker results may be seen by spraying a solution of sulphate of magnesium (commercial Epsom salts) at 1 oz. per gal. of soft water on the foliage and stems. In the case of chalk soils, too, where iron deficiency and lime-induced chlorosis can be difficult problems, it may sometimes be advantageous to spray the foliage with sulphate of iron in solution. But with the use of iron sequestrenes and chelates, which contain iron in such a form that it is made available to the plant despite the calcium present in the soil, even this does not provide a very convincing case for foliar feeding as such.

It may be that, living as I do in a very bad area for black spot and rust, I have a deep-rooted distrust of sprays, other than fungicides, which keep the rose foliage wet for long enough at summer temperatures for the spores of these diseases to germinate. Or it may be that, after several very wet seasons, having found it virtually impossible to keep the foliage of my roses protected against these diseases by preventive spraying – as heavy showers have washed off the fungicide almost as soon as it has been applied – I am rather sceptical about the value of trying to induce nutrient solutions to adhere to the foliage long enough to have any beneficial effect. I think this is a matter which each grower must decide for himself, weighing the possible advantages of foliar feeding against the additional labour involved, which is often badly needed elsewhere in the garden.

Liquid Feeding and its Effects

Any rose grower who goes in for liquid feeding his roses over many weeks of the season – say from early May to the end of July – may find it advisable at the end of the season to test his soil for excess acidity. This is because nowhere near all the liquid feed applied to the soil is taken up by the root tips. As many of these feeds have an acid reaction, there is a possibility of excess acidity building up. Much, of course, will depend on the rainfall and the original pH value of the soil; in a wet season most of this excess acidity will probably be leached away. Even so, it is a wise precaution to make some tests with a simple home soil-testing outfit and, if found necessary, to apply a dressing of ground limestone or magnesium limestone to the beds at 3 or 4 oz. per sq. yd. in November or December. This may be left on the surface for the winter rains to wash down to the roots. Dressings of this type should not be applied to excess – it should be borne in mind that it is still desirable for the soil to have a slightly acid reaction, say a pH not above 6·5, after the corrective has done its work. In practice it may be found that a dressing of ground limestone is necessary only every other year, and if supplies of dry wood ash are available, it will be beneficial to apply a dressing to the beds, up to 6 oz. per sq. yd., in late autumn of the year when calcium is not used. This could be pricked in at the same time as the remains of the spring mulch.

Bulky Organic Manures

Questions are sometimes raised regarding the advisability of using sewage composts in rose beds. Some local authorities with modern

Above: A typical bush rose before pruning. *Below left:* Removing unwanted wood completely. *Below right:* The bush after pruning

Opposite: Blessings (H.T.)
Top: Tradition (H.T.)
Bottom: Grandpa Dickson (H.T.)

Above: A hybrid musk rose before pruning
Left: Pruning almost completed. Much old wood has been removed in its entirety

specialised plant are now turning out a compost prepared from a proportion of sewage and vegetable matter collected by the household refuse collection department of the local Council, and this product resembles peat in appearance, with a slightly gritty texture and no objectionable smell. Such town composts may be used freely, both in making and feeding rose beds and I have used them with good results. But as they are low in food value they need supplementing with a compound rose fertiliser. Their main value lies in adding humus to the soil, and at a time when farmyard manure is becoming increasingly difficult to get, they are well worth trying.

It may be only of academic importance to the town and suburban rose grower to discuss the respective merits of the various animal manures. For those fortunate people who are still able to obtain supplies, and who, moreover, are able to exercise a choice, farmyard manure is generally preferable on a light or medium soil, and stable manure on a heavy clay soil. Pig manure is also valuable if it is well rotted, but poultry manure is too high in nitrogen to form a well-balanced manure. I have found it better to use it in its dried and ground form, mixed with granulated peat, as a light topdressing during the growing season. I once made the mistake of taking delivery of a large lorry load of turkey manure, but never again! It smelled to high heaven for weeks after it had been spread on the beds, despite liberal hosing. I wish I could say that it produced the most wonderful specimen blooms as compensation, but apart from pained expressions on the neighbours' faces, I cannot honestly say that it produced anything out of the ordinary.

Nor have I had any very favourable experience of fortified hop manure – not because this is not a valuable addition to most soils, but because of the very light and flaky texture of this material when applied as a mulch. With an extremely industrious blackbird and thrush population scattering the mulch almost continuously, I have come to the conclusion that this needs to be anchored with netting for it to have any opportunity to do the roses much good, although no doubt the lawn derives some benefit!

Some years ago I used to obtain old leafmould from woods and spread it over the rose beds. Used in conjunction with a reliable compound rose fertiliser this gave good results. It also yielded crops of oak, beech, yew, ash and other seedlings, which can be a source of embarrassment in the rose beds unless they are spotted and dealt with in the very early stages.

9

Aftercare

Looking after your roses – Special requirements during first season – Subsequent requirements – Mulching or hoeing – Spraying routines against diseases in districts with pure air – Spraying against pests – Disbudding – Removing dead blooms and trusses – Summer thinning and de-shooting – Cutting flowers for the house and for exhibition – Removal of suckers – Tying in new growth of pillar and climbing roses

It is not enough to plant your roses carefully and then to leave them to fend for themselves. Particularly during the first season, it is necessary to be satisfied that they are becoming established in their new quarters, and the evidence of this may be seen in the type of growth produced. If new strong basal growths start pushing up after the first flowers have faded, this is a very welcome sign that all is well. If, on the other hand, little or no new wood is being made, the grower should check that he has done everything possible to give the plants a flying start.

Encouraging New Growth
Sometimes there may be a dry spell in May, with cold east winds and perhaps frosts at night which give the young growths a scorched or shrivelled appearance. While there is little that can be done about May frosts, the plants should be firmed by treading over the roots near the stems, especially when, due to a wet winter, planting may not have been done as firmly as could have been desired. Unless there is firm contact between roots and soil, the growth will be unsatisfactory and may not appear at all in extreme cases, although the stems may remain green. If a plant does not start into growth normally, the soil around the stems should be trodden firmly and then at least 2 gal. of tepid water applied, to give the roots a soaking. If this does not start the plant into growth after 10 days or so, examine the stems carefully. If the bark is shrivelled, this might indicate frost

90

or other damage, and the stems should be cut back further until sound wood is reached. On the other hand, if the wood is plump and green and the pith white, give it a chance to start into growth. Where the wood looks unhealthy and a cross-section of the stem shows the pith to be discoloured, the likelihood is that there has been frost damage during the winter, and it is advisable to cut the stems down lower into healthy wood. Any wood which dies back from the pruning cut should also be removed before this travels further down the stem.

Watering

Dryness at the roots is the biggest single hazard with roses in their first season after transplanting. Even if the bed has been covered with a mulch of peat or compost it is advisable to water the surface thoroughly during any dry spells. The roots must be encouraged to

Figure 14. *Left:* De-shooting in spring. Only the strongest shoot should be left to develop from just below the pruning cut. Any others from the same point should be removed as early as possible. *Right:* De-shooting in summer. Pinching out any side shoots which appear before the terminal flower bud has opened will allow a finer bloom to develop and avoid overcrowding of the plant

Figure 15. Disbudding for exhibition. All side buds are pinched out as soon as they are large enough to handle without damaging the centre bud. (For clarity the buds are shown larger than they would be at normal time of removal)

establish themselves as quickly as possible, and provided that drainage is above reproach – and roses should not be planted unless it is – it is hardly possible to give them too much water during the settling-in period.

Multiple shoots will sometimes develop from the eye just below the pruning cut and it is advisable to limit these to one shoot only from each eye. This should be the strongest – normally the centre one of three, the two outer shoots being removed as soon as they are large enough to handle without damaging the one selected to remain. By using the point of the blade of a sharp pocket knife it is quite easy to remove the unwanted shoots while they are still very small.

No Cutting in the First Season

It is important to keep the plants growing and to ensure that every healthy leaf is left on the plant. This means that on no account should flowers be cut for house decoration or – worse still – for exhibition during the first season. This would deprive the plants of valuable leaves and retard their establishment. Disbudding will be advisable also, to reduce the strain on the root system of having to support numerous flowers, and faded flowers should merely be snapped off with an inch or so of the footstalk.

Pests and Diseases

In view of the importance of retaining all the leaves intact, a sharp lookout for any disfiguring diseases and insect pests is necessary. Caterpillars will quickly eat their way through a substantial part of the leaf area unless spraying with appropriate insecticides is undertaken in the early stages. Similarly, mildew, and also black spot in pure-air districts, may break out, and it is essential to spray with the recommended fungicides at the first sign of an attack. In fact, preventive spraying of the foliage is the only effective way of controlling black spot in districts which are prone to this disfiguring disease. This and other diseases are dealt with in the following chapter, but while on the subject of spraying, it is appropriate to mention here that efficient spraying equipment is indispensable to the keen amateur rose grower. It is false economy to buy the cheapest possible spray as, in the ordinary way, it will be brought into use perhaps at least a dozen times in an average season, even in built-up areas which are not susceptible to black spot attacks.

Spraying

All but those with only two or three dozen plants will find it an advantage to have a continuous-action sprayer—so much quicker and easier than the old-fashioned barrel and plunger type. Alternative nozzle ends should be available to enable either a coarse, drenching spray or a fine, mist-like effect to be achieved as required, according to the fungicide or insecticide being applied. The beginner is advised not to hold the nozzle end too close to the foliage when spraying – a safer and more effective coverage is obtained by standing a little distance away. He is also reminded that it is necessary to spray both the upper and under surfaces of the leaves – it is not enough to wet the upper surface thoroughly, as a heavy shower soon after spraying could largely undo the good work. By spraying underneath and using a bend attachment to enable this to be done easily, the spray is likely to be far more effective, especially if a little liquid soap is added to improve its powers of adhesion.

Quite often novices complain that a particular fungicide or insecticide has scorched the foliage on their roses. This may sometimes happen when spraying tender young foliage early in the season – say in late April or May, even though the maker's instructions may have been followed meticulously. The damage may be due to insufficient mixing of the liquid after dilution, or it could be caused by the sun shining on the wet leaves afterwards. Another possibility is that there may be some soil deficiency which renders

Figure 16. Types of continuous-action sprayer. *Top:* a bucket-type sprayer with extension lance. *Left and inset:* knapsack sprayer and its method of use. *Centre right:* a pressure hand sprayer

the foliage susceptible to spray damage, and there are some varieties with foliage somewhat sensitive to some sprays. A wise precaution is to mix the spray at half the recommended strength only for the first two or three occasions, while the foliage is maturing, to avoid possible damage. Furthermore, spraying should always be undertaken during the evening, when the sun has lost its strength and there is all night for the foliage to dry off to reduce the possibility of scorching.

Frost Damage

Late frosts can do a lot of damage to young shoots, and in some low-lying gardens this may be widespread nearly every spring. Late pruning is no answer, as there have been severe frosts as late as the third week in May in recent years. Making sure that each shoot is pruned to a dormant eye will help, but frosts in May can cripple growths starting even from dormant eyes. Many beginners have difficulty in recognising frost damage. Depending on its severity, it may take the form of shrivelled young shoots, with the edges and patches on the leaves turned brown and brittle. In the case of frosts occurring late in May when the flower buds may be well developed, the bud, shoot and foliage may be blackened and limp, with the bud pulpy to the touch instead of firm. If left on the plants these buds develop into malformed flowers, with full-petalled varieties showing perhaps only one or two rows of petals, and these often blackened or otherwise discoloured. Growths should develop naturally from lower down the stems, so there is no need to cut back the damaged shoots at this stage, but inevitably flowering will be delayed for several weeks.

Suckers

Suckers are sometimes a source of great perplexity to beginners. These are wild growths which spring from the rootstock and, if allowed to develop, they will divert the sap from the cultivated rose. It is vital to be absolutely ruthless with these sucker growths; they should be traced down to their point of origin, either on the main stem below the budding point or on the root system, and should then be pulled off. If cut, there is a danger of them re-appearing in greater numbers.

Some beginners and others with some years of experience seem to have difficulty in distinguishing between suckers and new basal shoots of the cultivated rose. If they will compare the colour of the wood and prickles, and the size, shape and colour of the leaves with those of the cultivated variety, they will find that they are easily distinguishable. Whether the rootstock used is *R. canina*, *R. multiflora japonica* or *R. rugosa*, the leaves will be found to be narrower, a paler green and usually with more numerous leaflets. *R. rugosa* in particular has leaflets with rounded ends, deeply veined (rugose) and a light green colour, carried on extremely prickly stems, with long narrow bristles all round them. The stems of *R. multiflora japonica* are normally slender and arching, with pairs of black prickles just below each leaf on the thorned variety (there is also a thornless variety sometimes used). Most of the trouble from suckering will come from plants budded on *R. canina* and from standards budded on Rugosa stems. Occasionally one has a troublesome plant which seems to devote its entire energies to suckering. If it is not too old, it is sometimes worthwhile lifting such a plant, removing all suckers very carefully by hand and re-planting rather shallowly in fresh soil. Sometimes it is suggested that injuries to the roots, such as might be caused during deep hoeing, may cause a plant to sucker, and in the case of rootstocks prepared from cuttings, failure to cut out all the eyes below the ground may lead to suckering. In the case of seedling rootstocks, suckers can arise from adventitious eyes on the root system. Declining vigour in the cultivated rose or scion also seems to make it necessary for the more vigorous alien root system to find an outlet or safety valve in suckering.

In the case of Rugosa standard stems, too-deep planting or inadequate staking will often be contributory causes. Even so, as the natural habit of the Rugosas is to spread by sending out suckers just below the surface, even with the strongest of staking and the shallowest of planting, suckers are always liable to develop and must be the subject of the utmost vigilance. They will appear anywhere on the Rugosa stem below the head, or anywhere on the extensive fibrous root system underground. They will sometimes emerge a yard or 6 ft. away from the parent stem, and may not be associated with it in the mind of the unwary. Unless they are traced to their point of origin – a trowel is useful for this detective work – and pulled off, they will soon deprive the cultivated rose head of nourishment and cause it to weaken and ultimately die. There must be many thousands of strong Rugosa bushes up and down the country,

Duke of Windsor (H.T.)

Left: The head of a
weeping standard after
pruning
Centre: Pegged down
roses, a form of training
suitable for very vigorous
varieties. Such training
provides a mass of colour
when the plants are in
flower
Bottom: The rambler
New Dawn trained over a
low wall. Note how the
growths have been spaced
out evenly

bearing their easily recognisable magenta-pink single flowers, followed by tomato-like heps, which started as stems of Rugosa standards but, through ignorance or neglect, were allowed to starve the cultivated head and take undisputed possession. One can sometimes come across them flourishing on waste land which used to be under cultivation as a garden.

Basal Shoots

Just as it is vital to remove suckers in the early stages, so it is essential to preserve and encourage new basal shoots of the cultivated variety. These are, indeed, 'succours', endowing the rose plant with renewed vigour and vitality. I have come across amateurs who have made a point of removing these under the mistaken impression that they are suckers, because they look different. It is tragic that such mistakes should be made. New basal growths in shades of red, crimson, bronze and russet are almost certain to belong to the cultivated variety if the leaflets are broad or rounded. The old belief that anything with seven leaflets is a sucker and anything with five leaflets is a cultivated rose is unreliable, as many varieties under favourable conditions will produce seven leaflets. A leaf comprising nine leaflets, though, is pretty certain to belong to a sucker if it appears among hybrid teas. The only infallible test is to trace the doubtful basal shoot to its source; if this is below the budding point, from which all the mature top growth emerges, then it must be a sucker. In case of any doubt, leave it a few days until you are certain, but do not forget about it.

Weeds

There used to be a widely held belief that keeping the hoe going was of great benefit to roses and one of the indispensable concomitants of success. The theory was that this disturbance of the top few inches of soil conserved moisture by, in effect, maintaining a surface mulch of loose soil, thereby reducing losses by evaporation. Today, it is felt that the main benefit from hoeing is to keep down the weeds – which in itself may be said to be conserving soil moisture which otherwise might have been lost by transpiration losses through the weed leaves – but, apart from this, mulching is probably equally beneficial and involves less labour. It is not every type of soil which lends itself to hoeing, either on flinty land and on some heavy soils I find that a small border fork is a much more practical tool.

Whether a hoe or a border fork is preferred it is obviously necessary to combat weeds in the rose beds as a matter of routine. Not only do these look untidy but, as already stated, they draw on the reserves of moisture, deprive the roses of light and air, and sometimes act as host plants for various insect pests. Ideally, of course, the weeds should be dealt with in the seedling stage, before there are such problems as deep tap roots and underground runners to contend with. But there must be few gardens of any size without some perennial weeds, such as docks, thistles, nettles, bindweed and ground elder. These are a very real problem when they become established among permanent plantings such as rose beds and borders. Although I have all of these to cope with I find that the bindweed and ground elder are particularly troublesome and cannot be dealt with really satisfactorily without lifting the roses. At one time I went to the lengths of unwinding the bines of the bindweed and dropping them in a jar half full of brushwood killer, which I would sink half in the soil to avoid it being overturned. Docks have a nasty habit of springing up just behind the main stem of a rose plant, in the one spot where it is almost impossible to uproot them intact without disturbing the rose roots. Annual weeds are no serious problem – it is the persistent perennial weeds which are a burden, and I am sorry to say that I have not found that paraquat-based weedkillers do much to lighten this burden, at least in my garden. My experience has been that they merely discourage the top growth for a few weeks, but do not kill and are therefore not a long-term solution.

De-shooting

Summer thinning and de-shooting are sometimes advantageous and are practised as a matter of routine by the keen exhibitor (see p. 130). It will often be found that, long before the terminal bud on a shoot has opened, side shoots will start into growth part way down the stem, and unless these are pinched out as soon as they are large enough to handle, the flow of sap to the terminal bud will be slowed down. In any case, unless these side shoots are thinned out, the plant will become a tangle of dense growth by the end of the season, most of which will have to be cut away when pruning the following spring. How much more sensible, then, to conserve this energy or to channel it where it will serve the plant best, by pinching out the unwanted side shoots in the first place. Usually all but one of these laterals should be pinched out and the main stem cut back to just above the one that has been allowed to remain when removing the faded terminal flower. Similar remarks apply to pinching or rubbing out new shoots which grow towards the centre of the plant. It is far better not to allow these to develop than to cut them right out later on when they have matured.

Removal of Faded Flowers
The removal of faded flowers from established plants is a subject well worth a little consideration. The procedure of merely snapping off the flower head, which is recommended for the first season after planting, need not be followed when dealing with established plants. The advice is sometimes given to cut the faded flower with a good length of stem, so that an equally fine flower can develop in succession to the first one. This is no doubt sound advice for the grower who insists on having his roses on long stems, but it is not the way to obtain plenty of colour in the garden. There are two disadvantages attached to removing the old bloom with a long stem: first, the plant is being deprived of several leaves on each such stem, which must have a weakening effect. Second, the longer the stem is cut, the less mature will be the bud to which it is cut back and, in consequence, the longer will be the interval before the next flower. Where garden display is of greater importance than the highest quality individual blooms, I would recommend cutting back the stem of the faded flower no more than half way, thereby reducing the flowerless interval. In fact, a practice I have followed for some years now is merely to snap off the faded flower and then wait for the laterals to start into growth before selecting the strongest one to bear the next flower.

Cutting Flowers of Established Plants
When cutting flowers for exhibition or even for the house, some loss of foliage is of course inevitable. Stems should always be cut with sharp secateurs – not torn off at the junction with the main stem; always leave at least one dormant eye pointing in the right direction, to replace the stem which has been removed. This is in the interests of maintaining the symmetry of the plant. Because of the length of stem which has to be cut when exhibiting at leading shows, it is strongly recommended that no single plant be called upon to contribute more than one such stem in any one season. Otherwise,

it is so easy to spoil one's plants if the practice is carried to excess in the scramble for trophies. In cutting for the house it is possible to make do with a somewhat shorter stem, and where this will allow an extra leaf to be left on the plant, such a compromise is earnestly recommended and will yield dividends in the following season. Some growers seem to be more ruthless in cutting their plants when they are in full leaf than they are when pruning them in a period of dormancy, which is clearly illogical.

Balling

In spells of wet weather in summer there is a tendency for the outside petals of some varieties to cling together instead of opening normally. This produces an ugly hard-boiled egg appearance, and unless these petals are stripped off the flower will rot instead of opening. This 'balling', as it is called, is not a disease, but merely the effect of excessive rain on usually very full-petalled varieties, mostly hybrid teas, with petals of a papery substance. It does not happen with moderately full varieties which have petals of a thicker substance, although a few of the full-petalled floribundas, such as Spartan and some of her progeny, are subject to this trouble. The only remedy, from the exhibitor's point of view, is to use bloom protectors (see Chapter 13). For general garden display the removal of the offending outside petals will sometimes allow the flower to open if done carefully and early enough, but this would be too laborious except where comparatively few plants are involved. It is always a relief to remove these ugly balled blooms.

Sometimes bedding roses and climbers will set heps or seed pods, but the keen amateur will go to some trouble to remove these in the early stages. Once they have reached an advanced stage of development it is very difficult to obtain further flowers from the plants in the same season. So long as the faded flowers are removed and the plant has adequate food, moisture and a reasonable temperature, it will usually continue to produce new growth, and this in turn will bear flowers except, of course, in the case of those climbers and ramblers, shrub roses and species which are summer flowering only.

Tying in Climbing Types

In the case of newly-planted and established climbing types, it is desirable to tie in new basal shoots as they grow and before the wood has hardened. In this pliable state it is easy to train them spirally round single pillars or tripods, tying them in position so that the wood hardens as one wishes them to grow. By this method there will not be the accidents and frustration associated with trying to bend brittle, hard-wooded stems at a later stage, and there will be a rewarding and prolific crop of flowers from the many eyes which will have been forced into growth by this form of training. Even when the climbers are trained on walls or fences there is an advantage in tying down the new canes while the wood is still pliable – otherwise accidents can and do happen.

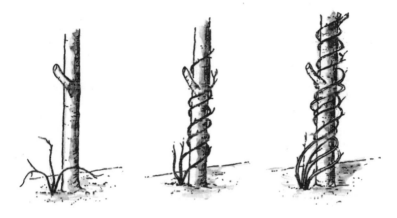

Figure 17. Training a single-pillar rose. *Left:* After planting, bend some of the shoots over to encourage new growth from the base. *Centre:* At the end of the first season, with new wood trained spirally in one direction only. *Right:* At the end of the second season. The canes are tied near the base of the pillar to avoid bareness

10

Pests and Diseases

Descriptions of individual pests and diseases of the rose and recommended control measures

INSECT PESTS

As soon as growth becomes rapid in the spring, under the impetus of milder weather conditions, insect pests seem to multiply alarmingly. Battle must be joined in earnest if they are to be prevented from ruining the display one has worked hard for through the stages of planting, pruning, weeding and general cultivation. A timely spray will often cope with an attack which, if left for a week or two, could become almost a plague.

It is well to bear in mind that not all insects are harmful to roses. Indeed, some are definitely beneficial, in that they prey on other insects which are properly regarded as pests. These predators include ladybirds and their slate-grey, yellow-spotted larvae shaped like tiny lizards, which feed on aphids, as well as the larvae of certain hover flies and of lacewing flies. It is an advantage to be able to recognise these predators, so as not to destroy them when going over the plants to remove a light infestation of aphids with the finger and thumb, which some amateurs do as a daily routine in early summer. Some other useful insects, such as the ichneumon fly, are parasites and deposit their eggs within the body of the host, whether aphid or caterpillar. The larvae live inside and feed on the body of the pest as internal parasites.

Some of the common pests of roses are referred to in the following paragraphs:

Aphids or Greenfly: There are several species of aphids which may be found on roses, and nearly everybody must be familiar with the colonies of these tiny insects which cluster beneath flower buds, on the growing tips of new shoots and on the underside of the leaves. They may be green, red, brownish or shining black, and are sap-suckers. It can be readily imagined how weakening it must be to have many hundreds of these creatures sucking the sap from a plant simultaneously.

While they have several natural enemies, such as sparrows and ladybirds, it is unwise to rely on these alone to avoid a large build-up in the population. As a by-product of sucking the sap from the plant, aphids deposit a sweet sticky fluid on the foliage called honeydew, representing sugar and other substances in excess of the insects' requirements. This may attract ants and flies, and it also sometimes has sooty mould growing on its surface.

Control. With a fine, mist-like spray, use a formulation of either malathion, gamma-BHC (lindane), derris or nicotine and repeat the spray after an interval of three days to deal with those aphids born after the first spraying. Make sure that the under surface of the leaves is treated as well as the upper surface, and follow the manufacturer's instructions exactly for mixing. As an alternative it may be desired to try a systemic insecticide. The term systemic means that the insecticide after being watered round the plant, is absorbed by the roots, whereupon the sap becomes poisonous to the aphids. A formulation of formothion could be tried in this form.

Capsid bugs: The green capsid bug does much more damage among roses than is commonly supposed. It is a bright metallic green, about ¼ in. long when fully grown, almost like a much enlarged aphis, but very much more active. It may be seen on the tips of shoots, usually sucking the sap from a young bud in the growing tip. If disturbed it either drops to the soil or hides under a leaf, moving very quickly. Leaves which have been attacked, apart from being punctured, have a curiously twisted and contorted appearance, caused by the capsid bug injecting a poison into the tissue, which often causes this to turn brown round the punctures. I have caught many of these pests between forefinger and thumb by approaching from behind, but a sudden snatch is necessary to be successful. Young buds which have been attacked turn brown and wither away. The pest attacks a wide range of plants, including blackcurrants.

Control. Spray the foliage, young growing tips and buds with gamma-BHC (lindane) or dust with pyrethrum early in the season, say, not later than mid-May in the south, and repeat the treatment about every 10 days or after heavy rain. Formerly the standard treatment was to spray the foliage and buds with wettable DDT, but recent research has indicated that the use of any insecticide which contains DDT, especially after the end of May, encourages attacks by the red spider mite. The Ministry of Agriculture have recommended that DDT should be used only where there is no effective and less persistent alternative. For this reason the use of DDT is not now recommended, especially in view of the increasing menace of the red spider mite on outdoor roses.

Caterpillars: By and large the caterpillars of quite a good number of butterflies and moths attack roses. As nearly all amateur growers will know, these are biting and chewing larvae which feed mainly on the leaves, but some of them will also attack the buds, including the sepals and the calyx. The shot-holed leaves are familiar to all, but some caterpillars feed on the edges of the leaves, when the damage may not be so conspicuous.

Control. In dealing with caterpillars in their widest sense, which includes the larvae of various moths, the most effective treatment is preventive, by spraying both surfaces of the leaves and also the stems, buds and growing points of young shoots with a protective coating of insecticide. Until very recently DDT emulsion was almost invariably recommended, but now that concern has been expressed officially about the persistence of this chemical, the alternative of trichlorphon is suggested for large outbreaks, repeating the spray after an interval of a few days. Where only a few bushes are affected, hand picking may be sufficient to control a localised attack. It is important not to neglect the warning signs of eaten foliage, as a severe attack may seriously weaken the plants, besides ruining the display.

Chafers: These beetles are largely a pest of the Home Counties, especially parts of rural Surrey with light soil. Four species may attack roses: (i) the cockchafer; (ii) the rose chafer; (iii) the garden chafer; and (iv) the summer chafer. The adults usually appear in May and June, attacking foliage, flower buds and open rose blooms. One-sided flowers may be the result of the garden chafer having attacked the other side at an earlier stage. The larvae of all four are large dirty white grubs about $1\frac{1}{2}$ in. long when fully grown, living in the soil and feeding on the roots of roses and other plants. The adult cockchafer – the largest of the four – may be recognised by its black head and reddish-brown wing cases with five raised lines on each. They fly at dusk from mid-May to early June and lay their eggs in the soil. The rose chafer is considerably smaller and has distinctive bright green wing cases and thorax. The adult appears from about the middle of May and damages the petals, anthers and leaves; its larvae devour young roots. Garden chafers, the smallest of the four, may reach ½ in. in length. The thorax is bluish-green and the wing cases reddish-brown. Unlike the other chafers the adults may be seen flying in bright sunshine during June; they feed on buds and open rose blooms as well as on other subjects. The summer chafer reaches about ⅔ in. in length and is reddish-brown, with a hairier body than the other chafers. Again, rose blooms figure in their diet.

Control. In areas where chafers are known to breed I would still favour spraying with a DDT emulsion to which pyrethrum has been added, as likely to prove the most effective control. If the grower feels strongly about using this extremely persistent insecticide, spraying with either derris or gamma-BHC might be tried.

Common garden frog-hopper or Cuckoo-spit insect: This pest can be easily identified by the spittle-like masses which may appear on the plants in June or thereabouts, often at the junction of the leaf and the stem, but also on the leaves themselves. Each mass contains a yellowish-green nymph and, as this is not active at this stage, it can be destroyed easily with the finger and thumb where there are only a few to be dealt with. The nymph sucks the sap of the young growth and leaves, and besides weakening the plant may cause the shoots or buds to wilt in cases of severe infestation. The adult is a very active, winged, frog-shaped insect, but does little damage.

Control. The nymph must be dealt with by spraying at high pressure with a contact spray to penetrate the spittle. Alternatively the spittle may be removed by spraying first with clean water and then following up with a contact spray, such as derris, gamma-BHC (lindane) or pyrethrum.

Gall wasps: Occasionally a curious ball of finely-divided, moss-like growth, with a reddish tinge, may be seen on a shoot of a cultivated rose. This is sometimes known as Robin's Pincushion, and is the nest of a gall wasp. Its presence seems to do little, if any, damage to the rose shoot on which it appears, and there is no need to take any remedial action. If objected to on the grounds of being unsightly the galls may be pulled off and burnt. They are much more commonly found on wild roses and their unusual appearance often provokes questions as to their nature and origin.

Leaf-cutting bees: These are very similar in appearance to normal hive bees. The female cuts semi-circular, clean-edged pieces out of the leaves for use in the brood cells of her nest. It is very difficult to do anything about this damage, which is seldom extensive. The only really effective control would be to seek out and destroy the nest, which may be in a rotting tree stump in the vicinity.

Rose leaf-hopper: This is a very small, pale yellow winged insect which sucks the sap and causes mottling to appear on the leaves during spring and summer. It can be identified by the presence of its white cast skins on the under surface of the leaves. The insect itself is very active, jumping high into the air when disturbed – hence its name.

Control. Contact sprays are only of limited value – a better control is to spray both surfaces of the leaves with malathion or gamma-BHC; alternatively a systemic insecticide, such as formothion, could be used to make the sap stream poisonous to the pest.

Sawfly, leaf-rolling: Although more than 20 species of sawfly attack roses in this country, it is necessary to know about only three of them. Probably the most destructive is the rose leaf-rolling sawfly, which lays its eggs in the margins of unfolding leaflets. At the same time it injects an irritant which causes the leaves to roll laterally downwards and inwards, thereby providing natural protection as well as food for the hatching larvae, which are pale yellowish-green and feed on the inside leaf tissue. They may move from one leaf to another, and late in the summer they descend to the soil where they pupate just below the soil surface. The adult female is black and shiny, not unlike a winged queen ant, and appears in May and early June to lay her eggs. The rolling of the leaves may check the plants badly as this substantially reduces the leaf area available for photo-synthesis.

Control. To be really effective, spraying should take place early in the season, before any rolling of the leaves has occurred, or at the first sign of rolling. Recent experiments suggest that trichlorphon may be the most effective spray, more so than gamma-BHC and malathion, and that it should be applied on at least three occasions between mid-May and mid-June, to both surfaces of the leaves.

Sawfly, rose slug: A shiny black fly, it appears from mid-May to mid-June and perhaps again in July and August. It lays its eggs in the edges of young leaves and, on hatching, the yellowish larvae feed on the leaves, eating the tissue and reducing them to a skeleton. On being fully fed they descend to the soil to construct cocoons in which they pupate.

Control. As for the rose leaf-rolling sawfly. The spray must be applied to both surfaces of the leaves.

Sawfly, shoot-borer: This sawfly lays its eggs in the growing tips of new rose shoots; on hatching, the larvae (pale brown in colour) bore down inside the shoot, feeding on the soft pith and thereby causing the tip of the shoot to wilt. Attacks are normally not widespread and damage is often restricted to only a few shoots.

Control. Pressing the affected shoot just below the wilting tip will often cause the grub to wriggle out backwards, when it may be dealt with quite easily.

Scale insects: The most common scale insect is the scurfy scale, which appears as flat, whitish scales on the shoots and stems. Eggs are laid during summer and the orange-coloured nymphs wander about freely for a time before starting to feed on the tissues of the stems by sucking the sap. Their bodies become gradually encrusted with a scaly structure, assuming a round or an elongated shape according to their sex.

Control. Spray with a formulation of malathion as soon as noticed.

Thrips or Thunder flies: These tiny pests cause most damage in hot dry spells. The most easily identifiable damage is along the margins of the petals, which become discoloured because of the action of the insect in breaking up the tissues and mashing them to a pulp for its food. They also attack the buds, leaves and young shoots, causing discoloration of the buds, mottling of the leaves and distortion of the young shoots. The adult is black or dark brown, seldom more than $\frac{1}{10}$ in. long, with two pairs of narrow wings. It overwinters under glass, in the crevices of bricks and woodwork and under the bark of old stems. The Ophelia group of roses is particularly susceptible to damage by thrips – and this includes Mme Butterfly, Lady Sylvia, Polly, Monique and Tiffany, as well as Ophelia herself.

Control. Spray the plants early in the season, from mid-May, paying particular attention to flower buds and young shoots, with a formulation of either derris, malathion or nicotine, and repeat at fortnightly intervals, or sooner on evidence of damage.

Tortrix moths or Rose maggots: These may be recognised by folded or rolled-over leaves, where the folding of the leaf is upwards, as distinct from downwards rolling by the leaf-rolling rose sawfly. The maggots feed from inside the rolled or folded leaves and are thus safe from contact sprays. The buds and flowers may also be injured, and the maggots are sometimes found in the bud between the sepals and the petals.

Control. A sharp lookout must be kept for the first rolled or folded-over leaves. Pressing these between the finger and thumb and then removing the leaf to save the labour of having to go through the same ritual again on future occasions is recommended. The leaves removed should be burnt. If this is done early enough in the season it should be possible to cope with a normal attack, but where large numbers of bushes have to be dealt with, nicotine dust applied at high air temperatures may be effective. Unfortunately the temperature has to be over 18°C. (65°F.) for the nicotine dust to volatilise, when the vapour will penetrate the folded or rolled-up leaves as nothing else will. It is not often that such high temperatures can be relied upon early enough in the season for this control to be effective, except in very favoured districts.

Four-footed rose pests: Apart from predatory insects, animals may do a lot of damage to roses. The worst, in my experience, are rabbits and moles. At one period the rabbits were so voracious in my garden that I had to surround my maiden rose plants with wire netting, 3 ft. high and sunk 9 in. below soil level – otherwise, they not only ate every new shoot, but often pulled the scion out at the union. Even now, after myxomatosis has reduced their numbers drastically, I still find it necessary to grow my established plants tall, to reduce the amount of damage. Apart from this, I have tried soaking small pieces of felt in rabbit repellent, and placing them between the stems at the base of newly-planted varieties. I have also tried enclosing entire beds with thick string tied to canes and soaked in repellent. This needs renewing periodically to remain effective.

Moles love to tunnel in newly-planted rose beds – sometimes they are so active that I am obliged to firm the roots daily. I have found the only effective control to be traps, set in the tunnels currently in use. I find the half-barrel type of trap fairly effective, but I do not pretend to eliminate the moles, only to keep down their numbers. It is advisable to wear gloves when setting the traps, to avoid the human taint, and to mark the site of each trap with a small stick which is easily recognisable. A popular mole run is along the extreme edge of a rose border, skirting the lawn; this raises the level of the soil and spoils the neat appearance of the lawn edging.

General: It is not suggested for a moment that all of the foregoing pests will be found in the one garden in the same season. Indeed, many amateurs may grow roses for years without having any pests to worry about, apart from a few greenfly and caterpillars now and then. The incidence of attack will vary from season to season, but apart from seasonal variations, the distance between the plants and methods of pruning may have a bearing on the degree of infestation, as well as the promptness with which control measures are taken in the early stages.

FUNGUS DISEASES

Black spot: Those resident in built-up or industrial areas seldom have much trouble with this disease, which flourishes in pure-air districts. I grew roses for 38 years in such areas without having any black spot at all – it is only since I moved to my present pure-air rural district that I have found this disease a serious problem. I am mentioning this because I am convinced that many thousands of amateur rose growers with gardens in built-up areas spend time and money quite needlessly spraying to protect their roses when conditions are such that the disease could not flourish in any case. It is believed that the sulphur and other impurities in the air are responsible for this state of affairs, which means that this disease should hold no terrors for the majority of amateur rose growers.

For those who do live in pure-air or fringe districts, the disease is characterised by the appearance on the leaves of black spots with fringed edges. These grow larger and eventually several of them may fuse together to form large and irregular-shaped patches. In the later stages the portions of the leaves between the spots turn yellow and the leaf falls prematurely – often as early as late July or early August. Where most, or all, of the leaves fall early, a further crop of leaves is usually produced from the shoot tips in the autumn, but the effort involved must weaken the plant.

Control. There is no cure for black spot as such – that is to say, once the black spots have appeared on a leaf, that particular leaf cannot be saved. The answer lies in controlling the spread of the disease by protective or preventive spraying, starting in April or early May in the south and continuing at fortnightly intervals throughout the season, renewing the protective spray more frequently after any heavy rain and applying it to both upper and lower surfaces of the leaves and to the stems. A formulation of either captan, maneb, zineb or ziram should be used. It is strongly recommended that special attention be given to spraying the lower leaves, as these are the first to be infected, the disease then spreading upwards to the younger leaves. As the spores remain active on leaves which have fallen, every effort should be made to collect and burn them as soon as possible.

When there has been a severe attack of black spot it is recommended that pruning be undertaken earlier than usual – say in December, and that afterwards the stems and the soil beneath the bushes should be sprayed with Bordeaux mixture, 1 gal. to 8 sq. yd. The plants should also be fed liberally in spring the following year to help them to overcome the debilitating effects of the disease. Finally, black spot should not be confused with purple spotting of the foliage, where the purple spots are much smaller, and do not have the characteristic fringed edges; they may be due to some lack of balance in the soil.

Canker: This can be caused either by wounds made by thorns, insects or implements, or by the breakdown of the tissue under the bark by unbalanced feeding. A sunken area is formed, brownish or purplish in colour, and the bark in the cankered area becomes cracked and loose and may be peeled off. The infected area becomes surrounded by a ridge of corky wound callus, and once the cankered area encircles the stem the latter will die, as the sap supply cannot extend beyond this point. Many cankers have fungi which invade the cracks in the stems but are not themselves the primary cause.

Control. There is no cure for cankered stems, which should be cut back cleanly below the lowest canker and burnt without delay. Prevention is the answer, by making all pruning cuts cleanly, with really sharp instruments, just above an eye, by careful use of cultivators, hoes, etc., to avoid physical damage, and by spraying against pests and diseases as necessary. It has been suggested that where cankers are numerous, calcium, magnesium and phosphate deficiency may be a cause. Ground chalk (4 oz. per sq. yd.) could be applied, together with superphosphate (1 oz. per sq. yd.) and sulphate of magnesium (commercial Epsom salts) at 1 oz. per sq. yd. The ground chalk needed will depend on the *p*H value of the soil and the recommended application of 4 oz. per sq. yd. is on the light side, as it is inadvisable to apply to excess.

Rose mildew: The only rose disease of much consequence which is common to all gardens, whether large or small, in all areas of the United Kingdom, whether rural or industrial, is rose mildew. This is a surface fungus, easily recognisable by the appearance of a white or grey mould in patches on the leaves and stems. The patches spread rapidly and eventually may cover nearly all the leaf surface, stems, prickles and buds, seriously checking growth in extreme cases. Attacks seem to be encouraged by extremes of temperature between day and night, or by dryness at the roots, particularly in places where air circulation is restricted, such as in a corner against a brick wall, or in the shelter of a dense hedge.

Control. The best treatment is preventive – to provide your roses with an open, well-drained situation, plenty of water, plenty of nourishment, and spacing them far enough apart to avoid overcrowding. It is also advisable, in gardens which are prone to attacks, to exclude varieties which are known to be particularly susceptible to mildew, and to avoid heavy dressings of nitrogenous fertilisers, which encourage vulnerable soft growth. Having said so much, one is left with a decision as to the best treatment when an attack has started. I must be honest and say that the only fungicide I myself have found very effective against mildew is a colloidal copper white oil spray no longer on the market. Some growers find dinocap effective as a spray, but I have not been so fortunate. Washing soda crystals (1 oz. dissolved in 1 gal. of rain water, plus a little liquid soap to act as a spreader) may be tried, and some growers claim good results. I find that this tends to make the foliage brittle after two or three applications, so that many of the leaves are shed in heavy rain. This is a point to bear in mind when considering the effectiveness of all fungicides – if the plants are defoliated prematurely, this may well be as weakening as the disease itself. For small outbreaks some growers still rely on sprinkling the foliage with flowers of sulphur or green sulphur, but this is unsightly and not very effective. A really active mildew preparation is still badly needed and long overdue. Systemic mildew fungicides are now being developed, although they are not yet at the time of writing available to gardeners in this country. They will be welcomed by most rose growers and should help to make effective disease control independent of weather conditions.

Rose rust: This is probably the most serious disease of the rose, as badly infected plants may die in the first year. The first stage of the disease may take the form of small, rust-coloured swellings on the under surface of the leaf in early spring. These contain spores which are dispersed when the leaf surface is ruptured. These swellings may also appear on the stems, due to the mycelium of the fungus remaining alive on the stems for some years; such stems become scarred with deep cracks and often die back to the base. More orange-coloured spores, of a different type, appear in summer, again as small raised spots or pustules on the under surface of the leaf. From about August a third kind of spore develops which is black and causes the pustules to change from bright orange to almost black in appearance. This type of spore has the capacity to withstand winter temperatures and can be called the over-wintering spore. It germinates in the spring and gives rise to further infection.

Control. As with black spot, rose rust cannot be cured, and control must take the form of protective spraying of the leaves and stems, and in particular the lower and older leaves which are the first to be attacked. Both surfaces of the leaves must be covered with a formulation of maneb, zineb or thiram, prepared strictly in accordance with the makers' instructions. In a pure-air district it is wise to keep a sharp lookout for the first sign of the disease, as it may then be possible to prevent it from spreading by cutting off the whole of the top growth, wrapping it in sheets of newspaper or a large paper bag, to prevent the spores being spread, and burning it straight away. Such prompt action is perhaps only possible with those who are

A rambler rose before and after pruning. The canes which have flowered are cut away as soon as the blooms have faded, and new canes from the base are tied in to fill the available space

Right: Mischief (H.T.)
Below: Percy Thrower (H.T.)

familiar with the symptoms of the disease. Where the orange spores have already appeared, despite spraying as a preventive, badly infected leaves should be removed and burnt in an effort to localise the attack. Leaves which are shed should also be burnt and any infected wood cut away and burnt as soon as possible. It is probably not worth trying to save a badly infected plant as it will remain a source of infection in future years and will be so weakened as to contribute little to the garden display.

MINERAL DEFICIENCIES

Chlorosis: This is the condition in which rose leaves will turn a sickly yellow, either entirely or in patches, and is due usually to a deficiency of one or more trace elements, i.e. those elements of which a very small amount is needed in the soil, such as iron, magnesium, manganese and boron. Iron deficiency is the most common cause of chlorosis. The leaves shrivel and eventually fall and the whole plant presents a weakly, unhealthy appearance, with thin flowers of poor quality borne on spindly shoots. Excess of lime in a soil reduces the availability of iron, as it becomes locked up in the form of insoluble iron salts. Clearly, unless an element can be reduced to a solution it cannot be of benefit to a plant, as it cannot then be absorbed through the root tips. On chalk soils, therefore, this particular problem is a common one.

Treatment. If the soil is alkaline it is useless to add a sprinkling of sulphate of iron to the beds (say ¼ oz. per sq. yd.), as is recommended for acid soils, since calcium would combine with it to form insoluble salts, as already mentioned. Spraying the foliage and stems with this quantity dissolved in a gallon of soft water will help and should be done at intervals of 10 days or so, until a marked improvement in leaf colouring is noticeable. A better treatment is to apply iron chelates to the soil. These have the property of holding the iron in a form available to the roots. They are dissolved in water and applied to the soil by a watering can at the strength recommended by the makers. A mixture of the sequestrenes of iron and manganese, plus active magnesium, is also available and is recommended for use on chalk soils.

VIRUS DISEASES

These have received greater attention in recent years and have been the subject of scientific studies in several countries in which the trouble appears to be much more prevalent than in the United Kingdom. Here the commonest rose mosaic virus disease is vein banding rose mosaic, in which the distinctly paler veins – often creamy-white or pale yellow – show in striking contrast in the leaflets during April and May and to a lesser extent in the autumn. They may not be noticeably abnormal during the summer months. There is not a serious loss of vigour in the affected plants and it is conceivable that many growers would not realise that anything was wrong.

A less common form of mosaic virus is the line pattern rose mosaic, producing narrow, pale wavy lines on the leaflets, sometimes forming an oak-leaf pattern. It has been identified on several American-raised roses in the United Kingdom. Here again, the symptoms are most noticeable in late spring, but the loss of vigour of the infected plants and the reduced flower production are much more serious than in the case of vein banding mosaic.

Control. If the rose nurseryman is careful to destroy any maiden plants showing the tell-tale mosaic pattern on any of the foliage, the trouble should not affect the average amateur who buys his plants from a rose specialist. Unfortunately, not all rose nurserymen have a sufficiently rigorous system of inspection to cull all infected plants, and some may be sent out to customers. Any plant showing a leaf infected with line pattern rose mosaic should be dug up and burnt, and it is important that no budwood be taken from the plant. While vein banding rose mosaic probably does not warrant such a drastic measure, again, no budwood should be taken from a plant which has shown the characteristic symptoms at any time. Amateurs doing their own budding are strongly recommended to use seedlings, rather than cuttings, as rootstocks.

General: Good cultivation, avoidance of overcrowding, care in the selection of the site so that the roses are not planted in draughts or corners or overhung by large trees or buildings, and constant vigilance, so that outbreaks are tackled in the early stages, will do much to reduce the incidence of disease in the rose garden. It may be asked why it is not possible to breed disease-resistant varieties. The trouble is that there may be many strains of the same disease, and although resistance to one strain may be bred into a variety, the same variety may fall a ready victim to another strain.

11

Propagation

Propagation – Methods of increasing roses – Cuttings – Layering – Seeds – Budding – Rootstocks for roses and their characteristics – Types in common use and their propagation – How to bud – Heading back and care of maiden growth

As hard-wooded shrubs, roses are not quite so easy to propagate as the soft-stemmed dahlias, delphiniums and chrysanthemums, or the annuals like sweet peas, which are so simple to raise from seed. Some of the less sophisticated groups of roses may be increased quite easily from cuttings, but this method is too slow and uncertain for application to most of the modern hybrid teas, although it can be practised successfully with the stronger-growing floribundas. The great advantage of roses raised from cuttings is that, as they are growing on their own roots, there is no possibility of suckers developing. On the other hand they do not often make such strong plants as the same varieties budded on a rootstock and the root system, as with most cuttings, is not as deep as on a seedling rootstock, and is therefore more vulnerable to the effects of severe frosts and prolonged droughts.

ROSES FROM CUTTINGS

Ripe, repeat ripe, shoots of the current season's growth are removed in September or early October, with or without a heel of the old wood attached. These should be about 9 in. long and are prepared by removing the unripe growing tip just above an eye, cutting the base of the shoot clean across, just below an eye, or in the case of those torn off with a heel of older wood, paring the heel smooth. The top two leaves should be left and all the others cut off. Half of the number of cuttings could be treated with a hormone rooting powder, as supplied for hardwood cuttings, the base of the cutting being moistened and then dipped in the powder. A narrow, V-shaped trench should be prepared in a sheltered part of the garden, about 8 in. deep with a couple of inches of sharp sand added. The cuttings are inserted upright, or nearly so, against one side of the trench, about 4 in. apart, and some fine soil added, mixed with moist granulated peat, firmed moderately and the remainder of the soil replaced and firmed. If it is at all dry it should be watered after firming. It is advisable to leave the level slightly below that of the surrounding soil, to save having to water the cuttings very often, as they must never be allowed to dry out. They should be left undisturbed until at least the October of the following year, when those that have rooted may be transferred to their permanent quarters.

The groups most easily raised from cuttings are those not many generations removed from the species, such as the Wichuraiana and Multiflora ramblers, the old garden roses, some of the early floribundas originally classified as hybrid polyanthas, and of course many of the species and their near hybrids. The miniature china roses are propagated from cuttings, too, on a large scale, but for a special reason – to keep them in character with their dwarf habit of growth. When budded on to rootstocks they tend to grow too vigorously.

ROSES FROM LAYERS

This method is only really suitable for groups with long, fairly flexible stems, such as those of the Wichuraiana and Multiflora ramblers and some shrub roses, such as the hybrid musks. Broadly, layering is possible with any of the varieties which produce long enough and flexible enough canes to be pegged down for garden display. These, of course, are very vigorous varieties capable of flourishing on their own roots. The procedure is quite simple: a stem is chosen which is near enough to the soil or flexible enough to be pegged down at a point two thirds along its length from the base of the plant. A slanting cut is made in the underside of the stem and about half-way through, so that it opens and forms a tongue, when a wooden peg is fixed over the stem to secure it in the soil. Sometimes a small pebble is inserted in the tongue to keep it open.

A mound of sandy soil, with perhaps some moist peat added, is heaped over the pegged tongue to encourage root formation, but the stem still draws sap from the roots of the parent plant. Layering may be undertaken from mid-summer onwards, but the layered stem should not be severed until some time after it is obvious from the new growth thrown up from the pegged point that it has its own root system. It is usual to sever the layer in the summer of the following season, preparatory to transplanting it in the autumn.

ROSES FROM SEEDS

While it is quite an easy matter to raise roses from seed, the ancestry of our modern bedding varieties is so complex that they do not come true, even under controlled conditions under glass. Rose breeders, of course, have to raise many thousands of seedlings from crosses between pre-selected parents – the pollen and the seed parent respectively – chosen for particular desirable qualities, in the hope of producing a seedling worth naming and introducing. But the modern rose has reached such a standard that the odds against any seedling being an improvement on existing varieties, sufficiently distinct, free flowering and not unduly prone to disease and weather damage, are astronomical – perhaps two or three seedlings will be of sufficient merit out of maybe 20,000 raised.

For the ordinary amateur who has neither the time, the glasshouse facilities nor perhaps the inclination to hybridise to produce new varieties, there are much simpler fields in which he can operate, merely for the interest and satisfaction to be gained in flowering roses from seed. Some of the cluster-flowered groups, such as the hybrid musks or the hybrid Rugosas, are very easy for the beginner. I have raised many hundreds of the former group and flowered many of them in about three months from sowing the seed. The heps or seed pods should be gathered as late in the autumn as is safe – say mid-October, and stored under cover in a box or a large flower pot of soil mixed with sand and peat, and kept moist. If a cool greenhouse is available, the heps may be removed from the soil mixture about the end of March, when it will be found that the pulp will have rotted and, by rubbing the hep between the palms of the hands, the individual seeds will separate from the pulp. These may be sown in boxes or pots, using a good compost, such as John Innes No. 3, and spaced about 1 in. apart each way and covered with $\frac{1}{2}$ in. of soil. Germination is irregular, and seedlings may be left in the boxes or transferred to individual thumb pots when one true leaf has formed. The little plants will often produce miniature flowers towards the end of June and may be carefully transferred soon afterwards to their permanent quarters out of doors. Alternatively, they are just as easy to raise in shallow drills outside, sowing the seed in April and applying a topdressing of moist peat to the drills to conserve moisture.

These three methods of raising plants will not produce any improved varieties as, with selection playing such an important part in the marketing of new roses, it follows that, from any chance fertilisation of seeds, the odds are all in favour of the seedlings being inferior to the parent varieties. Nevertheless, I have raised seedlings scarcely distinguishable in the garden from named hybrid musks, such as Prosperity and Cornelia. Some seedsmen offer seed of 'fairy' roses, *R. polyantha nana* or *R. chinensis minima,* producing flowers in various shades of pink on a dwarf plant in the first season.

ROSES FROM BUDDING

Budding, a form of shield or bark grafting, is the long-recognised method for the commercial propagation of roses and, apart from some of the old garden roses and the miniature china hybrids, it is the method used for virtually the whole of the roses propagated for resale in this country. It has been somewhat poetically described as 'the insertion of a bud of nobler race beneath a bark of baser kind', the bark of baser kind being that of the rootstock used to support the top growth of the cultivated variety. While nearly all modern roses are compatible with the various rootstocks now in use in this country, that is to say, when budding has taken place they make a perfect union with the stock, this was not always so before the Second War, when the Manettii stock and some others were still popular. I made a practice of using this stock for varieties in the Ophelia group which did very well on it, but it is not compatible with many modern roses.

ROOTSTOCKS

I suppose the ideal rootstock is like the ideal rose – a figment of the imagination. One that does splendidly on one type of soil may be mediocre on a different type. Theoretically one should have roses budded on the rootstock which is best suited to one's particular type of soil. This, though, implies that one must bud one's own roses, as nurserymen rarely offer a choice of bush roses budded on alternative rootstocks, although this is often available for standards. The qualities sought in a good rootstock are:

(i) that it will produce a fibrous root system which will enable the maiden plant to be transplanted readily to a wide range of soils and will support the plant over a long life

(ii) that it can be propagated readily, either by seed or from cuttings

(iii) that it will be reasonably free from suckering

(iv) that it will be absolutely hardy under normal winter conditions

(v) that it will have a bark thick enough to hold the bud firmly and that the sap will continue to 'run' to enable budding to extend over a reasonable period

(vi) that it is reasonably homogeneous so that all stocks of the same size will be ready for budding at the same time.

The rootstocks in general use in this country are summarised in the following notes:

Seedling Briar (*R. canina*). Probably more than 80 per cent of roses budded for resale are on this rootstock or one of its selected strains. The graded seedling briars are mostly imported from Holland where they are raised in enormous numbers. It transplants very well, has a deep root system, is long-lived and hardy and holds the bud well, but falls down a little on items (iii) and (vi) previously mentioned. It is an excellent stock for heavy or medium soils, but not as suitable for light soils. The maiden plants are only about two thirds the size of those on Multiflora or Rugosa, but catch up later. A number of selected strains are now widely grown and are sometimes preferred to the heterogeneous seedling briar. These include Broggs, Deegens, Schmidt's Ideal, Kokulinsky, Heinsohn's Record and Pollmeriana, among others. The only real difference, apart from their uniformity, is that some have fewer prickles and are easier to handle.

Cutting Briar (*R. canina*). While this stock used to be fairly popular on medium soils, it is probably little used today. Being propagated from unrooted cuttings, the root system tends to be shallower than that of the seedling briar and it is unlikely that the plants are as long-lived. Apart from this, *R. canina* cuttings do not root anything like as readily as some other stocks, and therefore an extra year is needed before they can be budded.

Laxa. The so-called Laxa stock is really *R. canina froebelii*. It used to be popular with Scottish growers and is still used to some extent. At one time it was believed that yellow varieties budded on Laxa developed a very rich colouring, but although I tried budding several of the leading yellows on both Laxa and seedling briar under identical conditions some years ago, I could find no real difference in the flowers. It is an extremely easy stock to handle, since it is practically thornless, with straight smooth necks and very thick bark which lifts readily. At one time it became unpopular as it is subject to rust disease, but it has since been claimed that the strain of rust which infects Laxa will not flourish on cultivated varieties. It is normally used as seedlings.

Multiflora (*R. multiflora japonica, R. polyantha multiflora, R. polyantha* Simplex). This vigorous stock, of Japanese origin, may be used as seedlings or as cuttings, and is very valuable on light, hungry soils which dry out quickly, as it continues to grow throughout the season. Unfortunately the bark is exceptionally thin and holds the bud insecurely – so much so that tying the maiden growth to a cane is essential to avoid losses from the scion blowing out in high winds. The cutting Multiflora is not at all easy to transplant if the roots are allowed to dry out, but the seedling is better in this respect. Neither, in my experience, is as hardy or as long lived as seedling briar. Cuttings about 9 in. long, with all but the top two eyes cut out, can be prepared in the autumn, placed in bundles of a couple of dozen in sandy soil with just the top 2 in. exposed. They remain there for the winter, and are planted out 3 in. deep in March, 8 in. apart. Most of them will have formed a callus by then and some may even have roots. They are earthed up like potatoes. Nearly all of them will root and may be budded at the end of July or in August when they are growing freely. The ideal is to insert the cuttings in their permanent beds, budding them *in situ*, and planting them farther apart for this purpose. I have had excellent results from this method on both light and heavy soils. It throws very few suckers, but the roots are rather thick and fleshy and inclined to be coarse. I prefer the variety with pairs of black prickles to the smooth-stemmed variety.

Rugosa (*R. rugosa* Hollandica). This stock is mainly valuable for the production of long stems for budding as standard roses. These are mainly imported from Holland where the soil is particularly favourable to their growth. Cuttings are easily rooted, prepared in the usual way about 9 in. long, with all eyes cut out except the top two and the base of the cutting cut straight across just below an eye. Rooting seems to be quicker if the bark is scraped for about an inch up one side of the cutting from the base. Such cuttings are used for budding with climbers, such as the difficult Mermaid and the climbing sports; they are also very good for potting up and budding

Left: The stems of faded flowers are cut back by not more than half to an outward-pointing eye
Below left: When blooms are required for exhibition it is necessary to reduce each cluster of buds to one
Below right: For garden display it is usual to leave two or three buds in each cluster

Roses used as a screen in the author's garden

Elizabeth of Glamis (Flori.)

Top left: Removing a sucker from the stem of a Rugosa standard rose flush with the stem. *Top right:* Root suckers must be pulled off at their junction with the rootstock or the root itself. *Bottom left:* The early removal of faded flowers is desirable. *Bottom right:* The flowers of some varieties are susceptible to 'balling' after prolonged rain in the pot for use as pot roses under glass. The rooted cutting makes a dense mat of fibrous roots, arranged in layers, and must be planted shallowly, as it is very prone to suckering. The sap stops running early, so it has to be budded as soon as the eyes are ready, preferably in June or early July. It produces large standard heads, but is not very long lived and must be securely staked.

Standard Briar (*R. canina*). This is the sturdiest stock for standards. Vigorous young stems, 5 or 6 ft. long, may be grubbed up from the hedgerows in rural areas in late autumn with a portion of root attached and planted in rows for budding during the following summer, if they are growing freely by then – otherwise they will be left until the next season. This stock is long lived and very hardy. Nowadays a selected strain, such as Pfanders, is often preferred, with excellent straight sturdy stems, and thick bark.

BUDDING YOUR ROSES

Remember that in budding one is really performing a surgical operation on a plant, so speed and cleanliness are essential. There is no real satisfaction in claiming that the operation was successful, but the patient died! Special budding knives are available with a single blade and a bone handle, tapering to a point for use in raising the bark of the stock. Select the variety you wish to propagate, choosing a shoot which bears a flower which is about to shed its petals. Cut the shoot about 6 or 8 in. long so that it carries several eyes, which may be identified as small knobs at the junction of leaf stalk and stem. An eye from the middle of the stem will be in the right condition – not too advanced and not immature. Cut off the leaves, leaving an inch of stalk to facilitate handling the budding eyes, and place the prepared stem in a jar with an inch of water in the bottom.

Prepare the rootstock by drawing the soil away from the stem as near the roots as possible and wiping it clean with a rag. Bending over the stock from the opposite side, make a T-shaped cut at soil level, the down stroke of the T being about an inch long. Reverse the knife and, using the end of the handle, gently raise the bark to form two flaps. It should on no account be forced – if the stock is ready the bark should lift cleanly and easily; forcing will only result in bruising and damage to the vital cambium layer. Press the flaps back in place to avoid drying out while you prepare the budding eye. This must be cut from the stem with a shield of bark, starting an inch above the eye, gradually deepening as the blade passes under the eye and becoming shallower so that it emerges an inch beyond it. This will produce a boat-shaped shield of bark containing an eye, a piece of leaf stalk and a thin sliver of wood behind the bark.

The Most Difficult Stage

The next step, perhaps the most difficult, is to remove the wood without damaging the eye. To do this, press the thumb nail firmly against the back of the eye, and with the forefinger and thumb of the other hand give a sudden sideways snatch at the sliver of wood at the top of the shield. This should come away cleanly. Reverse the shield and remove the wood from the lower half similarly. A little practice in advance will enable some proficiency and speed to be achieved. Trim the base of the shield with a cross cut about half an inch below the eye, lift the flaps of bark on the stock with the handle of the knife and, holding the shield by the leaf stalk, push it down the T-cut as far as it will go, with the eye pointing outwards. With a cross cut, trim the shield flush with the top of the flaps and bind firmly, but not too tightly, with moist raffia, leaving the eye itself exposed. Alternatively, rubber or plastic patent ties, with clips, are popular with the trade today, but raffia is probably simpler for the beginner.

Leave the budded stock for about three weeks. If the eye is then still alive and the shield green, all will be well. If the eye and shield have turned brown or black, try again on the other side of the stock, preferably a little lower down. Cut the tie on the stocks where the bud has taken and do nothing more until the following February, when the stocks should be headed back. This involves cutting away the whole of the top growth about an inch above the inserted eye. This should start into growth later in the spring, and the maiden growth should be tied to a small cane placed on the opposite side of the stock. The young plants should flower in July, about three weeks later than established plants. Cut back the stem fairly low after the first flowers to induce new growths from the union or budding point. Transplant the maiden plant to its permanent quarters in the autumn.

Standards and Half-standards

Standards and half-standards are dealt with similarly in the case of Rugosa stems, two or three budding eyes being inserted close together on opposite sides of the main stem, slightly staggered. Canina stems are budded into three of the strongest laterals (side shoots) as close as possible to the main stem.

In February Rugosa stems are headed back 2 or 3 in. above the highest inserted bud and all lateral growth is removed. The few inches left above draws the sap to the bud and provides something to which the maiden growth may be tied. All unbudded laterals on Canina stems are removed and the budded laterals are cut back to 2 or 3 in. beyond the inserted bud. The maiden growth must be tied to short sticks bound to the main stem for the first season. A bushy head is induced by pinching out the growing points of the maiden growths when two leaves are fully developed, and the same method is often adopted with bush roses, which do not then need such careful staking, except on Multiflora stocks.

12

Hybridisation

Rose hybridisation – New varieties obtained by cross-pollination under glass of selected parents – Selection of suitable parents – Potting up plants for flowering at end of May – Removal of petals and emasculation of bloom of seed parent – Protecting stigma until ready to receive pollen – Methods of transferring pollen – Labelling the cross – Ripening the pods and after-ripening – Rubbing out, testing and sowing seeds – Irregular germination – Transplanting seedlings – Budding on small rootstocks outside – Assessing quality

New varieties of roses are normally obtained from cross-pollination of two carefully chosen parents under controlled conditions and the sowing of the resultant seeds. It may not always be realised that roses are bisexual and, as such, may be self-pollinated unless steps are taken to prevent this happening. In this country the weather is such that it is normally necessary to cross-pollinate in a greenhouse, as the heps would be unlikely to ripen sufficiently out of doors. The first step is to select suitable varieties as parents, and these may be chosen for such qualities as disease resistance, freedom and continuity of flowering, compact and branching habit of growth, the ability to open freely in wet weather and the capacity to shed the petals cleanly before they become displeasing. For the seed parent it is desirable to select varieties which set seed freely, as evidenced by their behaviour in the garden. The pollen (male) parent will have to flower at about the same time as the seed (female) parent – otherwise it will not be possible to cross-pollinate.

Lift the plants in the autumn and pot into 8 in. or 10 in. pots, depending on their size and variety, using a compost which is not too rich, as rank growth is undesirable. The plants should be grown with little heat other than to exclude frost, the aim being to have flowers available by about the end of May when plenty of sunshine can be expected.

Ancestry

The ancestry of modern roses is so mixed that almost anything can happen in cross-pollinating two of these hybrids. Some years ago it was thought by some breeders that the qualities of the seed parent most likely to be transmitted to the progeny were growth and foliage, and that the colour tended to be inherited from the pollen parent, with fragrance not following any discernible pattern. This was clearly a very rough and ready generalisation which was based on the fundamental assumption that there is a significant difference in the progeny when cross-pollinating $A \times B$ as compared with $B \times A$, the seed parent being named first. On the other hand, some authorities maintain that the only difference lies in the setting of the seeds, some varieties being prolific and others sparing.

Preparing the Seed Parent

It is always advisable to do the cross-pollination on a sunny day. Not later than at the half-open stage and preferably a little earlier,

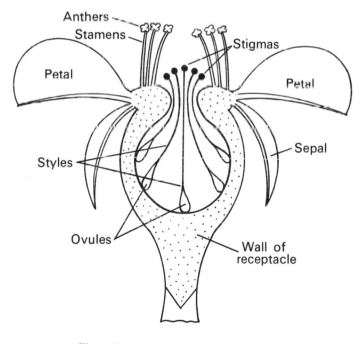

Figure 18. A cross-section of a rose bloom

the petals of the bloom chosen as the seed parent should be pulled off one by one, very carefully, making sure that no small piece is left to set up decay caused by botrytis. The next step is emasculation of the flower by the removal of all the anthers, to prevent self-pollination. A small pair of nail scissors or tweezers may be used, and if it is intended to apply the pollen from the anthers in another cross, the latter should be transferred to a small receptacle and suitably labelled, pending application at the right time a day or so later when the pollen is ripe.

Pollination

This leaves the stigma of the chosen seed parent, and if there is any danger of chance pollination by insects in the greenhouse (the ventilators being left open to maintain a buoyant atmosphere) a polythene cap should be placed over the flower head. Usually the prepared head will be receptive by the following day in fairly sunny

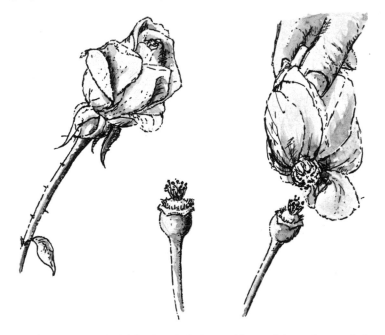

Figure 19. Rose hybridisation. *Left:* Young bloom of the seed parent before removal of petals. *Centre:* The seed parent after removal of petals and emasculation by removal of all the anthers, leaving the stigma. *Right:* Transferring pollen direct from the anthers of the pollen parent

126

weather, when the stigma will be seen to be shiny and sticky. For transferring the pollen of the pollen parent to the stigma of the seed parent, a small camel-hair paint brush may be used; alternatively, the forefinger will serve if the grower has the necessary delicacy of touch. The disadvantage of a camel-hair brush is the difficulty of ensuring that all the pollen grains are removed before it is used for the next cross. Perhaps the best method of all is to transfer the pollen direct from the anthers of the pollen parent, holding the petals well back while dusting the stigma generously. Then replace the polythene cap at once. The footstalk below the flower head should have a label tied to it, with particulars of the cross, giving the name of the seed parent first, e.g. Ena Harkness × Sutter's Gold.

Fertilisation

If everything goes well, the pollen grains will germinate and pollen tubes will grow down to the ovary inside the receptacle or seed pod, there fertilising the ovum in the ovule to form an embryo. Watering should be undertaken sparingly and the atmosphere kept dry at this stage, with ample ventilation being provided, to reduce the chance of botrytis infection.

The seed pod should begin to swell after a time, and when it is changing to orange-red in the autumn it may be cut off with a short length of footstalk for after-ripening. This after-ripening usually consists of storing the seed pods outside in a mouse-proof container, in moist granulated peat, for a period of at least three months, and ensuring that the peat never becomes dry.

Sowing Seed

By mid-February the fleshy part of the seed pods will have rotted and if they are rubbed with a circular motion between the palms of the hands, the seeds will separate cleanly. These will be of all shapes and sizes, and should be tested in water for viability. Those that float are unlikely to be fertile, but the sinkers should be sown under glass in boxes or sterilised seed pans or pots, about 1 in. apart and $\frac{1}{2}$ in. deep, in John Innes Potting Compost No. 1. After firming the surface, water well and apply about $\frac{1}{4}$ in. of coarse sharp sand to discourage moss. Some seeds may germinate in five to six weeks; others may lie dormant until the following year. A high temperature is not conducive to good germination, and one of from 13–16°C. (55–60°F.) is perhaps the most suitable.

Transplanting Seedlings

After the first true leaf has developed, transplant either to individual small pots or to deeper boxes, spacing the seedlings several inches apart; topdress them with moist granulated peat and grow them on until the first flower opens, when the plant may be from 4–6 in. high. Mildew must be watched for, and if it does appear dusting with flowers of sulphur will help to control it. The flower will, of course, be very small, but it will give an idea of the colour and fragrance. The number of petals will tend to increase later when the seedling is budded on small rootstocks, which may be done outside later, in August. Alternatively, the seedlings which show promise could be transferred to larger pots and budded on to rootstocks when the wood is stouter and the eyes can be more easily handled. Until the seedlings have been flowered on rootstocks outside for a couple of seasons it is not possible to say how they will stand up to varying weather conditions, or what major faults may be revealed. Some seedlings, while not good enough in themselves, may show useful qualities which might justify keeping them for use as parents.

Out of any batch of rose seedlings raised by cross-pollination commercially under carefully controlled conditions, perhaps not more than one in 20,000 of them will be considered good enough, after extended trials and observation, for naming and distribution. But this should not deter the keen amateur, as such prime favourites as Ena Harkness and Frensham were raised by an amateur.

Left: Joyfulness
(Flori. H.T. type)
Below: Circus (Flori.)

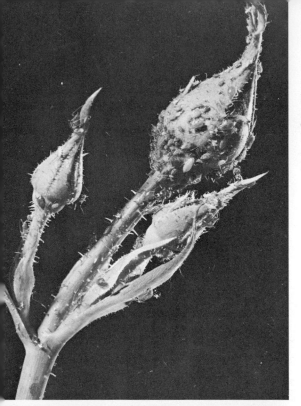

Top left: Rose buds and stems heavily infested with aphids
Bottom left: Cuckoo spit, another easily identifiable trouble caused by the common froghopper
Bottom right: The easily identifiable presence of the leaf-rolling sawfly

13

Exhibiting Roses

Planning and early care   Importance of timing – Tying stems to prevent damage – Procedure for three days before the show – Transporting blooms to the show – Staging in boxes, vases and bowls – Common faults – What the judges look for in the various classes

There is a fascination about exhibiting roses which tends to become even more absorbing with the passing of the years. The fact that the rose is one of the most tantalising of flowers to stage in perfect condition may be partly responsible   a matter of a couple of hours can make all the difference between a first-class, prize-winning specimen bloom and an 'also-ran'. With an interval of between 11 and 15 weeks elapsing between pruning and the opening of the bloom, it will be understood how important timing is. An unexpected warm spell or some May frosts can easily upset all one's calculations, based on experience gained over, perhaps, many seasons.

Planning Ahead

It goes without saying that the consistently successful rose exhibitor is the one who plans well ahead, and this is essential to success at the really large rose shows, such as those of The Royal National Rose Society. Preparation may be said to start with the carefully staggered pruning of the various varieties to ensure that, given normal weather conditions, they will open at or about the show date. Records are kept over several seasons of the interval between pruning and blooming for the varieties which it is intended to exhibit, and this may average from 10–11 weeks for a flower of moderate petallage to 15 or 16 weeks for an exceptionally full-petalled variety in all but very sheltered or unusually exposed gardens.

129

Care at an Early Stage

The keen exhibitor will give his plants daily attention as soon as active growth begins. It will be necessary to limit multiple shoots, which often develop from the eye just below the pruning cut, to one only—the strongest. Some varieties seem to make a particular habit of growing three shoots from the same eye. The two side shoots should be removed as soon as they are large enough to handle without risk of damaging the centre one which has to be left. Pests and diseases must be combated at an early stage to avoid unsightly eaten or diseased foliage. When the new shoot is showing a tiny bud in the growing point, side shoots may start to develop from the leaf axils along the length of the shoot, and unless these are pinched out in the very early stages they will deprive the terminal bud of nourishment (see p. 98).

In exposed gardens or in windy weather it will be advisable to tie each strong new shoot which bears a promising-looking terminal bud to a bamboo cane, to prevent damage from the thorns of nearby stems. Each stem should eventually be limited to one bud by removing the side buds as soon as they are large enough to handle, but leaving one extra in case of accident to the central bud. There is little point in leaving disbudding until the side buds are as large as peas, as by that time there is not much likelihood of increasing the size of the centre bud to any extent. It may sometimes happen that a spell of warm weather will bring the buds along earlier than had been planned, so that it becomes obvious that the centre bud will open at least a week before the show date. In such a case it is sometimes better to remove the centre bud and concentrate on the single remaining side bud which, being smaller because it is less advanced, will take longer to open and, with luck, may be just at its best on the day of the show. Decisions of this sort are largely a matter of judgment, based on previous experience of timing the blooms in the particular garden.

Liquid Feeding

Liquid feeding will be practised by the exhibitor, an application being made about every 10 days from the stage when the tiny bud first appears. There are many reliable proprietary brands of fertiliser on the market, but it is strongly recommended that one rich in potash be used, to improve the colour and substance of the petals. Each exhibitor has his own favourite formula, but nitrate of potash (1 oz. per gal. of soft water) is probably as good as anything for the beginner, using a gallon to feed two established plants of medium size. Further details are given in Chapter 8.

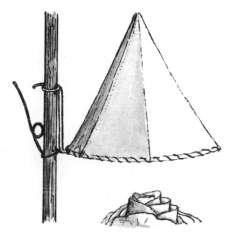

Figure 20. Using a bloom protector to shield an exhibition bloom against the effect of sun and rain. The base of the protector should be 2 in. above the top of the flower. The protector will normally be brought into use two or three days before the show

Grooming Before the Show

The serious preparation will start about three days before the show, when the plants are examined for full-sized buds on which the sepals have come away from the solid bud, revealing the colour, but without these petals having unfurled at all. Most varieties take about three days from this stage to the two-thirds open bloom. Ideally, a bloom protector should be placed in position over each such bud, so that the bottom of the protector is clear of the top of the bud. These bloom protectors are cone shaped, made either from oiled parchment or calico on a wire frame, and each is attached to a stake with a wire clip, so that the protector can be raised or lowered as necessary, according to the height of the bud.

At this stage a decision has to be taken as to whether or not to 'tie' the bud. A tie is a 9 in. length of thick soft wool which is placed inside the outside row of petals, about two thirds of the way down the bud from the point, and secured with a double twist. The object

131

of tying is to induce the petals to grow longer, as they are restricted by the wool from lateral development. A larger and shapelier bloom may sometimes be the outcome, provided that the ties are slackened slightly each day, to allow for natural growth. If this is not done grooves will be cut into the petals by the wool and these will look unsightly on the show bench.

If it is decided to try tying, it is important that the petals be perfectly dry at the time and that no insects are enclosed in the petals. Whenever a bud is tied a bloom protector *must* be used. There are certain disadvantages in tying, such as the danger of torn petals in inexperienced hands, and the false sense of security which it may induce. A certain proportion of tied blooms must be expected to fly open when the ties are removed just before judging, so spares should always be available. They also tend to lose some brilliance of colour compared with blooms allowed to open naturally. On balance I would not recommend tying for the novice, nor would I recommend it for the decorative classes, as distinct from the specimen bloom classes, except for safe transportation to the show, i.e. to avoid petals being accidentally torn in transit.

Apart from inspecting buds which have protectors over them each day, keeping a sharp lookout for any others which may have escaped attention previously, and adjusting any protectors which may have been blown at an angle in high winds, it will be desirable to remove

Figure 21. Tying rose blooms, before using a bloom protector. The woollen tie should be secured with a double twist inside the outside row of petals and about two-thirds down from the point of the bud

any greenfly or other pests as they appear. A small camel-hair brush, moistened with a little water, is excellent for removing these without damaging the petals. During the three days, the outside row of petals of any tied blooms will open out and perhaps fold back slightly, which is what is wanted, leaving the other petals enclosed by the woollen tie, but loosened slightly each day.

Cutting and Preparation for the Show

The blooms are usually cut the evening before the show, after the sun has lost its heat, or very early on the show day if this is a local event, allowing several hours for the stems to absorb water in a cool place before the staging begins. For vases and bowls they must be cut with as long stems as possible, merely leaving an inch or so of the current growth on the plant to provide for a replacement stem in due course. For exhibition in the box classes the stems need not be more than 6 in. long. When cutting it is worth while carrying a bucket with a few inches of water in the bottom and placing the end of each stem in the water immediately it is cut. When all likely blooms have been cut, much time will be saved at the show if the stems are prepared at home later in the evening. For this purpose it is a good plan to have two or three clean, pint-sized milk bottles available, filled with water. Place the stems, one at a time, in a milk bottle, leaving both hands free to remove the woollen tie without tearing the petals. If the centre of the flower holds – that is, if it retains its conical shape, without flying open to reveal the stamens – and it is free from any blemish or malformation, replace the tie carefully, then wash each leaf under a running tap, rubbing it gently between the finger and thumb to remove any insecticide or fungicide deposit. Then remove the thorns from the lower half of the stem, or at least the sharp points. If any leaves or outside petals are slightly damaged at the edges, these may be trimmed carefully, using a small pair of nail scissors.

Some varieties suffer from a weak neck, which means that the flower is too heavy for the footstalk to support. If such varieties are to be staged in vases or bowls they will need wiring, and it will save time, and perhaps accidents, if this is done at home. There are two methods of wiring roses: one is to use stiff florists' wire to pierce the seed pod at an angle, and then to secure the stem to the stiff wire at several points with finer gauge wire. The easier method is to use a length of less rigid wire and to form a small ring round the stem

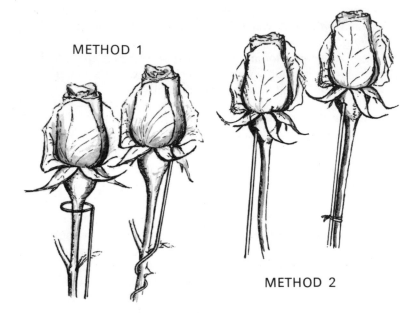

Figure 22. Two methods of wiring roses. Method 1 involves forming a small ring fitting round the seed pod. Method 2 uses stiffer wire to pierce the seed pod at an angle. The support wire is then secured to the stem with finer gauge wire

under the flower at right angles to the length of the wire which, when pushed up under the sepals, will just encircle the seed pod. The wire is then run behind the footstalk to just below the first leaves, where it is twisted round the stem twice and any surplus length run down further behind the stem. The second method is recommended for the beginner, as it is very easy to decapitate flowers when using the first method.

Having prepared the stems in this manner, they should be grouped together as far as possible to form each separate exhibit, to save too much handling and risk of petal damage at the show. Thus, for a bowl of 12 decorative hybrid tea roses the 12 stems selected, together with a few spares, should all be kept in the same bucket, which is filled with cold water to within a few inches of the flowers and left in a cool place. Each stem should be cut on the slant to expose as large a surface as possible to absorb water, and a small piece of bark should be removed about an inch up one side of the stem from the cut end.

If a box of specimen blooms is being staged this must be of the regulation size and type, i.e. 18 in. × 12 in. for six blooms or 18 in. × 24 in. for 12 blooms. It should have the base covered with fresh green moss between the water tubes. It is a help to arrange the specimen blooms in the box before leaving home, as this will allow more time for staging the bowl and vase classes at the show, as well as ensuring that the large specimen blooms, which are inclined to be top-heavy, do not meet with an accident in transit. I remember an occasion when, travelling by car to Westminster, I had to brake hard for another car emerging without warning from a side street, and found my best blooms decapitated in consequence. Fill each water tube and cut the stem of the rose so that it reaches the bottom of the tube when the base of the bloom rests on the metal ring forming the top of the stiff upright wire soldered to the back of the water tube. Twist some fine wire round the stem and the upright to hold the former in position, leaving the woollen ties round the blooms. In a box of six, have the two largest blooms in the back row, the next largest in the middle row and the smallest in front. They should all be as evenly matched as possible for size, age and condition and the colours should be arranged so that adjacent blooms form a contrast, if possible. Insert variety name cards in the wire card holders attached to the water tubes and be sure that distinct varieties have been used if the schedule requires them. Then lock the lid in position, making certain that you take the key with you.

Figure 23. An exhibition box for six rose blooms

135

Transportation

Before embarking for the show, see that you have everything you will need: a supply of reeds or long stalky grass for packing the vases; florists' wire; nail scissors; secateurs; a small camel-hair paint brush for dressing the blooms; a small flower pot; a sharp pocket knife; a copy of the show schedule; a pen, and some stiff paper for the variety name cards. If the schedule allows exhibitors' own vases and bowls, these also must be taken.

It is an advantage to transport the roses in water, either by car or van, in which case all but a few inches of water should be emptied from the containers. If the roses have to be taken by public transport, dry-packing in a large cardboard box may be unavoidable. Pack the roses in layers, using plenty of tissue paper between, and make a roll of newspaper for wedging across the box for the neck of the flowers to rest on, to avoid friction and bruising of the petals. Finish off by wedging a thin cane across the middle of the box to hold the stems firmly in place.

Staging

The first task on arrival at the show is to place any dry-packed roses in water, cutting a little off the end of each stem in case it has become sealed. Then collect the class cards from the show secretary and any bowls and vases required. Place the box entry in the appropriate class with the entry card in front of it, face downwards. Unlock the box, lower the struts attached to the inside of the lid so that air is admitted, but the blooms are shaded from direct sun by the lid. Then fill the bowls with water up to the grill, pack the vases with reeds or stalky grass brought for the purpose, trim them flush with the top of the vase and fill with water. Arrange the vases of specimen blooms first, as this is quicker than arranging a bowl. Vases are usually of three or six blooms: for three blooms an inverted triangle is best as an arrangement, using the shortest stem for the bottom of the triangle. For a vase of six, three tiers, with two in the top, three in the middle and one below look most effective. The packing will hold the stems in any desired position. Specimen blooms in vases will be tied, if only for safe transit, and the ties should be carefully removed at this stage to test whether the centre of the flower is holding. If it is, replace the tie until a few minutes before judging; if the petals fly open, revealing the centre, the flower is useless for showing and should be replaced with a younger bloom from the spares, which should always be taken.

For bowls of decorative hybrid teas or floribundas, select young, fresh flowers of brilliant colouring with healthy foliage in preference to insipid blooms. Note whether an all-round or a frontal effect is stipulated in the schedule. Usually the former is required where the bench is accessible from both sides, and the latter where there is a back cloth or wall behind. In arranging the stems in the bowl try to achieve pleasing contrasts between adjacent flowers, such as orange or deep yellow next to rich crimson, and avoid placing a deep pink, carmine or cerise next to scarlet or crimson. Make sure that the required number of stems has not been exceeded and that the minimum number of varieties has been used.

Floribundas should have as many flowers as possible open in the truss. If a flower has become spotted with age or has lost one or more petals it is usually better to remove it, together with the footstalk supporting it, using a fine pair of nail scissors. In the decorative classes it is particularly important that the foliage be healthy and free from disease or insect damage. Place the entry card face downwards and leave a further card, face upwards, listing the varieties.

Shortly before the time for judging, remove the ties from the specimen blooms in vases and boxes and 'dress' the flowers, using the camel-hair brush. This technique consists of opening out the two or three outer rows of petals so that they reflex, forming a background for the central cone or spiral, which must be symmetrical, firm and free from any cleft or quartering. This dressing must not be overdone, causing the petals to be forced back unnaturally, or the blooms will lose points. In the box classes the lid will be removed and placed under the staging, the base will be raised at the back by supporting it with a small flower pot and the water tubes in the back and middle rows will be raised in their sockets, as far as they will go in the back row and half way only in the middle row. This will ensure that every detail of each bloom can be seen by the judges without handling them. Foliage does not score points in a box class – the blooms count for everything, but specimen blooms in vases do receive points for healthy foliage, for the exhibit as a whole.

Common Faults

A common fault with novices is to show their blooms overblown or immature. The correct stage for most varieties is when the bloom is two-thirds open or slightly beyond this stage in the case of very full-petalled varieties. Perfecta, for example, is at its best when nearly three-quarters open, as it holds its form until a late stage. I have noticed, too, that Peace is nearly always shown at its blowsy, blown stage at local shows, when it has completely lost its shape and richest colouring. I am convinced, after many years of judging rose classes, that most amateurs leave better roses behind in their gardens than those they take along to the show – they seem to have little idea of what constitutes a good show bloom. Split (those with a cleft in the central cone), quartered (those with two clefts) and blown blooms (those opened out to reveal the stamens) will never be awarded prizes by a competent rose judge. The condition of the blooms at the time of the judging is the sole consideration.

WHAT THE JUDGES LOOK FOR

(1) *Specimen Bloom Classes*

(a) A full-sized flower, representative of the variety, with petals of firm substance, free from weather or insect damage or discoloration and of typical colouring, with freedom from 'blueing' in the case of red or deep pink varieties.

(b) Freedom from coarseness and from splitting, quartering or other malformations of the centre petals. These must form a symmetrical cone or spiral shape, with two or three rows of petals opened out around it.

(c) Where specimen blooms are arranged in vases, the stems must be long and strong, holding the flower erect and furnished with healthy, attractive foliage.

(2) *Decorative Classes Generally*

(a) The flowers must be fresh and brilliantly coloured, so as to catch the eye.

(b) The foliage must be clean, healthy and abundant and hide the wire grill of the bowl, while stems must be long and strong.

(c) The arrangement must be tasteful and effective as a complete unit within the limits imposed by the Schedule.

(3) *Decorative Hybrid Tea Classes*

The size of the flower is less important than shapeliness and brilliance, combined with freshness. Each flower must be of full size for the particular variety and free from splitting, quartering, weather damage or insect damage.

(4) *Floribunda Classes*

(a) The trusses must be large and have as many clean, open flowers as possible, free from spotting or burning. Dark-centred flowers which have shed their pollen are too old to impress.

(b) Faded flowers and those which have lost one or more petals should be carefully removed with the footstalk; traces of mildew must be removed from the calyx and footstalks of buds and flowers.

14

Roses in Pots under Glass

Suitable plants – The first potting – Cultural programme for a complete year – The best varieties

If there is a drawback to concentrating on roses, to the exclusion of all other flowers from the garden, it arises from having to wait until early summer for the first blooms of the hybrid teas and floribundas, although the climbing sports of these types will produce flowers in May in sheltered gardens. I have even had flowers as early as 14th April from Cl. Shot Silk in a warm sunny corner near the house. The flowering season can, however, quite easily be made to start in mid-April every year by growing roses in pots in a heated greenhouse. This is not a difficult matter, as is sometimes assumed. All that is needed is a greenhouse heated sufficiently to provide early-June average temperatures in April, and, of course, to exclude frost on cold nights. Roses can be grown successfully, too, in a cold greenhouse, when they will come into flower some time in May, depending on the district. But this is not early enough for many growers, who understandably prefer to enjoy the blooms produced in a heated greenhouse well before any can be expected in the open.

Suitable Plants

The best time to make a start is in late October, when some fairly small plants may be lifted from the garden with a view to accommodating them in 8-in. pots. This is the most convenient size of pot and, while very vigorous varieties may need to be repotted into the 10-in. size in a few years. others will be quite happy to remain in an 8-in. pot for many years. Alternatively, some dormant budded stocks may be lifted and potted up or, better still, individual stocks may be potted up and budded in the pot outside during the following summer. The dormant budded stock, already established in its pot,

140

could be brought into the greenhouse during the following December. While seedling briar stocks are quite satisfactory, cutting Rugosa is particularly valuable for pot work, with its very fibrous root system which soon fills the pot.

Where the third method of budding the stocks in the pots is adopted, the latter must be sunk up to their rims outside after the stocks have been potted up, and care taken to see that the compost in the pots never dries out. It is a good plan to apply a thick mulch of peat over the surface of the sunken pots, and to give them regular thorough soakings during dry weather. Budding will be undertaken just as if the stocks were planted in the garden, but it will pay to insert the bud as close to the roots as possible to avoid trouble with suckers.

Compost and Potting

Much has been written about the ideal compost for pot roses. There is no doubt that top-quality fibrous loam, obtained from a pasture in good heart, is excellent, and a mixture of 5 parts of this (by weight) with 1 part each of sharp sand and dried pulverised cow manure, together with 2 or 3 handfuls of meat and bone meal, a handful of coarse hoof and horn and a handful of sulphate of potash per half dozen pots, will give satisfactory results. These ingredients should be mixed really thoroughly to ensure uniformity throughout. As loam is such a variable material and some amateurs may not wish to prepare their own, a reliable proprietary compost, such as John Innes Potting Compost No. 2 or 3, may be used instead.

If they are new, the pots should be soaked thoroughly before use. There should be an inch of crocks at the bottom of each, then a $\frac{1}{2}$ in. deep layer of $\frac{1}{2}$ in. bones. Some small pieces of fibrous turf come next, then compost is added to about one third of the way up the pot, firmed with a potting stick (a small length of old broom handle will serve admirably), and the plant or stock stood on this to test for height. The budding point should be about $1\frac{1}{2}$ in. below the rim of the pot after planting to allow for it being just covered and still leave the rim an inch above the final soil level to allow for watering and feeding.

Trimming

If the plant has been lifted from the open garden, the roots will probably need severe cutting back to fit into the pot without curling them round. Try to have plants with a well-balanced root system so that roots can point in all directions. Firm planting is important, using the potting stick to firm the compost several times while it is being added over and around the roots. Any long straggling growth should be shortened and all the leaves and flower buds cut off, but pruning will be left until Christmas or the beginning of January. The pots may be left outside in a sheltered corner until early December, when those containing plants (as distinct from stocks, which will be left outside for another year) will be transferred to the greenhouse. The top ventilators should be kept open and no heat introduced at this stage. Newly-potted roses must on no account be forced in their first year, as they have not had time to fill the pot with roots.

Figure 24. Pruning roses in pots. A bush rose before and after pruning
and a standard rose before and after pruning

Pruning

Pruning will be undertaken about the end of December, and it is essential to be drastic. Weak growth should be removed entirely and the strong shoots all cut back to within two or, at the most, three eyes from the base. It must be remembered that not only do pot roses have a restricted root run, but that they must not be allowed to become too tall – otherwise in a few years' time they will not fit into some greenhouses, as they tend to be longer jointed under glass than out of doors. The rule must therefore be to prune hard every year, back to two eyes from the point of origin of new shoots.

Heating, Watering and Ventilation

After pruning leave the plants for at least a further week before introducing a little heat. If it is turned on before the pruning cuts have healed, loss of sap by bleeding may be excessive. When growth has begun, spraying the plants with lukewarm water will help them, but once the foliage has developed only rainwater should be used for spraying in hard water districts, as tap water will leave an unsightly lime deposit on the leaves. Watering should not be excessive until rapid growth indicates that plenty of water is required. It should never be applied cold, straight from the tap, but at approximately the temperature of the greenhouse. Damping down several times daily by watering the floor on warm days will help to maintain humidity, especially in April when the sun can be strong when shining through glass.

Temperature control, ventilation and shading are interdependent and will require care. Indeed, these and watering will largely determine the success of the venture. The air must be kept buoyant at all times and a night temperature not below 5° C. (40° F.) should be aimed at. During the day, fluctuations will be unavoidable, and when the sun is strong outside the temperature can soon rise to over three figures, especially in a small greenhouse. Some form of shading will be needed to avoid scorching from such extremes, and this could take the form of slatted blinds, limewash applied to the glass of the roof and upper sides, or curtains, either of fabric or green polythene sheeting. Roof ventilators only should be used, as side ventilation usually produces draughts which encourage mildew. Day temperatures to be aimed at may be 10° C. (50° F.) during February, 13–16° C. (55-60° F.) during March, 16-18° C. (60–65° F.) during the first half of April and 18–21° C. (65–70° F.) in the second half of April. Night temperatures may be about 5° C. (10° F.) below these day temperatures for the respective periods.

While the pots should receive a thorough soaking at approximately weekly intervals when the plants are growing freely, the actual quantity of liquid required may vary considerably between individual pots. The old method of tapping the outside of each pot with a mallet, made from a 4-in. length of broom handle in the middle of which a hole is drilled to fit a bamboo cane to form a handle, is still useful. If a dull, heavy sound is produced by tapping, the soil is moist enough, but if a ringing tone is emitted, more water is needed. If a pot is cracked, though, it will never emit a ringing tone when tapped, even if the soil is bone dry!

Feeding and Spraying

Watering may be combined with liquid feeding from late February. Very weak manure water may be applied about once a week, and towards the end of March, when the flower buds should be forming, 1 oz. nitrate of potash dissolved in 1 gal. of soft water may be used as a supplementary feed.

Insect pests and mildew should be tackled in the early stages. Normally, greenfly and caterpillars are the only insects likely to give trouble. The former can quite easily be controlled by hand in a small structure or by spraying with a BHC or derris formulation, and the latter can be dealt with by finger and thumb. Mildew will be no problem if top ventilation, rather than side ventilation, is given, and extremes between day and night temperatures are avoided. If any does appear, spray with a dinocap preparation at the first sign.

Flowering

Disbudding may be necessary, as normally only one bud should be allowed to each shoot on hybrid teas, so that a really top-size flower may be enjoyed free from the blemishes which often afflict outdoor roses. After the first flush of flowers has finished, remove the dead flowers with a few inches of stem and start hardening off by turning off the heat and opening all ventilators. Remove the pots from the house about mid-June, either sinking them up to their rims in ashes or standing them along the side of a hard path in a sheltered position. I sink mine up to their rims in sandy soil on the north side of the house and apply a mulch of granulated peat to the surface to save

Right: Leaves damaged on their underside by leaf hopper
Bottom left: Scurfy scale, a scale insect which occasionally infests the shoots and stems of roses
Bottom right: Robin's Pincushion, the nest of the gall wasp

Left: Manx Queen
(Flori.)
Bottom: Orange
Sensation (Flori.)

frequent watering in dry weather. If there have been any casualties among the outdoor bedding roses I remove the dead bush and sink a pot rose up to its rim to fill up the gap for the summer. An occasional application of liquid fertiliser may help to stimulate new basal shoots, but these should not be allowed to flower freely, or it may affect the flowering under glass in the following spring.

Re-potting

During the early part of October, before the weather becomes too bad, the drainage of the pots should be checked and any worms and suckers removed by knocking the plant out of the pot with the ball of soil intact. Remove the top inch or so of soil, first loosening it carefully with a small fork to avoid damage to any surface roots. Replace it with some new compost, enriched with dried cow manure, bonemeal or a little fish manure, and then leave the pots outside until early December, when they are again brought into the greenhouse and the cycle is repeated as already outlined. The glass of the house, both inside and outside, and the whole of the interior should be thoroughly cleaned just before the pots are brought in.

Varieties

The main attraction, to me at any rate, of growing roses in pots under glass, is to enjoy the perfection of the very full-petalled hybrid teas when grown in this way. In a small greenhouse it seems rather a pity to devote valuable space to the floribundas, although these will do well enough under glass. Some full-petalled hybrid teas which will please the connoisseur of perfectly formed blooms are given below, but there are many others:

Shades of red: Christian Dior, Ena Harkness, Fragrant Cloud, Josephine Bruce, Karl Herbst
Shades of pink: Ballet, Eden Rose, Gavotte, Margaret, Pink Favourite, Sarah Arnot
Pink and white blends: Isabel de Ortiz, Perfecta, Stella
Pink and yellow blends: Gail Borden, My Choice
Off-white, flushed pink: Memoriam
Yellow and yellow flushed pink: Dorothy Peach, Grandpa Dickson, Peace
Vermilion: Princess, Super Star
Salmon red: Montezuma
Cerise: Wendy Cussons

15

Labour Saving in the Rose Garden

Labour saving for the busy amateur – Rose groups demanding much labour –
Labour-saving equipment – Beds rather than borders – Wide spacing of plants –
Avoidance of disease-prone varieties and those of sprawling or lax habit –
Exclusion of standard and pillar roses from windswept gardens – Width of paths
to suit the mower – Hard pruning to reduce labour – Combined operations after
pruning – Labour-saving rootstocks – Weeding – Mulching with peat – Chemical
weed control among roses

In these days of scarcity of labour, with few people with horticultural
knowledge willing to work part time in somebody else's garden, it
becomes necessary in larger gardens – say of half an acre or more –
to plan the lay-out, equipment and cultural programme with an eye
to saving as much labour as possible.

Roses Requiring Much Work

Some groups of roses seem to be very demanding in labour requirements and I would place the old Wichuraiana ramblers high on this
list. When one considers the work entailed every year in cutting out
all the canes that have flowered and tying in the new canes to take
their place for flowering in the following year, and all for a prodigal
display over a mere three or four weeks, it would seem that the owner
of a large garden with little or no assistance ought to think twice
before including them in any quantity. It is true that there are places,
such as steep banks, where they may be allowed to ramble more or
less at will, but if they are not to become a thicket of tangled growth,
a lot of attention will still be needed.

One might also begrudge the time spent in training some of the
very vigorous climbing sports of bush hybrid teas. Although these
do not involve the wholesale removal of old canes like the
Wichuraiana ramblers, the new canes have to be bent over and

146

trained as horizontally as possible to induce them to flower with reasonable freedom, and all the lateral growths on the older canes have to be shortened, quite apart from the periodic renewal of rustic fences and other supports. It is evident that for anybody afflicted with labour shortage, the modern recurrent-flowering climbers are a far better proposition than the two rampant groups already mentioned. Apart from the more prolonged periods of flowering, they are more restrained in growth and much less demanding in their pruning requirements.

Pruning

Pruning, of course, is one of the seasonal tasks most demanding of labour and, unfortunately, it cannot be deferred after the sap has started to rise. I normally stagger the operation over as long a period as possible by starting on the hardier groups towards the end of November if I should be held up by wet weather for planting. In this connection I treat the pruning of these groups as a stand-by task, to be tackled when the soil is in no condition for digging, weeding or planting.

When considering whether to practise light or moderate pruning, always bear in mind that the pruning itself will take longer when light, because perhaps three or four laterals will have to be shortened for every main stem that is cut back lower down with fairly severe pruning. This is a lot of extra work when 500 or 1,000 plants may be involved. Moreover, lightly pruned plants will naturally be taller and more susceptible to gale damage, and may even need some support in exposed gardens.

After pruning, it is a great labour saver if the topdressing of meat and bone meal, combined with hoof and horn, is applied as soon as the prunings have been raked together and removed. Only one pricking over of the beds is then required to make good the trampling down associated with pruning and to incorporate the dressing of fertiliser with the top inch or two of soil.

Equipment

Labour-saving equipment and appliances are an obvious means of getting through the chores more quickly. Powered mowers, rotary cultivators, electric hedge trimmers, powered edging tools, lawn fertiliser spreaders and the like spring readily to mind. So do continuous-action sprayers and automatic sprinklers.

147

Lay-out of Rose Garden

Probably a less spectacular, but nonetheless effective, field for economising in labour is in the lay-out of the garden. Rose beds always require less labour than long borders, with a boundary fence or wall at the back. The beds may be tackled from both sides, unless they are very wide, without trampling down the soil in the process, whether planting, pruning, pricking over, mulching or the removal of suckers is involved. On the other hand, if wide borders are planted with roses and there is only a frontal approach, there is no alternative to moving about between the plants and becoming impaled on the thorns and scratched frequently, thereby slowing down the main operation. Ideally the beds should be about 6 ft. wide to accommodate three rows of plants spaced 2 ft. apart, with 1 ft. to spare between the two outside rows and the edge of the bed. This fairly wide spacing for varieties of only average vigour will enable weeding to be tackled with greater ease and will also tend to reduce the incidence of disease as compared with closer planting.

The width of the paths between the rose beds and the length of the beds will also have a direct bearing on the labour required for mowing grass paths and trimming the edges. Sharp corners should be rounded off and the cutting of numerous small beds in a lawn should be avoided, since they require a disproportionately large number of man-hours in keeping the edges tidy, as well as slowing down mowing. Crazy paving, stone or brick paths instead of grass will eliminate the weekly chores of mowing and trimming, although they are less attractive as a setting.

Excluding Disease-prone and Lax-growing Varieties

Quite apart from the spacing of the plants affecting the incidence of disease, it is highly desirable that varieties known to be particularly disease prone should be excluded from the garden where labour is at a premium. The same may be said of those with a sprawling or lax habit of growth, which makes cultivation more difficult and, when these varieties have been planted in beds cut in the lawn, interferes with the mowing and trimming of the edges. In windswept gardens standards and pillar roses are very doubtful assets, as the supports are so vulnerable to damage in gales and high winds generally, especially where the soil is fertile and cultivation thorough, so that there is a lot of growth to support. Renewal of broken posts and stakes, not to mention the ties, takes up a lot of time in such gardens. Standard roses with large heads impose a great strain on even stout stakes in exposed gardens, and frequent renewal, even when oak stakes are used, seems to be inevitable.

Labour-saving Types of Roses

Another obvious saving in labour is to grow floribundas and the decorative type of hybrid teas, which do not often need a lot of disbudding, for garden display. It is the exhibitor of specimen blooms who finds it essential to disbud, to de-shoot, to feed with liquid manures and to shade with bloom protectors, all of which is very time consuming. Growing for general garden display, on the other hand, necessitates far less effort per dozen plants.

Those who do their own budding will also find that it pays to use a rootstock which does not sucker freely, as this will save a great deal of labour which would otherwise be spent in removing suckers from established beds in later years. For instance, Rugosa cutting stocks throw a tiresome succession of suckers, whereas Multiflora cuttings, if carefully prepared, seldom produce suckers. This advice, though, must be read in conjunction with the section of Chapter 11 (p. 118) dealing with the various types of rootstocks and their suitability for different soils. The labour required for budding standard and half-standard Rugosa stems can be reduced by inserting buds exactly opposite each other in the main stem and using one length of raffia to bind them simultaneously.

Weed Control

Weeding and weed control perhaps offer the greatest possible scope for labour-saving practices. Mulching the beds with a thick layer of granulated peat – a sterile material – discourages the germination of weed seeds, although perennial weeds usually manage to emerge through the mulch. There are some encouraging reports, too, where chemical weed control in rose beds has been tried. This may take the form of a pre-emergent weedkiller, such as simazine, which is applied to the soil surface after the bed has been entirely freed from weeds. To be effective, the soil must not be disturbed after the weedkiller has been applied.

Alternatively, a paraquat weedkiller may be sprayed or applied, through a special sprinkler bar attached to a watering can, to the leaves and stems of weeds when they are growing freely in the rose beds. Care must be taken not to apply the liquid to the leaves or soft growing shoots of the roses, as it does not discriminate between weeds and roses. A home-made portable screen is useful when applying the liquid, to protect the roses from any drift. I am afraid that my own experiments with paraquat during the two wet seasons of 1965 and 1966 were disappointing, possibly due to the excessive rain encouraging the weeds even more than usual. I found that although the leaves would be turned brown and growth would be inhibited for a few weeks, the weeds of a perennial type would grow with their pristine vigour apparently unimpaired a few weeks after application of the liquid. It may be, however, that in many gardens paraquat will be much more effective, so I think that each grower should experiment and decide thereafter whether chemical weed-killers are likely to cut down labour appreciably under his own particular growing conditions.

Figure 25. Applying paraquat weedkiller around rose bushes with a dribble bar fixed to an ordinary watering-can

16

Roses for Fragrance

Fragrance and your roses – The different types of rose fragrance – Planting fragrant varieties near windows – Selections of highly fragrant varieties – Old garden roses and fragrance – Cutting roses for the house

It is sometimes said that beauty is in the eyes of the beholder; so, also, there may be justification for remarking that fragrance is in the nose of the smeller. Certainly, sensitivity to fragrance varies enormously between individuals. Nasal catarrh and heavy smoking will surely impair the ability to appreciate fragrance in full, and to distinguish between its many types, as exuded by modern and old garden roses.

Perhaps the most powerful and distinctive fragrance is the rich damask aroma of some old garden roses, and such crimson varieties as Hugh Dickson, Crimson Glory, Papa Meilland and Chrysler Imperial. There are many roses with this glorious perfume, including a number in shades of pink, but unfortunately the most fragrant are not always first-class garden roses in other respects, notably resistance to disease. When Pernet-Ducher introduced the Pernetiana roses (now merged with the hybrid teas) early in the present century, many of these in shades of yellow, orange and flame, and other crosses introduced in the years between the wars, had a distinctly fruity fragrance, reminiscent of ripe apples. Betty Uprichard, introduced in 1921 and still available, has a distinct verbena perfume, while some other hybrid teas like Ophelia and Shot Silk, to name two famous introductions, are credited with a sweet honey scent. Some of the modern floribundas – Spartan and Dearest are good examples – have a definite spicy scent which has been identified more specifically with cloves, and I would certainly not disagree. Some enthusiasts with unusually keen olfactory organs say they can isolate the fragrance of ripe raspberries in Tzigane, of apricots in

Marcelle Gret and of myrrh in Magenta. While I would not presume to be so definite, although a non-smoker and endowed with a nose of generous proportions, it is true that there are many variants among the fruity, citrus, sharp and spicy scents in modern roses.

The 'tea' scent is more widely acknowledged and identifiable. Many of the old tea-scented roses, contemporaries of the hybrid perpetuals, had this curious fragrance, so called because of its resemblance to that of a freshly-opened tea chest. Golden Dawn, among modern roses, has this character in marked degree. The musk scent is also widely recognised and identifiable in the hybrid musks, such as Penelope, Cornelia, Moonlight and Felicia, although difficult to define. A delicate wild rose fragrance is attributed to the floribunda Fashion, and I have always found the sweet briar fragrance of the Wichuraiana rambler François Juranville most refreshing and noticeable after warm rain in early summer. The hybrid sweet briars, of course, all have this character highly developed, with the fragrance exuded by the foliage resembling that of ripe apples. I once had a hedge of these hybrids round three sides of my front garden, and the scent after rain was almost overpowering at times.

Whatever the subtle qualities identified by connoisseurs of rose fragrance, it is a fact that this arises from certain essential oils, contained mostly in the petals. These oils are highly volatile, but require a temperature probably over 18° C. (65° F.), and sufficient humidity in the air to develop their full potential of fragrance. This is one reason why the scent of some varieties seems to be capricious, sometimes strong, and at other times – possibly with lower temperatures – hardly detectable. When some roses credited with only a slight fragrance are cut and arranged indoors, they may develop quite a heady perfume, with the warmth of the room and the still atmosphere providing the right conditions.

It is this unstable character in rose fragrance which accounts to some extent for differences of opinion concerning the scent of even well-known varieties, when grown and tested under varying conditions. How much more difficult, then, must it be to assess the fragrance of an unnamed new seedling undergoing its trials and probably not grown anywhere except on the raiser's nursery, apart from the few plants sent to the Rose Society's Trial Ground.

However easy it may sometimes be to fall into the habit of denigrating modern varieties, there are sufficient powerfully scented

Left: Rose slugworm damage caused by larvae of the rose slug sawfly
Left centre: Leaf-cutter bee damage
Bottom: Green capsid bug damage. This is a more menacing pest than is often thought

Opposite page: Evelyn Fison (Flori.)

Left: Shepherdess (Flori. H.T. type)
Below: Golden Slippers (Flori.)

Top: Black spot on rose leaves, an extremely common trouble in rural districts
Bottom left: Symptoms of rust, probably the most serious disease of the rose
Bottom right: Vein-banding mosaic, in which the pale yellow or creamy-white
veining is clearly visible

roses which are highly desirable in other respects – free flowering, vigorous and healthy and attractive in form of flower, colouring and foliage – to justify making special arrangements to plant them in beds near the house, where their perfume may be wafted in through open doors and windows on warm summer days and evenings. In the main the hybrid teas carry the strongest perfumes among modern groups and some of these, arranged for convenience under broad colour groups, are mentioned below. For more detailed descriptions the reader is referred to Chapter 20.

FRAGRANT HYBRID TEAS

Shades of crimson and scarlet: Ernest H. Morse, Fragrant Cloud, Chrysler Imperial, Ena Harkness, Josephine Bruce, Lancastrian, Mme Louis Laperrière, Papa Meilland

Cerise, carmine and deep pink: June Park, Prima Ballerina, Wendy Cussons

Medium pink and pink with lighter shadings: Belle Ange, Eden Rose, Grace de Monaco, Lady Sylvia, Monique, Tiffany

Pink and yellow blends: Elsa Arnot, My Choice, President Herbert Hoover, Teenager

Pale pink and pink and cream blends: Angel Wings, Ophelia, Polly, Silver Lining

Flame, coppery-pink and gold: Signora

Pure vermilion: Super Star

Yellow, buff, etc: Diamond Jubilee, Golden Melody

Orange-yellow, shaded pink: Diorama, Sutter's Gold

Lavender and mauve: Blue Moon, Sterling Silver

Cherry-red and gold bicolor: Westminster

The above named include some of the most sweetly-scented hybrid teas in cultivation. It would have been very easy to extend the list by including more of the crimson varieties descended from Crimson Glory, but the temptation has been resisted, as nearly all of them succumb rather easily to mildew and can look a sorry sight late in the season when spraying of the soft new growth has been neglected.

FLORIBUNDAS

It seems rather a waste to plant beds and borders close to the windows with floribundas, as the vast majority of them just cannot compete with the best hybrid teas for fragrance. It may be, though, that some growers with an eye to maximum colour over the longest period, coupled with a moderate fragrance, may prefer to plant some of the fragrant floribundas near the house where eye appeal may sometimes take precedence over nose appeal. The following varieties are recommended with every confidence where this is the objective:

Shades of pink and salmon-pink: Charm of Paris, Dearest, Pernille Poulsen, Scented Air
Shades of orange-salmon and salmon-red: Elizabeth of Glamis, Spartan
Orange-vermilion: Orange Sensation
Golden-yellow, shaded flame-red: Lucky Charm
Cream, amber and pink blend: Sweet Repose
Pink and silver bicolor: Daily Sketch
Deep golden-yellow: Arthur Bell
Orange-yellow: Copper Delight
Lavender-mauve: Magenta

STANDARDS, HALF-STANDARDS AND CLIMBERS

Height could be added to the beds of the foregoing selections by planting a few standards or half-standards of the same varieties. Where fragrance is the prime consideration this will have the advantage of raising some of the blooms to a height convenient for savouring their perfume as individuals. If the lay-out allows a few tripods to be introduced near the house without obscuring the vista from the windows, or if it is practicable to train a few fragrant climbers on trellis-work against the walls of the house, round the windows, Maigold (bronzy-yellow), Aloha (deep rose-pink, suffused salmon), Cl. Shot Silk (orange-carmine, salmon and yellow), and Cl. Etoile de Hollande (crimson) would be suitable varieties, flowering early in the season, with some flowers later. New Dawn (flesh pink), while excellent for a pillar or tripod in the open garden, would not be suitable for planting against the house wall, but as it is sweetly scented, recurrent flowering and not rampant, few would begrudge it the space it takes up on a tripod.

OLD GARDEN ROSES

I have not even touched on the wealth of fragrance to be found among the old garden roses and many will regard this as a grave omission. It is not easy to blend the old and the new into a harmonious entity in a small garden; the colours, form, foliage, habit of growth and recurrence of the old roses are so different from the modern hybrids that segregation may be the safest rule. The enthusiasts who make a feature of the old favourites will need no recommendation from me, but the beginner might do a lot worse than try half a dozen, to see whether their old-world magic casts a spell on him. Where fragrance is of paramount importance I would suggest the bourbon Mme Ernst Calvat; the bourbon climber Zéphirine Drouhin; the hybrid Rugosas Conrad F. Meyer and Blanc Double de Coubert; the Chinensis shrub Gruss an Teplitz and the hybrid perpetual Reine des Violettes.

RULES FOR CUTTING

When cutting roses for the house it is desirable to follow one or two elementary rules to ensure that their fragrance is retained as long as possible. Cutting should be done either in the cool of the early morning or in the evening when the sun is no longer blazing in the sky. Single or semi-double roses should always be cut in the bud stage, when the sepals have parted from the petals, so that their fragile beauty and fragrance may be enjoyed without risk of damage from handling. Other roses are best cut when in the buttonhole stage and not more than half expanded.

17

Standards, Half-standards and Weeping Standards

Standard and weeping standard roses – The roles of the standard rose – Providing an extra dimension – Uses in small gardens – Isolated specimens – Recommended varieties – Half-standards for a small garden – Recommended floribunda half-standards – Weepers and those of stiffer growth – Stocks for standard roses – Special problems of planting, staking, suckering and pruning

Standard roses are similar to bush roses budded on a tall stem, except that they are normally double-budded, and bush roses are only single-budded. The object of double-budding is to form a symmetrical head in the first season, whereas a single-budded standard will take more than one season to do this. Weeping standards are produced by budding one of the Wichuraiana ramblers of lax growth on to a 5–6 ft. stem, so that the pendulous canes trail gracefully and naturally towards the soil, forming a head resembling a huge bouquet when it is in full flower.

Uses of standard roses

The role of the standard rose is normally to provide an extra dimension in an otherwise flat lay-out. This is particularly important in large rose gardens, where it is customary to plant an entire bed of perhaps 150 bushes with one variety. Where the variety is bushy and compact in habit, the general effect is improved by introducing a number of standards to provide some elevation. These may be full, half or even quarter-standards, depending on the vigour of growth of the variety. Full advantage is taken of this type of planting for maximum display in Queen Mary's Garden in Regent's Park.

Another role of the standard rose is to provide a colourful avenue of approach to the front door of the house. If the standards are well-grown specimens with balanced heads, and are to the same scale as the rest of the garden, they can be most effective. They also enable the

156

blooms to be admired at eye level and tested for fragrance as the visitor walks up the path. If bush roses also are planted in the borders flanking the path the standard stems will not be obtrusive or regimented in appearance. Standard roses have a special value in small gardens which may be hemmed in by walls, outhouses or hedges. While bush roses would tend to be deprived of light and air in such gardens and would become drawn, standards would start with a $3\frac{1}{2}$ ft. advantage and be that much closer to the light and free air circulation which are so necessary to healthy growth. I have seen standard roses flourishing in tiny patches in front of houses in the inner suburbs of London, often in competition with a nearby privet hedge, although every effort should be made to prevent encroachment by the voracious privet roots, if the experiment is to succeed over the years.

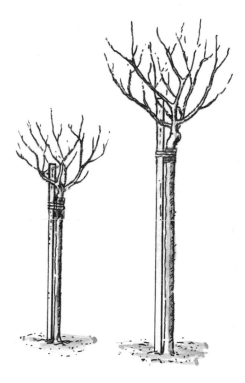

Figure 26. Half-standards *(left)* are budded at 2 ft. 4 in. above soil level and full standards *(right)* at 3 ft. 6 in.

Less usual is the planting of standard roses in place of climbing or pillar roses, to screen the top of an ugly boarded fence in the small garden where climbers would be too rampant, besides taking up too much time in pruning and training. If a row of full standards is planted just in front of the fence, the heads will disguise the upper portion and provide a pleasing background to the border. Individual stakes may be dispensed with if brackets are screwed to the fence posts, and a length of old insulated cable is secured to the brackets at a height of 3 ft. or slightly more, so that the standards can be tied to the cable just below the head. There should be a clearance of at least 15 in. between the cable and the fence and it should be stretched taut, so that friction is avoided. If a row of half-standards is planted in front of these full standards, and bush roses in front of the half-standards, it is quite easy to produce the effect of an amphitheatre of bloom, with the front rows concealing the leggy stems of standards.

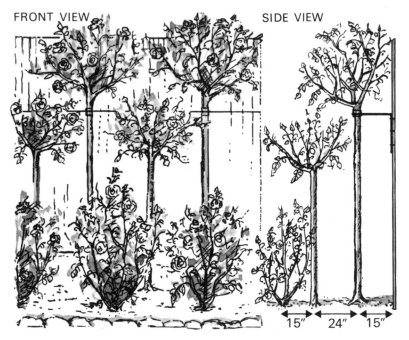

FRONT VIEW   SIDE VIEW

15"   24"   15"

Figure 27. A method of using standard roses in a small garden to screen the top of a close-boarded fence, with half-standards in front and bush roses to provide colour down to soil level

Another popular role for standards, and especially for weeping standards, is as single specimens on a lawn. It is usual to plant each one in its own circular bed, and a particularly fine specimen with a well-developed head can look impressive in splendid isolation when in full bloom. Unfortunately the flowering period of the true Wichuraiana ramblers is of short duration, although a symmetrical specimen can still be an object of interest as a focal point throughout the year.

Suitable Hybrid Tea Varieties

Not all varieties make suitable heads as standards. Some are too tall and upright and do not branch sufficiently, while a few are not vigorous enough to develop a satisfactory head. The best heads are formed by varieties which make short-jointed, branching growth and strong but sturdy bushes. Some hybrid teas which normally should give satisfactory results in this form are tabulated in the following list by main colour groups:

Shades of red: Champs Elysées, Dame de Coeur, Fragrant Cloud, Hugh Dickson, Josephine Bruce, Karl Herbst, Red Devil
Vermilion: Super Star
Salmon-red: Montezuma
White: Frau Karl Druschki
Shades of pink: Eden Rose, Margaret, Michèle Meilland, Mme Caroline Testout, Pink Favourite
Cerise: Wendy Cussons
Pink and yellow blends: Chicago Peace, Gail Borden, Helen Traubel
Yellow: Dorothy Peach, Lydia, Peace, Spek's Yellow
Orange, shaded yellow: Beauté
Bicolors: Grand Gala (scarlet and silver) Kronenbourg (crimson and gold) Lady Eve Price (cerise and ivory), Miss Ireland (salmon-orange and peach), Piccadilly (scarlet and gold), Rose Gaujard (pink and silver)

Half-standards

It seems likely that owners of small gardens are rather prone to plant full standards when half-standards are really what they require. These are budded about $2\frac{1}{3}$ ft. above soil level, compared with $3\frac{1}{2}$ ft. for standards, and are much more appropriate for a small garden than the latter. They may be expected to form at least as good heads as standards and perhaps better, as the sap has not as far to travel from the roots. Many of the larger rose specialists will be able to supply some hybrid tea varieties in half-standards, and most of them offer floribunda half-standards which are, of course, excellent for providing plenty of colour over an extended period. Most of the strong-growing modern floribundas will form large heads and, on the whole, are easier to grow than the hybrid tea standards.

Some suitable recommended floribundas are set out in the following list, grouped broadly by colour:

Shades of red: Ama, Evelyn Fison, Frensham, Independence, Paprika, Red Dandy
Orange-vermilion: Orangeade
Salmon-red, shaded scarlet: Spartan, Toni Lander
Orange-salmon: Fashion
Red, yellow and pink blends: Circus, Lucky Charm, Masquerade
Flame, orange and yellow blends: Shepherd's Delight
Golden-yellow: Allgold
Yellow, flushed pink: Faust
Shades of pink: Dearest, Vera Dalton
Pink and silver bicolor: Daily Sketch
Pink, cream and amber: Chanelle, Sweet Repose
Lavender and mauve: Africa Star, Magenta
White: Iceberg

Weeping Standards

True weeping standards of pendulous growth are not available in a very wide selection today, but all except the most ardent enthusiast – and he would most probably bud his own in any case – should find enough to satisfy them in Crimson Shower; Dorothy Perkins (bright pink); Excelsa (rosy-crimson); François Juranville (coppery-pink, shaded orange); Lady Godiva (flesh pink); Sanders' White and White Dorothy. Apart from these, though, the practice has developed of offering tall standards of many climbers and ramblers of stiffer growth. These cannot by any stretch of imagination be described as weeping standards, although many people plant them and fix an 'umbrella' trainer just below the head. The new canes are tied down to the trainer as they grow, while they are still pliable, so that a type of trained head is developed which can make an impressive display of colour. Varieties with this stiffer type of growth include Albéric Barbier (yellow buds, opening to cream); Albertine (reddish-salmon to coppery-pink); Crimson Conquest; Dr W.

Sir Lancelot (Flori.)

Right: Leaves severely affected by mildew
Bottom left: Die-back on a stem caused by the infection of an open wound
Bottom right: If stubs are left when pruning, these invariably die back and may attract disease

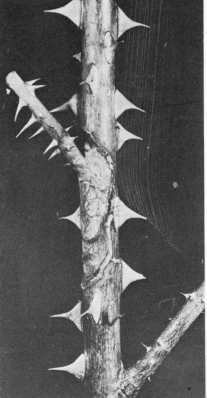

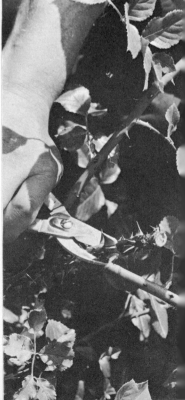

Van Fleet (flesh pink); Easlea's Golden Rambler; Emily Gray (rich golden-buff) and Paul's Scarlet Climber. Like the true weepers, these are not recurrent flowering, although it is quite usual for some of them to produce a few trusses after the main flush of bloom has finished. While, to me, these lack the grace and elegance of the true weepers when budded as standards, without having the compensation of being reliably recurrent flowering, many people like them and the fact that they continue to be offered is sufficient indication that they satisfy a demand.

Figure 28. An 'umbrella' trainer used for training a weeping standard rose

A third group comprises more recent introductions which are recurrent flowering, but of the somewhat stiffer growth which really requires tying down to some form of trainer. While not as graceful as the true weepers these do provide colour over an extended period and are therefore worthy of consideration on their merits as a separate group. All of them have most attractive and healthy foliage and some are hybrids of *R. kordesii*, raised by Wilhelm Kordes, of Germany, and notable for their exceptional winter hardiness. Recommended varieties include Danse du Feu (orange-scarlet); Dortmund (single, crimson, with white centre); Golden Showers; Hamburger Phoenix (crimson); Leverkusen (pale yellow); New Dawn (flesh pink); Parkdirektor Riggers (crimson-scarlet) and Ritter von Barmstede (deep pink).

Planting of Standard Roses

General care of standard roses, so far as preparation of the soil and feeding are concerned, is the same as for bush roses. What is different is the planting, which needs to be very shallow, especially with Rugosa stems, as these have a natural tendency to throw up suckers. If the root system of a well-grown Rugosa standard is examined, it will usually be found to consist of two or three flat layers of fibrous roots. Unless the upper layers are removed it is almost impossible to plant them so that the bottom layer is close enough to the surface. This may sound rather drastic treatment, but if the soil is reasonably light, further roots will soon develop and, what is more important, trouble from suckering should not be anything like as great as when all the roots are left intact and the bottom ones are planted too deeply. On a really heavy soil the Rugosa stems are less satisfactory, especially if the soil is cold, and it would be better in the long run to plant standards budded on English briar (*R. canina*) or one of its selected strains, such as Pfanders, on such soils, leaving Rugosa stems for lighter soils.

Staking

Staking of standards and half-standards is a first priority. A stout oak stake should be driven into the hole before the roots have been covered during planting. It should be long enough when driven firmly into place for the top to come well up into the head, to give firmer support. There should be two ties – one just below the head and the other a foot or so lower down. Thick felt or an old nylon stocking should be wrapped round the stake and also round the standard stem before tying the two with either tarred string or old insulated electric cable. This protection against chafing is very important, as a well-developed head offers considerable wind resistance and the vital dormant eyes near the budding points can be ruined by friction.

Pruning and Removal of Suckers

Pruning must aim at keeping the centre of the head open and developing both sides so that they are symmetrical. This may seem obvious, but it is not always as easy as it sounds, as the individual scions are not necessarily of equal vigour. The closer together the buds are inserted on the standard stem, the closer the scions should resemble each other in growth. A few nurserymen insert the buds

162

exactly opposite each other in Rugosa stems, but this is seldom possible with English briar stems, as these are budded in the lateral growths which are normally staggered on the stem. Pruning weeping standards will aim at cutting out the canes that have flowered, leaving only the vigorous new canes which start developing from the budding points in summer. Where there are insufficient of these, one or two of the canes which have flowered may be kept for a further season, but all the laterals on these should be cut back to two or three eyes from the main stem.

Sometimes suckers will start to grow on the standard stem below the head, and these must be removed while very small. Most of the trouble with suckers, though, will be from those springing from the root system. These may appear several feet away from the stem and must not be allowed to develop to any great size – otherwise the standard head will be weakened and may eventually be starved to death.

18

Autumn in the Rose Garden

*Seasonal tasks – Preparing for the winter – Shortening extra-long growths –
Cleaning up operations – Ripening off the wood – Limiting the number of late
flowers – Winter protection – Outstanding autumn varieties*

With modern roses 'the last rose of summer' has become an
anachronism, when magnificent displays often delight the eye in
mid-October, or even later, in the absence of severe frosts. It is no
exaggeration to say that the modern hybrid teas and floribundas –
and many modern shrub roses and recurrent ciimbers, for that
matter – will go on flowering as long as the weather remains open,
but once the sap has been frosted no further worthwhile blooms of
typical colouring will open outside.

Cultivation of a routine nature, such as weeding and spraying,
particularly spraying against disease, should continue during the
autumn, both to enable the rose beds and borders to look their best
and to prevent black spot getting out of hand in pure-air districts.
Very often the richest colours of the entire season appear in the
autumn – shades of a purity and intensity seldom matched in the
more torrid 'dog days' of June. Not only is there the wealth of colour
normally associated with the season of mists and mellow fruitfulness
– the glistening tawny-gold, the opulent orange, russet and coppery-
bronze; the glowing crimson, fiery scarlet and flamboyant vermilion;
the vivid orange-salmon, flame, reddish-apricot and scarlet and gold
bicolors – there is also the richly-hued foliage of many of the rose
species, with their quota of scarlet heps, to add colour to the scene.
Some near hybrids of species, the hybrid Rugosas, for example, have
foliage which assumes glorious gold and copper tints just before
leaf-fall.

Autumn Fertilising

While enjoying a fine show of colour, assuming one is blessed with a dry autumn, one should not forget that preparations must be made for the approaching winter. If it has not already been applied, a dressing of sulphate of potash at the rate of 2 oz. per sq. yd. will materially assist the ripening and hardening of the new wood, and this is particularly important following a wet season with below-average sunshine, which may have encouraged a lot of lush growth. No liquid stimulants should be given at this time of year, as there is no point in encouraging soft new wood to develop, only to have it killed back by the first really severe frosts.

Cleaning Rose Beds

Cleaning up the rose beds will help to present a cheerful front, whatever the weather. In most autumns there will be sodden, rotted or 'balled' blooms to snap off, or diseased leaves, as well as the occasional entire shoot which has died back, to remove. I can never see any point in leaving masses of immature buds on the plants when a severe frost can be expected almost nightly. It seems better to compromise by disbudding quite severely in the hope of obtaining two or perhaps three respectable blooms, rather than have hundreds which are frosted before they even show colour. This is a tremendous waste of plant energy – just as allowing every sappy new growth to develop late in the season is wasteful, as the soft wood just will not survive the first severe frost. Far better to rub these out in the early stages, if one can so harden one's heart.

Preparing New Beds

The preparation of new beds, to receive plants for which orders have already been placed, is another autumn task which is better tackled early, before the heavy rains of November make the soil unworkable. The transplanting of maiden plants from their nursery rows to their permanent quarters is also best done in October, before plants can reasonably be expected to be lifted and delivered by the rose specialist. Mid-October is sometimes ideal for this operation, but all the leaves, buds and soft growth should be removed, as well as the stub beyond the inserted bud. This stub should be pared off smoothly with a sharp knife.

It is surprising how much damage rose shoots will inflict on each other during the autumn and winter gales, and everybody who has had to sacrifice very promising shoots because of severe lacerations caused by the prickles of adjacent plants will need no exhortation from me to shorten any extra-long growths in advance. It is so fatally easy to overlook this, or to postpone it until working conditions are less unpleasant, by which time the damage may have been done. Similar remarks apply, too, to the climbers and shrub roses which can produce enormous autumn shoots. If these cannot be tied in to their supports, then it is better to shorten them in good time – otherwise they are likely to be little use after having been lashed about like whips for days on end.

Removing Unnecessary Wood

Much cleaning up can be done in the autumn among the Wichuraiana ramblers and the weeping standards of these ramblers. Nearly all the canes which have flowered may be cut right out in September. This will assist the ripening of the new canes which, in the case of the rambling forms, may be tied in to the supports for flowering next season. The true weeping standards will not really need an umbrella trainer, so no tying in of the new canes is necessary. The removal of the old canes will be far easier in the autumn as, if left over until spring, it will be found that, even when the canes are cut into sections, it will be almost impossible to remove them without damaging a lot of early new shoots on the young canes.

It is a valuable time-saver to go over the plants in mid-October to remove any dead, decadent, damaged or badly diseased wood. This will save much time when pruning later. Where black spot and rust have been troublesome during the season it will probably be found that there are a number of stems which have died back to an intermediate point. Where these diseases have not been fully controlled by earlier spraying, it is worth trying spraying the wood after most of the leaves have been shed with a weak solution of disinfectant or Bordeaux mixture, taking care to spray the surface of the soil under the plants as well. The fallen leaves should be raked up and burnt.

Winter Protection

As part of the routine preparation for the winter months, some growers with very exposed gardens, particularly in the north, make a practice of earthing up with loose soil round the base of their bush roses. Others like to apply a thick mulch of animal manure to the beds in the late autumn, arguing that this will protect the roses from the most severe frosts. I must say that I have not much faith in either of these practices. Earthing up may conceivably save some pithy wood from the worst effects of icy winds and may enable it to survive a mild winter, but it certainly will not protect it from severe frosts such as were experienced in the winter of 1962–63. What I would recommend, though, in particularly exposed gardens, is the protection of the heads of standard roses by wrapping straw round the scions near the budding points and tying it down to the main stem, so that it is held firmly in place over the vital union. But the straw should be removed as soon as the sap rises in the spring, to avoid forcing the wood into premature growth.

Applying a thick mulch of animal manure in the autumn seems to me to be largely a waste of a valuable and scarce material, as most of the nutrients will be washed away during heavy winter rains. I have heard it described as tantamount to pouring beer over a sleeping man! I would have thought that a mulch saturated with icy rain would tend to lower the soil temperature, rather than to

Figure 29. Protecting the head of a standard rose with straw during the winter. Care should be taken to see that the budding points are well covered and that the ends of the straw are tied down to the main stem

167

afford winter protection. On a cold heavy soil it is not a practice I would advocate, but on light soils which need to be made more retentive of moisture, it probably does no harm, if little good, compared with the practice of applying the mulch about the end of April.

SOME OUTSTANDING AUTUMN-FLOWERING ROSES

A. Hybrid Teas

Shades of crimson and scarlet: Ena Harkness, Ernest H. Morse, Josephine Bruce, Lancastrian, Lucy Cramphorn

Vermilion: Super Star

Scarlet and yellow bicolor: Piccadilly

Cerise: Wendy Cussons

Cerise and ivory bicolor: Lady Eve Price (Caprice)

Coral-salmon: Mischief

Coral-salmon, with peach reverse: Miss Ireland

Burnt orange and flame: Mojave

Orange and yellow shaded: Beaute, Diorama, Sutter's Gold

Apricot centre, shading to cream: Anne Watkins

Shades of yellow: Dorothy Peach, Grandpa Dickson, Parasol, Peace, Spek's Yellow

Yellow, pink and orange blend: Signora

Yellow and pink blend or bicolor: Chicago Peace, Gail Borden, My Choice

Carmine-pink, paling to cream in centre: Stella

Carmine-pink, shading to silver: Rose Gaujard

Shades of pink: Eden Rose, Pink Supreme, Prima Ballerina

B. Floribundas

Shades of scarlet and crimson: Evelyn Fison, Lilli Marlene, Paprika, Red Dandy

Orange-scarlet: Fervid, Korona, Meteor, Orange Sensation

Orange-yellow and orange: Amberlight, Copper Delight, Golden Slippers, Vesper

Shades of yellow: Allgold, Arthur Bell, Chinatown, Faust, Goldgleam

Coppery-salmon, shaded scarlet: Toni Lander

Salmon-red: Arabian Nights

Salmon-pink: Pernille Poulsen, Scented Air

Orange-Salmon: Elizabeth of Glamis, Tombola

Cream, amber and pink blends: Mandy, Sweet Repose
Pink, orange and yellow blends: Circus, Travesti
Rose-pink: Vera Dalton
Pink and silver bicolor: Daily Sketch
Orange-flame and yellow: Shepherd's Delight
White: Iceberg

19

Renovating the Neglected Rose Garden

Dealing with sucker growth – Re-budding, where possible, using strongest sucker to make a standard rose – Getting rid of beds which may not be worth reclaiming – Pruning to bring plants back into shape and to encourage new basal shoots – Treatment of bush and shrub roses – Gradual elimination of old stems on which the bark has thickened – Treatment of ramblers and climbers – Rose hedges – Neglected standard roses – Perennial weeds and their destruction

It must often happen that force of circumstances may compel a keen amateur to purchase a house, perhaps in a different area, the garden of which has been neglected for several years. Little imagination is needed to envisage the wilderness which may confront him where roses have been neglected for even a couple of years.

Removal of Suckers

Perhaps the most urgent task is the removal of sucker growths from the rootstock, as these will be depriving the cultivated rose of food. As already indicated in Chapter 9 these should be pulled off at their junction with the rootstock or the root itself – it is not sufficient to cut them off just below soil level. Before going to this trouble, though, it will be advisable to check that the cultivated variety is still alive and worth keeping, as it does not take long, with suckers growing freely, to kill the cultivated rose by starvation. If this has happened, or growth is too weak to warrant the trouble of reclaiming the variety, the complete plant should be dug out and burnt.

Exceptionally it may be decided in such a case, where there is a particularly strong sucker, to try budding this to form a standard or half-standard *in situ*. All other growths should be cut away to concentrate the strength of the roots on this one sucker, which should be budded in June or July, as explained in Chapter 11.

Sometimes a complete bed may have to be scrapped, where,

170

perhaps, the variety may have been none too vigorous in the first place, and the rootstocks with their suckers will have taken control with little competition. In such a case the bed should be dug over thoroughly after the plants have been dug up, given a dressing of animal manure if available, or failing that, one of peat and a complete fertiliser, and some other crop grown for several seasons to bring the soil into good heart before attempting to grow roses on it again.

Where only some of the plants are worth keeping, there is a natural tendency to try to economise by filling the gaps with young, newly-purchased plants. In general, this practice is not to be recommended, as the young plants rarely catch up with their elders. The main objection, though, apart from the patchy effect, is that the soil will most likely have become 'rose sick' by having grown roses for many years. If, therefore, replacements in established beds are essential, because no other site is available, then it is most important to replace at least a cubic foot of the soil in which the roots will be planted. This need not be replaced with fresh soil purchased from an outside source. Provided that it has not grown roses before, soil from the vegetable plot, for instance, which has yielded good crops, should be quite adequate.

Pruning

Assuming that the rose beds are not too far gone and that reasonable plants of the cultivated varieties still exist, treatment will be aimed at pruning so as to eliminate hard, woody stems on which the bark has thickened, and to rejuvenate the plants by encouraging the production of new shoots from the base. The dormant buds there will have more difficulty in breaking into growth through the thickened bark of the old stems, and the choice may lie between cutting back all the old stems in the first season – thus running the risk of the plant dying under this drastic treatment – or cutting back only one or two of them hard. The remainder could then be carefully bent over and tied to canes, to encourage the new basal shoots to develop. I rather favour the second treatment, which may allow the remainder of the old stems to be cut away in the second season, when all the new basal shoots produced in the first season will be retained. This applies to both bedding and shrub roses. The latter will also probably need a considerable amount of thinning out of the growths and shortening of those which are retained to ensure symmetrical specimens.

Ramblers and Climbers

Neglected rambling and climbing roses are rather a different proposition. When the main canes have been allowed to grow vertically, this results in a tangled mass of growth 8 ft. or more above the ground, with bare stems at a lower level. The first step is to untie the canes from their supports so that they lie flat on the ground. It is then much simpler to sort out the healthy young wood and to cut out all dead, exhausted and twiggy wood, than when standing precariously on top of a ladder.

In the case of ramblers cut out the canes which have flowered; these are the ones with numerous twiggy side shoots. Tie the young canes to the supports without delay and make sure, by watering the base of the plant thoroughly, that it is not short of moisture – otherwise mildew will almost certainly give trouble.

In the case of climbers, including the climbing sports of bush hybrid teas, the problem is to encourage the production of new wood from the base of the plant. This is best ensured by leaving the canes lying prone on the soil for a few weeks before re-tying them to the supports, and then bending them over by attaching them to horizontal wires, if growing against a wall. Similarly, the laterals from the main canes should be bent over and tied down, and also any new growths from the base of the plant. The effect of all this is to force the dormant lower buds into growth.

Rose Hedges

Rose hedges which have been allowed to get out of hand will need trimming and any dead wood cutting out. The extent of the trimming necessary will depend on the groups to which the roses belong and on whether a boundary or an internal hedge is involved. A boundary hedge planted with some of the hybrid Rugosas, for example, will probably not need a lot of trimming except where there may be danger to pedestrians from projecting prickly stems. Internal hedges comprising floribundas and floribunda shrubs may need the removal of a lot of dead and twiggy wood and the healthy stems cut back to ensure some semblance of uniformity.

In all cases a thick mulch with organic manure or peat will be beneficial after weeds have first been removed from round the base of the plants. This should be supplemented with a dressing of a complete rose fertiliser during the spring or early summer.

Standards

Neglected standard roses often pose a problem. Where these are budded on Rugosa stems, suckering is likely to be so prolific after even a couple of seasons of neglect that the head may be in a sorry condition, and gale damage, due to the stakes or the ties having ceased to be effective, may have aggravated the problem. Suckers must be removed completely, not only from the main stem but also any springing from the root system. It is unlikely that many Rugosa standards will be worth keeping after several years of neglect, as they do not normally have as long a life as standards budded on English Briar. A common sight in neglected gardens is the legacy from Rugosa standards, where the head of the cultivated rose has died and suckers from the rootstock have produced a strong Rugosa bush, bearing magenta-pink single flowers in clusters, with light green foliage supported on very prickly stems. These bushes should be dug out or transplanted to form a boundary hedge, as they are out of place in a bed or border alongside a path.

Weeds

The weed problem in neglected rose beds may be acute. Where persistent perennial types, like docks, thistles, bindweed, nettles, ground elder and couch grass have taken charge it may be more satisfactory in the long term to lift the best of the roses between October and March and to replant them elsewhere, so that the weeds can be treated with an effective but non-selective weedkiller. This will mean leaving the bed unplanted for at least six months after treatment, but the alternative of attempting to eliminate bindweed and ground elder, for example, when growing among the rose roots, demands years of patience and persistence, and even then may not be successful. At least, that has been my experience.

Finally, it is advisable to have the soil in a neglected garden tested for lime and other possible deficiencies, and to apply a dressing of ground limestone (calcium carbonate) to the surface in November or December to remedy any deficiency indicated.

Part Two

A to Z Guide to
Varieties

Descriptive lists of
Hybrid Tea, Floribunda, Climbing, Rambling and
Pillar Roses, Shrub and Hedging Roses
and Miniature Roses

Key to List of Varieties

When describing the varieties selected for inclusion in the following chapters it has been found convenient to adhere to a uniform pattern.

They have been listed alphabetically in each chapter, because this is the orthodox practice which the reader expects, besides being the best method of enabling a variety known by name to be found quickly. In addition, those described in each chapter have been listed as well at the end of each chapter, in broad groups according to colour. This should be helpful to the reader in selecting, for example, pillar roses to plant towards the back of a deep border of floribundas; or to plan beds or borders of varieties within the same group, supplemented by the broad indications of the habit of growth incorporated in the individual descriptions.

Raisers and Parentage

After the name of the variety, any alternative name is shown in brackets. The name of the raiser follows and the year when the variety was introduced in this country, which may differ from the year of introduction in the country of origin in the case of some foreign varieties. Then follows the parentage, where known, the seed parent being named first.

Colour

The colour of the flower is then given, and the expert on colour will not agree with some of the terms used. Throughout the descriptions the layman – and not the colour expert – has been kept in mind, it being recognised that the vast majority of amateurs who grow roses are laymen. If the use of such terms as 'apricot' or 'salmon' enables the beginner unfamiliar with the variety to visualise the approximate colouring, then it is felt that the end justifies the means, even though these are not technically correct colour descriptions.

The budding sequence. *Above left:* The chosen bud or 'eye' is removed, leaving the propagator with a boat-shaped piece of bark. *Above right:* The sliver of wood is removed from behind the 'eye'. *Below left:* The flap of the T-shaped cut made in the bark of the rootstock is opened up. *Below centre:* The bud is inserted. *Below right:* The bud is tied in with moist raffia

Molly McGredy (Flori. H.T. type)

A further complication is that the colour of most varieties tends to vary according to the climate, the soil, the time of year and whether the plant is growing in full sun or partial shade. Frequently, the autumn crop will reveal noticeable differences from the first flush of June. A young bloom will often be more intense in colour than one which has passed its peak. It is because of these influences, among others, that it has been felt necessary to add the warning that all colour descriptions can only be approximate.

Flower Shapes

In reference to the flower shape or form various terms are used to indicate petallage or degrees of fullness. These are explained as follows:

Single: The bloom has only one row of five petals, although sometimes two or three extra petals inside the main row may be seen
Semi-double: The bloom has two or three complete rows of petals
Moderately full: There are 15-25 petals
Full: The bloom has from 26-40 petals
Very full: There are over 40 petals

Fragrance

Fragrance is difficult to assess, not only varying with climatic conditions, temperature and humidity, but also with the stage of development of the flower. The sensitivity of individuals to fragrance also varies enormously; the heavy smoker, for instance, other things being equal, will not normally have as keen an appreciation of fragrance as the non-smoker. Scented varieties have been described as 'slightly fragrant', 'fragrant' or 'very fragrant', but in many instances, particularly among the floribundas, no reference has been made to fragrance. It may be assumed that, with these varieties, such fragrance as there is will not be perceptible to the average grower under normal conditions in the open air. This is not to say that under ideal conditions of temperature and humidity there may not be some fragrance released. It may often happen, too, that when blooms which seem to be scentless outside are cut and arranged indoors, there may be a perceptible fragrance.

Growth

Growth will vary according to the climate and the type of soil, the cultivation and feeding programme, the method of pruning and

177

whether thorough watering is resorted to in dry weather. The terms used to describe the type of growth of the different varieties are self-explanatory and should help the reader when considering planting distances. Thus, varieties of tall, upright growth may normally be planted closer together than those described as branching or spreading. The abbreviations T, M and L (tall, medium and low growing) should also be helpful as a broad indication of the height, always subject to the reservations concerning the type of soil, feeding and pruning methods already mentioned.

Susceptibility to Disease

Remarks on susceptibility to disease are based primarily on the author's own experience of growing the variety in a pure-air district in which trouble with black spot and rust is experienced every year. Where the remarks 'May need protection from black spot' or 'May need watching for mildew' appear, the former is a warning to the grower in a pure-air district to practise preventive spraying against black spot; the latter indicates that a mildew fungicide should be used at the first sign of this disease. In this connection the reader is referred to Chapter 10, which deals with diseases and their treatment. Probably the great majority of amateur rose growers, and certainly most of those whose gardens are in industrial or densely populated areas, will rarely have trouble with black spot or rust, although the increasing insistence on smokeless fuels may well extend the areas in which trouble may be expected. Certainly up to the past year or two mildew has normally been the only disease for which vigilance has been necessary in such areas. The incidence of disease will vary from year to year according to weather conditions; overcrowding, or planting beneath overhanging forest trees, may encourage attacks, and neglect to spray at the first sign may lead to epidemics. It cannot be too strongly emphasised that preventive spraying is the only method of controlling black spot and rust in pure-air districts, but may not be necessary in industrial and densely populated areas.

20

Descriptive List of Hybrid Tea Roses

Hybrid tea roses – Recommended varieties and their descriptions – 'At-a-glance' Colour Chart of varieties described

Few will dispute that the hybrid teas are the aristocrats of the rose world. Many of them have high-pointed blooms of classic symmetry, with gracefully reflexing petals, delightful at the half-expanded stage and still pleasing when fully open. They may be carried singly or in clusters of three or more, according to the variety, and depending also upon the extent of disbudding practised by the grower. Nearly all the modern varieties are sufficiently free flowering to make a fine garden display when only moderately disbudded, while the same varieties, with more severe disbudding, are often ideal for exhibiting.

Where large, high-quality flowers, rather than mass displays of colour, are the first consideration, then the hybrid teas will be chosen by the connoisseur; not only are the flowers superior in size, form and colour range to those in any other group, but their fragrance in general is more pronounced. What, then, are their disadvantages? They are not so quick to repeat as the floribundas, because high-quality blooms require a longer period in which to reach maturity. In consequence, a bed of hybrid teas is not colourful on as many days in the season as a bed of floribundas. Also, while by no means fastidious in their requirements, they will not tolerate as much neglect as the floribundas. The very full-petalled varieties are also at a disadvantage in wet weather, when some of the buds may 'ball' badly instead of opening normally.

Nevertheless, and despite some views that they have passed the peak of their popularity and may be superseded eventually by the hybrid tea type floribundas, I cannot see this happening for many years, if at all. The rose enthusiast who prefers quality to quantity,

179

whether in the garden or as cut flowers for the house, will undoubtedly plant the hybrid teas and, given a modicum of attention, they will amply reward him with a lavish display year after year.

In making a selection, such matters as colour preferences or prejudices, the emphasis placed on a rich fragrance, and the form of the flower will tend to influence the beginner more than such practical points as freedom of flowering, colour stability, disease resistance and tolerance to wet weather. In describing the following varieties any known weakness has been mentioned, but it must not be assumed that this will be revealed under all the varying conditions in which roses are grown. In restricting this selection of varieties a certain ruthlessness has been necessary, as it would have been so easy to have included many more. The name and date given after the varietal name indicate the raiser and the date of introduction.

Explanatory Note: The following abbreviations have been used:

T = growth taller than average
M = growth about average in height
L = growth below average height

DESCRIPTIVE LIST OF HYBRID TEA ROSES

Allegro: Meilland, 1962. (Happiness × Independence) × Soraya. Bright geranium red. Long, pointed buds, opening to full blooms of medium size, carried erect on very vigorous, tall growth with glossy dark green foliage, crimson when young. Good for cutting and does not mind rain. No scent. T.

Amatsu-Otome: Teranishi, 1960. Chrysler Imperial × Doreen. Golden-yellow, fading paler. The flowers are full, shapely at first, opening loosely, and are carried erect on stout, branching, claret-coloured stems, with large, glossy, dark green foliage. Free flowering in clusters and quick to repeat. M.

André le Troquer: Mallerin, 1950. Orange and yellow shades, apricot in the heart. Moderately full, cupped flowers with large petals; very fragrant. Growth is moderately vigorous, sturdy and upright, with large, dark green, tinted bronze, leaves. May need watching for mildew and not too hardy in severe weather. M.

Angel Wings: Lindquist, 1958. Golden Rapture × Girona. Creamy-white, deepening to yellow at the base, flushed cyclamen pink on each petal. The long, shapely buds, moderately full, open quickly but are exquisite in the early stages and very fragrant. Growth is tall and upright with long stems ideal for cutting. While too tall for formal beds, it is useful at the back of a border. T.

Anne Letts: Letts, 1953. Peace × Charles Gregory. Delicate pink, with a silvery-pink reverse. The flowers are pointed, mostly of pleasing form, full and fragrant. Growth is vigorous and branching, very thorny, with glossy, dark green foliage. The flowers dislike rain and the foliage may need protection against black spot and mildew. T.

Anne Watkins: Watkins Roses Ltd., 1963. Ena Harkness × Grand'mère Jenny. Deep cream, intensifying to apricot in the heart and flushed pink on the outside petals. Moderately full, of pleasing regular shape, the flowers are carried on vigorous, upright, thorny growth, with dark, rather small glossy leaves. May need protection from black spot. M.

Apricot Silk: Gregory, 1965. Souvenir de Jacques Verschuren seedling. Deep apricot tinted red. Long, pointed buds, opening to pleasing flowers, moderately full, carried on tall slender growth, with glossy dark green, bronze-tinted foliage. May need watching for mildew. T.

Baccara: Meilland, 1956. Happiness × Independence. Vivid deep vermilion with blackish shadings on the outer petals; full, well formed, but scentless. Growth is vigorous and upright with glossy reddish-green foliage, red in early stages. Lasts well as a cut flower and excellent for forcing under glass. Dislikes rain. M.

Bacchus: Dickson, 1951. Deep carmine-red, shaded scarlet. Full, fragrant flowers carried on rather weak footstalks. Growth is tall and vigorous, upright, with semi-glossy dark green foliage. Does not mind rain, but may need watching for mildew. T.

Ballet: Kordes, 1958. Florex × Karl Herbst. Deep pink, very full and shapely blooms carried upright on vigorous growth, with light green, semi-glossy foliage. No scent. May need protection from black spot. M.

Bayadère: Mallerin, 1954. R.M.S. Queen Mary × unnamed seedling. Rich pink suffused orange, with a yellow base. Large, very full, rather short-petalled blooms, giving a quartered effect in the later stages. Growth is vigorous, tall and branching, with matt, dark green foliage. A robust variety requiring plenty of room. T.

Beauté: Mallerin, 1954. Mme Joseph Perraud × unnamed seedling. Long-pointed buds opening into moderately full flowers of light orange, intensifying in the heart. Slightly fragrant. The growth is vigorous and branching, with dark green semi-glossy foliage. M.

Bel Ange: Lens, 1962. (Independence × Papillon Rose) × (Charlotte Armstrong × Floradora). Rosy-salmon on the inside with a carmine-pink reverse. The flowers are large and well formed, fragrant and borne very freely on strong, upright growth, with abundant dark green foliage, tinted red. Very good for garden display. M.

Belle Blonde: Meilland, 1955. Peace × Lorraine. Bright golden-yellow, centre deeper. Full, fragrant flowers of medium size; free flowering on bushy growth, with plentiful dark green glossy foliage. May need protection from black spot. M.

Bettina: Meilland, 1953. Peace × (Mme Joseph Perraud × Demain). Orange, with golden base, heavily veined and flushed salmon and red. Full, regular form; fragrant; vigorous growth, with glossy, dark green bronze-tinted foliage. May need protection from black spot. M.

Blessings: Gregory, 1968. Queen Elizabeth × unnamed seedling. Soft coral pink, deeper in the centre. Large, full, fragrant flowers, usually produced in small clusters. Growth is upright but bushy, with ample semi-glossy foliage. A promising variety for bedding and for cutting. M.

Blue Moon (Mainzer Fastnacht, Sissi): Tantau, 1964. Unnamed seedling × Sterling Silver. Silvery-lilac, full, shapely flowers; very fragrant. Vigorous upright growth, with semi-glossy medium green foliage. May need protection from rust. Good for cutting and artistic work. M.

Bonsoir: Alex. Dickson, 1968. Peach-pink, shaded deeper pink. The flowers are very full, shapely, fragrant and borne freely on vigorous, upright growth with glossy, large, dark green foliage. A promising new variety. M.

Brandenburg: Kordes, 1965. (Spartan × Prima Ballerina) × Karl Herbst. Deep salmon, shading to rich salmon-red. Full flowers, shapely at first, carried freely on tall upright growth with abundant, matt, medium green foliage, red when young. Little scent. Opens freely in all weathers. Good for cutting. T.

Brasilia: S. McGredy IV, 1968. Perfecta × Piccadilly. Light scarlet on the inside of the petals, with pale gold reverse. The flowers are shapely at first, moderately full, opening loosely and do not mind rain. Growth is vigorous and upright, with abundant semi-glossy medium green foliage, crimson when young. An attractive new bicolor. T.

Bridal Robe: McGredy, 1955. McGredy's Pink × Mrs Charles Lamplough. White, shaded ivory. The flowers are large, very full and pointed, with attractive reflexing petals, and fragrant. They are carried freely on sturdy, vigorous growth, with large, glossy, dark green foliage. Dislikes rain. Useful as a pot rose under glass. M.

Brilliant (Brillant, Schlösser's Brillant, Detroiter): Kordes, 1952. Poinsettia × Crimson Glory. Rich scarlet, full, high-centred flowers, with little fragrance, produced on vigorous, upright growth, sparsely furnished with semi-glossy, dark green foliage. Needs watching for mildew. M.

Buccaneer: Swim, 1953. Golden Rapture × (Max Krause × Capt. Thomas). Buttercup yellow, non-fading, medium-sized flowers, moderately full, carried in clusters on very tall upright growth with matt, medium green foliage. Too tall for formal bedding, but useful for the back of a border. Does not mind rain. T.

Camelot: Swim and Weeks, 1964. Circus × Queen Elizabeth. Rosy-salmon, fragrant full flowers of cupped formation, carried both singly and in clusters on tall, upright growth. The foliage is glossy, dark green and abundant. A healthy rose. T.

Caramba: Tantau, 1967. Parentage unknown. Light crimson inside the petals, with a silvery reverse forming a striking contrast. Very full, shapely flowers of medium size, carried upright on stout stems, with abundant semi-glossy medium green foliage, red when young. Strong healthy growth. No scent. This is a very promising novelty. M.

Carla: De Ruiter, 1963. Queen Elizabeth × Sweet Repose. Delicate camellia pink, with a slight suffusion of pale salmon. Full, rather globular flowers, carried upright on sturdy growth, with dark green, crimson-tinted foliage. The petals are rather soft and will not stand much rain. May need protection from black spot. M.

Champs Elysées: Meilland, 1957. Monique × Happiness. Deep crimson with scarlet shadings and non-fading. Full, cupped flowers with little scent, produced freely on branching growth with matt, rather small foliage. Does not mind rain. L.

Charles Mallerin: Meilland, 1947. (Glory of Rome × Congo) × Tassin. Deep velvety crimson with blackish shadings. Full, very fragrant blooms, opening rather flat. Growth is vigorous, upright, but uneven, often with one extra-strong shoot dominating the plant. Dark green foliage, needing watching for mildew. Not very free flowering. M.

Cherry Brandy: Tantau, 1965. Light vermilion, shading off to gold at the base of the petals. The flowers are shapely, moderately full, opening wide later, fragrant, and mostly carried singly on stout stems. Growth is free and branching, with healthy, bronze-tinted foliage. Best in cool weather. M.

Chicago Peace: Johnston, 1962. Sport from Peace. Orange and yellow shades, heavily overlaid with cyclamen pink. Very full, large flowers, carried on very vigorous tall branching growth, with large, glossy, dark green foliage. T.

Christian Dior: Meilland, 1959 (Independence × Happiness) × (Peace × Happiness). Rich velvety scarlet, paler on the reverse. Very large, full, well-formed but scentless blooms, carried erect on tall, strong growth, with medium green, semi-glossy foliage, red when young. Needs watching closely for mildew. T.

Chrysler Imperial: Lammerts, 1952. Charlotte Armstrong × Mirandy. Rich dark crimson, tending to 'blue' in the later stages. Full, well-formed, very fragrant flowers, borne on moderately vigorous upright growth, with semi-glossy, dark green foliage. May need protection from rust and mildew. M.

City of Hereford: Le Grice, 1967. Medium rose-pink, shading off to pale orange at the base and somewhat deeper pink on the reverse of the petals. The full blooms, of rather globular formation, are very fragrant and produced freely on branching growth of useful bedding habit. The foliage is matt, light green and needs watching for mildew. Good in autumn. M.

Cologne Carnival (Kölner Karneval, Blue Girl): Kordes, 1964. Silvery-lilac. The flowers are moderately full, well formed at first, opening loosely. Growth is vigorous and bushy, with dark, glossy foliage. Free flowering. M.

Colour Wonder Königin der Rosen): Kordes, 1964. Perfecta × Super Star. Orange-salmon on the inside of the petals, the reverse being pale yellow. Very full, small-petalled blooms, shapely and lasting longer than most in good condition. Slightly fragrant. Growth is vigorous but short and upright, with rather small dark green glossy foliage, bronze tinted. An unusual colour break. L.

Crimson Brocade: H. Robinson, 1962. Rich scarlet-crimson, very large-petalled, full flowers, with rather weak footstalks. Slightly

Orange Silk (Flori.)

Top left: The standard briar *(Rosa canina)*, the sturdiest stock for standard roses, is obtainable with roots attached or as a 4-ft. cutting. *Top right:* A standard briar pruned ready for planting. *Bottom left:* A briar stock showing (top right) a bud being tied in; centre left, a bud in a T-cut; and, bottom right, another prepared T-cut. *Bottom right:* Maiden growth of standard rose tied to bamboo cane

Top: Suitable growth from which to prepare cuttings. *Bottom left:* Preparing a cutting. This should be 9 in. long when prepared and the cut is made just below an 'eye'. *Bottom right:* Inserting cuttings 4 in. apart in a trench. Fine soil and peat are added and the soil moderately firmed

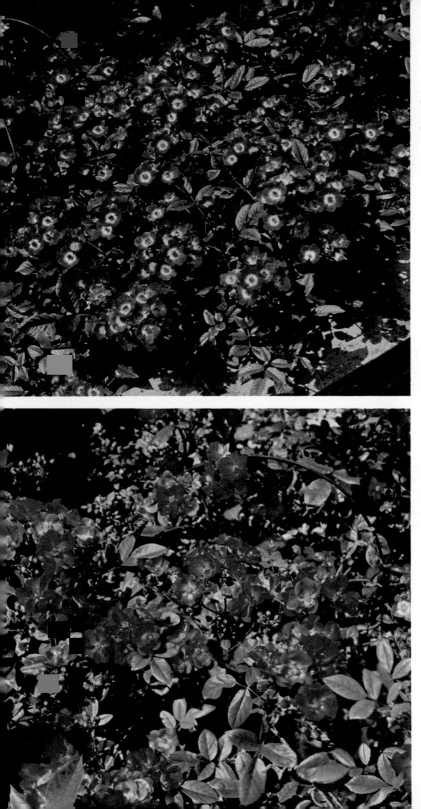

Left: Bashful
(Flori. dwarf)
Below: Dopey
(Flori. dwarf)

fragrant. Very vigorous branching growth. Semi-glossy dark green foliage, tinted red, which needs protection from mildew and rust. Does not mind rain. Good in autumn and repeats quickly. T.

Crimson Glory: Kordes, 1935. Cathrine Kordes seedling × W. E. Chaplin. Deep, velvety crimson, tending to turn brownish or rusty looking in the final stages. Very fragrant and free flowering, with spreading thorny growth, but with rather weak footstalks unless well grown. Semi-glossy foliage, medium green, tinted red when young, and subject to mildew. The parent of many fine roses. L.

Criterion: De Ruiter, 1966. Rich cerise, fragrant, shapely flowers, full, but opening quickly. Very free flowering on vigorous branching growth, with abundant glossy, bright green foliage. Good in autumn, but may need protection from black spot. M.

Dame de Coeur (Queen of Hearts): Louis Lens, 1959. Peace × Independence. Cherry-red, full, large flowers, borne very profusely on tall, branching growth with plentiful glossy, medium green foliage. Not subject to disease and makes a fine specimen bush. A splendid rose for garden display. T.

Diamond Jubilee: Boerner, Jackson and Perkins, 1947. Maréchal Niel × Feu Pernet-Ducher. Deep buff, shading off to cream at the petal edges. The flowers are large, very full, shapely and very fragrant; they are carried on upright growth, with semi-glossy foliage. Free flowering, considering its size and petallage. M.

Diorama: De Ruiter, 1965. Peace × Beauté. Apricot-yellow, shaded orange and flushed pink in the young flower. The blooms are large, high centred, full and fragrant, but open quickly. Vigorous, branching growth, with semi-glossy medium green foliage, shaded bronze. May need protection from black spot. Good in autumn and opens freely in the rain. M.

Doreen: Robinson, 1950. Lydia × McGredy's Sunset. Orange-yellow, shaded rich orange and flushed scarlet. Moderately full, fragrant flowers, produced very freely on vigorous branching growth, clothed with glossy, dark green, bronze-tinted foliage. Excellent in the autumn and does not mind rain. Needs protection from black spot. M.

Dorothy Peach: Robinson, 1958. Peace × Lydia. Soft yellow, sometimes tinted peach and flushed red. Well-formed, full flowers, borne very freely on strong, branching growth, with medium-green, semi-glossy foliage. May need protection from black spot. Very suitable for a small bed where Peace would be too tall. M.

Dr A. J. Verhage: Verbeek, 1960. Tawny Gold × Baccara seedling. Golden-yellow, shaded apricot. Flowers are rather small, moderately full and fragrant. Growth is moderately vigorous, with small, dark green, glossy leaves. A good forcing rose but it needs generous treatment and warm weather in the open garden. L.

Dr Albert Schweitzer: Delbard-Chabert, 1961. Chic Parisien × Michèle Meilland. Cerise, slightly paler on the reverse. Large, full but loosely-formed flowers, slightly fragrant, carried upright on stout stems. Vigorous, bushy growth with large, glossy, medium green leaves. Good in autumn. May need watching for black spot. M.

Duke of Windsor: Tantau, 1968. Orange-vermilion, rather more orange than Super Star. The blooms are of medium size, moderately full, of spiral formation at their best, but not always of good shape, opening loosely. Fragrant. Growth is bushy and compact, ideal for bedding, well furnished with healthy, dark green, semi-glossy foliage. Some petal damage in wet weather. L.

Eden Rose: Meilland, 1950. Peace × Signora. Deep madder pink with a silvery-pink reverse. Full, globular, very fragrant flowers, sometimes of excellent form but tending to open quickly. Very vigorous, tall and branching growth with large, glossy, medium green foliage, bronze tinted when young. May need watching for mildew. T.

Elida: Tantau, 1966. Dark vermilion with an orange tone which imparts extra brilliance. The flowers are full, shapely and of medium size but scentless, carried on rather tall, upright growth with semi-glossy, dark green foliage, dull red in the early stages. A vivid splash of colour, especially in the autumn. M.

Ellen Mary: Le Grice, 1963. Wellworth × Independence. Dark crimson with blackish shadings, developing a purplish bloom with age. Very fragrant, well-formed, full flowers carried freely on vigorous growth, and good in the autumn. T.

Ellinor Le Grice: Le Grice, 1950. Lilian × Yellowcrest. Golden-yellow. The flowers are large, full, globular, with a distinct fruity fragrance. They are borne very freely on strong, upright growth with glossy, rich green foliage which needs protection from black spot. M.

Elsa Arnot: Croll, 1958. Ena Harkness × Peace. Soft pink, flushed cerise and shading to yellow at the base, with a pale yellow reverse. Moderately full blooms opening loose, but very fragrant. Sturdy upright growth with plentiful, glossy, dark green foliage. L.

Ena Harkness: Norman, 1946. Southport × Crimson Glory. Rich crimson-scarlet. Full, shapely, very fragrant flowers of superb velvety texture carried on vigorous branching growth, with semi-glossy, medium green foliage. A delightful rose in cool weather, but the footstalks are often weak, causing the blooms to hang their heads. Still the best in its colour group. M.

Ernest H. Morse: Kordes, 1965. Bright turkey-red, with full flowers, usually well formed, but opening quickly and sometimes confused. Very fragrant. A vigorous, upright grower, with healthy semi-glossy, dark green foliage. One of the best of the recent introductions. T.

Ethel Sanday: Mee, 1954. Rex Anderson × Audrey Cobden. Medium yellow, flushed apricot. Full, well-formed blooms, produced very freely on vigorous, branching growth, with small, matt, dark green leaves, bronze-tinted. Needs protection from black spot. M.

Eve Allen: Allen, 1964. Karl Herbst × Gay Crusader. Cherry-red inside the petals with old gold on the reverse, forming a pleasing bicolor. Moderately full, fragrant flowers, opening quickly and borne on branching growth, with semi-glossy, medium green foliage. May need protection from black spot. M.

Evensong: Arnot, 1963. Ena Harkness × Sutter's Gold. Warm, rosy salmon, intensifying towards the base. Full, rather globular flowers carried erect on tall, vigorous growth, with healthy medium green foliage. T.

Femina: Gaujard, 1963. Fernand Arles × Mignonne. Coppery salmon pink, deeper in the heart. The flowers are of medium size, full, but open quickly and are carried erect on vigorous growth. Semi-glossy foliage, tinted bronze, which needs protection from black spot. M.

First Love: Swim, 1952. Charlotte Armstrong × Show Girl. Pale pink with deeper shadings. Unusually long-pointed buds and young flowers, opening moderately full. They are borne freely on wiry stems and are excellent for cutting. Growth is tall and rather spindly, with pointed, semi-glossy foliage. T.

Flaming Sunset (Beryl Formby, Sunset Glory): Eddie, 1947. Sport from McGredy's Sunset. Deep orange, veined and flushed vermilion, with a paler reverse. The flowers are full, with small petals giving a low-centred shape, opening loosely. Fragrant, free flowering.

Growth is moderately vigorous, bushy and branching, with small, bronze-tinted, glossy foliage. L.

Fragrant Cloud (Duftwolke, Nuage Parfumé): Tantau, 1964. Seedling × Prima Ballerina. Orange-red, paling with age to coral-salmon. Large, full, well-formed flowers with a delicious fragrance and produced freely on upright, strong growth, clothed with large, glossy, dark green foliage. May need protection from black spot. M.

Francine: Kriloff, 1961. Crimson, with a distinct silvery reverse. The flowers are of medium size, full, shapely, opening loosely, and carry a pleasing fragrance. Growth is vigorous and branching, with glossy, copper-beech coloured foliage. Free flowering. M.

Frau Karl Druschki (Snow Queen): Lambert, 1900. Merveille de Lyon × Mme Caroline Testout. Pure white with pink-tinted buds, opening into well-formed, full but scentless flowers. Needs disbudding to produce high-quality blooms. Growth is very vigorous with matt, light green foliage which needs watching for mildew. Suitable for pegging down or growing as a specimen bush. Makes a fine head as a standard. T.

Fred Gibson: Sanday, 1968. Gavotte × Buccaneer. Amber and pearly cream, flushed pink on the outside and intensifying in the heart to rich apricot. The beautifully modelled blooms are large and full, with shell-shaped petals, and borne singly on long stems in the first flush, in small clusters later. Growth is tall and upright, with dark green, semi-glossy foliage, reddish when young. A promising new rose for the exhibitor. T.

Fritz Thiedemann: Tantau, 1960. Horstmann's Jubiläumsrose seedling × Alpine Glow seedling. Deep vermilion, without shading. The flowers are of medium size, full, fragrant, sometimes with split centres. Growth is moderately vigorous, branching, with glossy, dark green, leathery foliage. L.

Gail Borden: Kordes, 1956. Mev. H. A. Verschuren × Viktoria Adelheid. Deep rose-pink shaded orange-yellow, with buff-yellow on the reverse. Large, full, globular flowers, carried profusely on vigorous and robust growth, forming a tall and well-branched bush, with large, handsome, glossy dark foliage. Opens well in all weather and is a trouble-free rose for the beginner. T.

Garvey: McGredy, 1960. McGredy's Yellow × Karl Herbst. Peach-pink, deepening to rosy-salmon. Full, globular blooms carried on very strong and thorny upright growth with large glossy leaves, tinted bronze. Does not mind rain. T.

Gavotte: Sanday, 1963. Ethel Sanday × Lady Sylvia. Warm rose-pink, with a silvery-pink reverse. Large, very full flowers, of classical form, borne freely on vigorous, spreading growth with semi-glossy foliage. Will not stand much rain. M.

Gertrude Gregory: Gregory, 1956. Sport from Lady Belper. Bright golden-yellow, medium-sized flowers, full and slightly fragrant. Growth is moderately vigorous and branching, with dark green, glossy foliage, tinted bronze. M.

Gold Crown: Kordes, 1960. Peace × Spek's Yellow. Deep golden-yellow, sometimes flushed or tinted pink on the outer petals. Full, fragrant flowers, often borne singly on very tall strong growth, with large, glossy, bronze-tinted dark leaves. The flowers often develop with split centres. Too tall except for large beds. T.

Golden Giant: Kordes, 1960. Parentage unknown. Golden-yellow in the heart, paling to cream towards the edges of the petals. Exceptionally free flowering, needing much disbudding to produce high-quality flowers. Very tall and sprawling growth, of shrub habit, with matt, small, medium green foliage, needing watching for mildew. An ungainly grower, best at the back of a border. T.

Golden Melody (Irene Churruca): La Florida, 1934. Mme Butterfly × Florence L. Izzard. Buff-yellow in the heart, paling to cream towards the petal edges. Full, very fragrant flowers of exquisite shape, borne on vigorous, branching growth. Foliage dark green, bronze tinted and needs watching for mildew. M.

Golden Splendour: Kordes, 1962. Buccaneer × Golden Sun. Light yellow, deeper in the heart. Very full, globular, fragrant flowers produced very freely on vigorous branching growth. Good in fine weather, but unhappy in the rain. M.

Gordon Eddie: Eddie, 1949. Royal Visit × Cynthia Brooke. Buff, deepening to fiery apricot in the heart, and normally richer in the autumn. Large, well-formed, full flowers, inclined to be globular; fragrant. Vigorous, bushy growth, with the flowers carried freely on strong stems, with glossy, dark green foliage. Needs protection from black spot. M.

Grace de Monaco: Meilland, 1956. Peace × Michèle Meilland. Clear rose-pink without shading. Full, globular, very fragrant flowers, carried in profusion on tall but angular growth with matt, large leaves. The weight of the blooms and the angle at which growths are produced may mean that they have to be supported when in full flower. T.

189

Grand Gala: Meilland, 1955. Peace × Independence. Scarlet inside the petals, with a contrasting silvery reverse. The blooms are very full, globular and low-centred and are carried in clusters on strong, tall growth with glossy, dark green foliage tinted crimson. Very free flowering, but except in hot sunny weather the blooms look rather rough. T.

Grand'mère Jenny. Meilland, 1950. Peace × Signora. Light yellow, flushed peach and cyclamen pink towards the petal edges. Long-pointed buds opening into elegant flowers with long petals, carried erect on firm, upright growth. The glossy, medium green foliage may need protection from black spot. T.

Grandpa Dickson: Dickson, 1966. (Perfecta × Governador Braga da Cruz) × Piccadilly. Lemon yellow, fading to creamy-yellow, flushed pink at the petal edges with age. Very full, shapely flowers held erect on tall, upright growth with abundant glossy, dark green foliage. Early flowering, quick to repeat and good in autumn. T.

Greetings (Gruss an Berlin): R. Kordes, 1963. Rich scarlet without shading. Large, high-centred, full flowers, slightly fragrant, carried on strong, bushy growth, with large abundant, glossy leaves, tinted red. A healthy, trouble-free variety of strong constitution. T.

Guinevere: Harkness, 1967. Red Dandy × Peace. Light rose pink, medium-sized, full-petalled flowers, symmetrical but somewhat low-centred. No scent. Moderately vigorous growth, of branching habit, suitable for bedding, with small, light green foliage. M.

Hawaii: Boerner, Jackson and Perkins, 1960. Golden Masterpiece × unnamed seedling. Coral-salmon, shaded orange. The shapely, full blooms develop from very long-pointed buds and carry a pleasant fragrance. Growth is vigorous, upright, inclined to be spindly, with copper-green, semi-glossy foliage. The flower opens quickly in warm weather. T.

Helen Traubel: Swim, 1951. Charlotte Armstrong × Glowing Sunset. Soft coppery-pink, suffused apricot, the latter colour predominating in the autumn. Full, very fragrant flowers with rather weak footstalks, carried on tall, very vigorous growth, with matt, dark green foliage. The flowers open quickly in hot weather. T.

Heure Mauve: Mallerin, 1962. Simone × Prélude. Lilac-mauve. The flowers are full, slightly fragrant, shapely at first and do not mind rain. Growth is vigorous and bushy, with semi-glossy, medium green foliage. M.

Ideal Home (Idylle): Laperrière, 1960. Monte Carlo × Tonnerre.

Rich carmine-pink, shading off to ivory-white towards the base. Full, globular, fragrant flowers of medium size, produced in clusters on vigorous upright growth. Very large, dark green foliage, crimson when young. T.

Intermezzo: Dot, 1963. Grey Pearl × Lila Vidri. Deep lavender-mauve. The flowers are of medium size, rather low centred and globular, fragrant, borne freely on compact, branching growth, with rather small, glossy, dark green foliage. Needs protection from black spot. L.

Invitation: Swim and Weeks, 1961. Charlotte Armstrong × Signora. Coppery-salmon-pink, veined scarlet, with yellow base. Long-pointed buds open into shapely, full, high-centred, fragrant flowers, developing quickly, on vigorous, branching growth. The foliage is glossy, medium green and healthy. Good in autumn. M.

Isabel de Ortiz: Kordes, 1962. Peace × Perfecta. Deep pink with a silvery-white reverse. The blooms are large, very full, of great depth and fragrant. Growth is tall and upright, with ample dark green, glossy foliage. Best in fine weather. A popular variety with the exhibitor. T.

Isobel Harkness: Norman, 1957. Phyllis Gold × McGredy's Yellow. Deep yellow, moderately full, with few but large petals, opening quickly. The growth is moderately vigorous, with dark green, glossy foliage. May need protection from black spot. M.

Jean Campbell: Sanday, 1964. Ethel Sanday seedling × Lady Sylvia. Blush pink to pearly-cream, suffused apricot. The medium-sized flowers are full, shapely, fragrant and borne profusely on long stems with few thorns. The foliage is dark green, semi-glossy and abundant. Good for cutting. T.

John S. Armstrong: Swim, 1961. Charlotte Armstrong × seedling. Dark crimson, with scarlet highlights. The flowers are full, rounded and of medium size, borne in clusters. Growth is strong and branching, with abundant, healthy, dark green, semi-glossy foliage. Very free flowering and excellent in autumn. Does not mind rain. A trouble-free variety. T.

Jolie Madame: Meilland, 1958. (Independence × Happiness) × Better Times. Bright vermilion, fading with age. The petals are short but numerous, forming a cupped, full flower, carried in clusters on vigorous, upright growth. Very free flowering. The foliage is glossy, reddish-green, crimson when young. T.

Josephine Bruce: Bees, 1952. Crimson Glory × Madge Whipp.

191

Deep crimson, sometimes flushed scarlet. Full, shapely, very fragrant flowers carried on robust spreading growth, with dark green, semi-glossy foliage, which needs watching for mildew. Should be pruned to inward-pointing eyes, to correct a sprawling habit. Makes a good head as a standard. M.

June Park: Bertram Park, 1958. Peace × Crimson Glory. Deep rose-pink, almost carmine. Full, shapely blooms, very fragrant, carried on vigorous spreading growth, with dark green, semi-glossy foliage. May need pruning to inward-pointing eyes. M.

Karl Herbst: Kordes, 1950. Peace × Independence. Dark scarlet, lighter on the reverse. Very full, well formed and floriferous, but there is only a slight fragrance. Growth is very vigorous, tall and branching, with large, glossy, dark green foliage, tinted red and resistant to disease. The flowers are held upright on stout stems. Needs dry sunny weather to give of its best. T.

King's Ransom: Morey, 1961. Golden Masterpiece × Lydia. Rich golden-yellow. Full, well-formed flowers of medium size, borne in profusion on vigorous growth, with attractive, glossy, dark green foliage. M.

Klaus Störtebeker: Kordes, 1962. Scarlet-crimson. The flowers are large, full, but often coarse, slightly fragrant and carried on very vigorous growth, with ample dark green, semi-glossy foliage. Good in autumn, but may need watching for mildew. Will not stand much rain. T.

Konrad Adenauer: Tantau, 1954. Crimson Glory × Hans Verschuren. Crimson, sometimes lighter on dry soils. Full, cupped flowers, very fragrant and free flowering. Vigorous, branching growth. May need watching for mildew. M.

Kronenbourg: McGredy, 1965. Sport from Peace. Scarlet on inside with old gold reverse to the petals. As the flowers age the scarlet deepens to crimson and finally to purple. Large, full flowers, similar in size and form to those of the parent. Very vigorous, strong growth, with large, glossy, dark green leaves. A colourful variety, but the faded flowers need removing to avoid clashing with the young blooms. T.

Lady Belper: Verschuren, 1948. Mev. G. A. Van Rossem × seedling. Light orange, shaded bronze on the outer petals. Full, well-formed fragrant flowers, with classically pointed centres. Moderately vigorous growth with bronze-tinted, semi-glossy dark green foliage. Free flowering, but needs watching for mildew. M.

Left: A standard specimen of the popular variety Peace

Below: Certain conifers, especially golden-leaved ones, associate well with roses. This group of floribundas is in the author's garden

Left: A rose shoot which is being layered

Below left: The roots formed by a layer. The layer should not be severed from the parent plant until such a root system has developed

Lady Eve Price (Caprice): Meilland, 1946. Peace × Fantastique. Bright cerise on the inside, with a cream reverse. Moderately full, rather formless flowers, which open with great prodigality in all weathers. Vigorous, dense, branching growth, with abundant, glossy, dark green foliage. A colourful variety, and an ideal one for the beginner. T.

Lady Seton: McGredy, 1966. Ma Perkins × Mischief. Deep rose-pink, suffused salmon-pink. Full, pointed, shapely flowers, fragrant, opening quickly in warm weather and crowning tall growth, well furnished with medium green, semi-glossy foliage. Conspicuous in the autumn and useful for cutting. T.

Lady Sylvia: Stevens, 1927. Sport from Mme Butterfly. Light rose-pink, shading off to pale apricot-yellow at the base. Shapely, very fragrant blooms of medium size, carried on strong, almost thornless stems with matt, rather small foliage. An excellent, vigorous variety for cutting and all decorative work. M.

La Jolla: Swim, 1954. Charlotte Armstrong × Contrast. A pleasing blend of soft pink, cream and gold, sometimes flushed and veined carmine. Of medium size, the flowers are well formed, fragrant and borne in the greatest profusion so as to cover the whole plant. Upright vigorous growth, with dark green, glossy, rather small foliage. M.

Lancastrian: Gregory, 1965. Ena Harkness × seedling. Rich crimson-scarlet. Large, double, very fragrant flowers, with a velvety texture, carried erect on strong stems. Vigorous and upright, with medium green glossy foliage, tinted crimson. Free flowering and excellent in the autumn. May need watching for mildew. M.

Lilac Rose: Sanday, 1962. Karl Herbst × Chrysler Imperial. Soft pink, shaded lilac. Full, shapely flowers carried singly early in the season and in clusters later. Growth is tall and upright with plentiful large, dark green foliage. T.

Lucy Cramphorn (Maryse Kriloff): Kriloff, 1960. Peace × Baccara. Vivid geranium red. The flowers are very full, well formed and fragrant, with tightly packed petals, and borne freely on very vigorous, tall, branching growth, with luxuriant, large, glossy dark green foliage, tinted red. An excellent healthy variety for garden display, with rather brittle footstalks. T.

Lydia: Robinson, 1949. Phyllis Gold × seedling. Intense golden-yellow. Full, medium-sized flowers, rather formless, produced in great profusion on compact, branching growth with bright green, glossy, holly-like foliage. Does not mind rain, but may need protection from black spot. L.

Majorette: Meilland, 1967. Orange and bronze, shaded peach. The medium-sized, full-petalled flowers are rather globular and low centred, with some splitting early in the season. Later they appear in trusses of 5 or 6 blooms and are smaller. Growth is upright with dark, coppery-bronze, glossy foliage needing protection from black spot. Very free flowering. M.

Marcelle Gret: Meilland, 1947. Peace × Princess Beatrix. Rich saffron yellow, paling somewhat with age. Globular, full flowers, borne freely on upright growth, with glossy, dark green foliage. May need protection from black spot. Does not mind rain. M.

Mardi Gras: Jordan, 1952. Crimson Glory × Poinsettia. Scarlet-crimson. The flowers are full, fragrant, well formed and borne freely on vigorous upright growth, with semi-glossy, dark green foliage. Somewhat similar to Ena Harkness. M.

Margaret: Dickson, 1954. May Wettern seedling × Souvenir de Denier van der Gon. Bright pink with a silvery reverse, 'blueing' slightly with age. Very full, fragrant, perfectly-formed flowers carried early in the season and quick to repeat. Vigorous, tall growth, furnished with abundant, large, matt foliage with unusually pointed leaflets. Impatient of rain. T.

Maria Callas: Meilland, 1965. Carmine, with lighter shadings. The flower is very full, but low centred and rather formless, with little scent. Growth is vigorous and branching, with large, glossy, dark green foliage. M.

Marjorie Le Grice: Le Grice, 1949. Mrs Sam McGredy × Président Plumecocq. Tangerine-orange and flame on the inside, with a pale yellow reverse. The flowers are fragrant, shapely at first, opening loosely, and carried on rather weak footstalks. Growth is vigorous and upright, with coppery-bronze foliage. May need protection from black spot. T.

Mary Wheatcroft: Robinson, 1945. Mrs Sam McGredy × Princess Marina. Coppery orange-flame to salmon-red – a wonderfully rich colour. Only moderately full, the flowers open quickly and are carried on moderately vigorous growth, with abundant glossy copper-beech coloured foliage. May need protection from black spot. M.

McGredy's Ivory: McGredy, 1929. Mrs Charles Lamplough × Mabel Morse. Creamy-white, tinted yellow at the base. Large, full,

194

high-centred flowers, with elegant, shell-shaped petals, forming a bloom of great depth. Vigorous growth, with dark green, glossy, pointed foliage. Impatient of rain and may need watching for mildew. M.

McGredy's Yellow: McGredy, 1933. Mrs Charles Lamplough × (The Queen Alexandra Rose × J. B. Clark). Creamy-yellow. Long-pointed buds, opening into full, beautifully-formed flowers, carried upright on vigorous thorny wood. Dark green, glossy foliage, bronze tinted. May need protection from black spot. M.

Memoriam: Von Abrams, 1960. (Blanche Mallerin × Peace) × (Peace × Frau Karl Druschki). Off-white, tinted pale pink, deeper in the heart. The flowers are large, very full and of immaculate form, and carried erect on sturdy growth. Vigorous, with very dark green, semi-glossy foliage. Impatient of rain. Good in dry weather–otherwise mainly for the exhibitor. M.

Message (White Knight): Meilland, 1956. (Virgo × Peace) × Virgo. Pure white. The flowers are high centred, full and shapely and carried erect on long stems. Vigorous growth, with light green matt foliage. Impatient of rain and may need protection against rust. M.

Michèle Meilland: Meilland, 1945. Joanna Hill × Peace. Soft pastel shades of pearly-pink and amber, flushed salmon, deeper in the heart. Moderately full flowers, delightfully formed, carried on wiry stems and excellent for cutting. Very prolific on moderately vigorous, branching growth, with abundant matt, light green foliage. Good in autumn. M.

Milord: McGredy, 1962. Rubaiyat × Karl Herbst. Crimson-scarlet. Full, globular blooms, making a bright display, but carrying little scent. Vigorous, tall, upright growth with medium green foliage, reddish when young. T.

Mischief: McGredy, 1960. Peace × Spartan. Coral-salmon flowers of medium size, full, usually well formed, fragrant. Unless disbudded they may be borne in large trusses. Vigorous, branching growth, with plentiful light green, semi-glossy foliage, reddish when young. Does not mind rain. May need protection from rust. A very attractive and floriferous variety. M.

Miss Ireland: McGredy, 1961. Tzigane × Independence. Coral-salmon on the inside, with peach or buff reverse, giving a delightful bicolor effect. Full, shapely flowers carried freely on wiry red stems suitable for cutting. Vigorous, upright growth with dark green, crimson-tinted foliage. May need watching for mildew. T.

Mister Lincoln: Swim and Weeks, 1964. Chrysler Imperial ×
Charles Mallerin. Dark crimson, suffused scarlet. The flowers are
large, full, well formed at first opening loosely and are very fragrant.
Vigorous growth, with dark green, matt foliage. Fairly free flowering. T.

Mme Butterfly: Hill, 1918. Sport from Ophelia. Pale pink, suffused
apricot, shading to yellow at the base. The flowers are medium
sized, full and shapely, very fragrant and carried on stiff, almost
thornless stems. Very floriferous, needing much disbudding.
Vigorous upright growth, with small, matt, medium green leaves.
Good for cutting. M.

Mme Caroline Testout: Pernet-Ducher, 1890. Mme de Tartas ×
Lady Mary Fitzwilliam. Satin rose-pink. Very full, globular flowers,
with little scent, borne on vigorous, branching growth, with matt,
medium green foliage. Free flowering. Makes a fine head as a
standard. Inclined to 'ball' in wet weather. M.

Mme Louis Laperrière: Laperrière, 1952. Crimson Glory × seedling. Deep velvety crimson. The blooms are of medium size, full,
symmetrical but rather globular, highly fragrant and produced in
abundance on bushy, branching growth, with small medium green
foliage. Keeps its colour and does not 'blue'. M.

Mojave: Swim, 1954. Charlotte Armstrong × Signora. Rich burnt
orange and reddish-flame with darker veining. Moderately full
flowers of medium size, carried erect on long straight stems. Growth
is very vigorous, tall and upright, with glossy, bronze-green foliage.
A very healthy variety, excelling in autumn. T.

Monique: Paolino, 1949. Lady Sylvia × seedling. Rose-pink,
shading to silvery-pink. The flowers are full, opening loosely, and
very fragrant, and are borne on very vigorous, tall growth. The
foliage is matt, light green and may need watching for mildew. T.

Montezuma: Swim, 1956. Fandango × Floradora. Deep salmon-
red, fading to deep salmon-pink with age. The scentless flowers are
large, full, high centred and produced very generously in clusters
unless disbudded. Growth is very vigorous, tall and upright, with
plentiful semi-glossy, medium green foliage, tinted red when young.
Impatient of rain and needs watching for mildew. A variety much
favoured by exhibitors, but it needs cutting when young. T.

Mrs Sam McGredy: McGredy, 1929. (Donald Macdonald ×
Golden Emblem) × (seedling × The Queen Alexandra Rose). Bright

coppery-scarlet to salmon-red. The full flowers are exquisitely formed, carried on long slender stems, with lovely copper-beech coloured foliage and wood. Moderately vigorous and requires generous treatment. May need protection from black spot. M.

My Choice: Le Grice, 1958. Wellworth × Ena Harkness. Light pink, shaded yellow, with pale yellow reverse. Large, full, shapely flowers, slightly globular, very fragrant and floriferous. Vigorous upright growth with light green semi-glossy foliage. T.

New Style: Meilland, 1962. (Happiness × Independence) × Peace. Bright crimson-scarlet. The flowers are full, shapely at first, opening loosely, scentless and carried on robust stems. Growth is vigorous and branching, with large, glossy dark green foliage, copper tinted when young. M.

Numéro Un: Laperrière, 1962. Parentage unknown. Intense vermilion. The flowers are very full and globular, and carried singly and in trusses on tall, branching growth. The foliage is semi-glossy and medium green. This seems to be very close to the floribundas. T.

Opera: Gaujard, 1949. La Belle Irisée seedling. Bright coppery-orange-scarlet, shading to orange-carmine, with yellow base. Full, well-formed flowers, slightly fragrant, produced freely on vigorous growth, with large, semi-glossy, medium green foliage, tinted bronze. May need protection from rust and black spot. M.

Ophelia: Paul, 1912. Parentage unknown. Delicate pearly-pink, blush and cream, shading to amber at the base. The flowers are full, classically formed, exceptionally fragrant and carried erect on long, almost thornless stems. Growth is vigorous, with matt, medium green foliage. The early flowers are liable to attacks by thrips and may be malformed as the result of late frosts and cold winds. Excellent for cutting and in the autumn. T.

Papa Meilland: Meilland, 1963. Chrysler Imperial × Charles Mallerin. Dark velvety crimson. Full, very fragrant flowers, carried on vigorous upright growth with glossy dark green foliage. May need protection from mildew. M.

Parasol: Sanday, 1964. Peace × Ethel Sanday seedling. Rich golden-yellow, paling somewhat with age. The flowers are full, of medium size, opening many at a time and making a striking display. Growth is vigorous and branching, with glossy dark green foliage. A free-flowering bedding rose which repeats quickly and is quite trouble-free. M.

Paris-Match: Meilland, 1956. Independence × Grand'mère Jenny. Deep carmine-pink. Full, well-formed blooms, with only slight scent. Growth is vigorous, tall and branching, with abundant dark green, large, semi-glossy foliage. T.

Pascali: Lens, 1963. Queen Elizabeth × White Butterfly. White, sometimes shaded peach at first. The scentless flowers are of medium size, moderately full and carried freely on tall, upright growth with dark green, semi-glossy foliage. Although having comparatively few petals, it dislikes rain, like all the white varieties. T.

Peace (Mme A. Meilland, Gioia, Gloria Dei): Meilland, 1942. Joanna Hill, Charles P. Kilham, Margaret McGredy, and *R. foetida bicolor* are included in the pedigree of this famous rose. The flowers are exceptionally large and full, with slightly frilled petal edges, basically yellow, splashed crimson on the guard petals, opening yellow, tinted cerise-pink at the edges. As the flower ages, a soft pink suffusion spreads across the petals. Growth is very vigorous and branching, with massive stems and huge leathery foliage, dark green and glossy. A wonderful variety which does best with light pruning, grown as a specimen bush. It also makes a wonderful head grown as a standard. T.

Peer Gynt: Kordes, 1968. Colour Wonder × Golden Giant. Canary yellow, tinged orange pink on the outer petal edges, intensifying with age. Full, slightly fragrant flowers, rather globular in shape. Compact, bushy form of growth, with large, abundant, medium green, semi-glossy leaves. M.

Percy Thrower: Lens, 1964. La Jolla × Karl Herbst. Clear pink, full blooms, shapely at first, opening loosely. Only slight fragrance. Vigorous, branching growth, with glossy, dark green foliage. May need protection from black spot. M.

Perfecta (Kordes Perfecta): Kordes, 1957. Spek's Yellow × Karl Herbst. Cream, deepening to yellow at the base, flushed pink and tipped crimson. The flowers are large, very full, shapely, with quilled petals and fragrant, but the first flowers usually look rough in the early stages. Growth is vigorous, tall and upright, with glossy, very dark green foliage, tinted purple. The cut flowers last an unusually long time, but the footstalks are brittle and liable to break in rough weather. At its best in fine weather. T.

Pharaoh: Meilland, 1967. (Happiness × Independence) × Suspense. Vivid orange-scarlet which retains its brilliance to the end. The flowers are fairly large, of regular form, but the large petals do not reflex. They are held erect on stout stems, clothed with dark green, semi-glossy, leathery foliage. There is no scent. Growth is vigorous and upright and the blooms last well on the plants. May need protection from black spot. M.

Piccadilly: McGredy, 1959. McGredy's Yellow × Karl Herbst. Scarlet, merging gradually into yellow towards the base, with a pale yellow reverse. The medium-sized flowers are moderately full, shapely at first, opening wide quickly. Growth is vigorous and upright, with very attractive dark green glossy foliage, heavily shaded bronze. Very free flowering and quick to repeat. A delightful bicolor. M.

Picture: McGredy, 1932. Parentage unknown. Clear pink, deeper in the heart with a tinge of yellow at the base. The medium-sized flowers have a most appealing camellia formation and are produced freely on short, bushy growth, with matt, medium green foliage. Free flowering and good in autumn, but it may need watching for mildew. L.

Pilar Landecho (Marquesa de Urquijo): Camprubi, 1939. (Sensation × Julien Potin) × Feu Joseph Looymans. Exceptionally long-pointed buds, opening into high-centred flowers in orange-yellow intensifying to reddish-orange in the heart, with reddish veinings, shaded coral-orange on the reverse. Very vigorous and tall, with glossy, dark green leathery foliage. Flowers dislike rain and often develop split centres. T.

Pink Favourite: Von Abrams, 1956. Juno × (Georg Arends × New Dawn) Deep rose-pink, paling towards the petal edges. Large, full, well-formed blooms, carried freely on tall, branching growth, with beautiful glossy, oval, medium green foliage. Slight fragrance. One of the healthiest varieties ever introduced, seemingly disease proof. Good in autumn. T.

Pink Peace: Meilland, 1959. (Peace × Monique) × (Peace × Mrs John Laing). Deep pink. The flowers are full, but open quickly and are borne on very vigorous, tall growth with semi-glossy, medium green, bronze-tinted foliage. The blooms do not resemble those of Peace in shape, but are fragrant. T.

Pink Supreme: De Ruiter, 1964. Amor × Peace. Soft pink, deeper in the centre. Rounded flowers of medium size, moderately full, opening quickly in warm weather; fragrant, and carried several on a stem. Vigorous and tall, with glossy, medium green foliage. Very free flowering. May need protection from black spot. T.

199

Polly: Beckwith, 1928. Ophelia seedling × Mme Colette Martinet. Pearly-cream, suffused pink and amber and intensifying to apricot at the base. The large, beautifully-formed flowers are full, very fragrant and carried upright on long, almost thornless stems, with semi-glossy dark green foliage. Good in autumn and a delightful rose for cutting. T.

President Herbert Hoover: Coddington, 1930. Sensation × Souvenir de Claudius Pernet. Deep pink, orange and gold blend, stained crimson on the outside petals. The full, medium-sized flowers are fragrant, with attractive whorled centres. They are carried on extra-long upright growth, sparsely furnished with small, semi-glossy foliage. A very vigorous but leggy grower, which may need watching for mildew. T.

President Pats (Staatspräsident Päts): C. Weigand, 1937. Ophelia × Souvenir de Claudius Pernet. Off-white, pearly-cream and amber shades towards the base. The flowers are large, beautifully pointed, full and very fragrant. Vigorous, upright growth with medium-green, large foliage. Best in fine weather. T.

Prima Ballerina (Première Ballerine): Tantau, 1958. Unknown seedling × Peace. Deep pink, almost carmine buds, opening to deep cherry-pink flowers, full and shapely, but opening quickly. Very fragrant. Very vigorous, tall and upright, with luxuriant dark green, semi-glossy, red-tinted foliage. Does not mind rain. T.

Prince of Denmark: McGredy, 1964. Queen Elizabeth × Independence. Deep rose-pink to carmine in the heart. Full, medium-sized flowers of pleasing form are borne in profusion on bushy, branching growth, with glossy, dark green, red-tinted foliage. Very good in autumn. A healthy, prolific variety which repeats quickly and gives no trouble. M.

Princess: Laperrière, 1964. (Peace × Magicienne) × (Independence × Radar). Clear vermilion. Large specimen blooms, with high-pointed centres, are borne on short stout stems. Growth is moderately vigorous and bushy, with matt, medium green foliage. Good for exhibition. L.

Red Devil: Dickson, 1967. Silver Lining × Prima Ballerina. Deep glowing scarlet with a distinctly lighter reverse. Large, very full blooms, of symmetrical form, are carried on very vigorous, tall and upright growth. The foliage is particularly handsome and abundant— glossy and rich green, tinted crimson. Excellent in dry weather but very impatient of rain. Fragrant. T.

Regalia: Robinson, 1964. Rose Gaujard × seedling. Wine-red on the inside, with a distinct silver reverse. The full, fragrant flowers are of cupped formation and carried freely on branching, spreading growth, with dark, bronze-tinted foliage. Quick to repeat and good in autumn. L.

Rose Gaujard: Gaujard, 1958. Peace × Opera seedling. White ground, flushed, shaded and edged rich carmine, with a silver reverse. The large, full flowers are frequently of excellent form but sometimes split, and last a long time on the plants. Growth is very tall and branching, with plentiful large, glossy dark green foliage, tinted bronze. Exceptionally profuse and quick to repeat. A very healthy and easily-grown variety, outstanding in the autumn. T.

Royal Highness (Königliche Hoheit): Swim, 1962. Virgo × Peace. Soft pink. A very full-flowered, high-centred and fragrant variety, much sought after by exhibitors. Vigorous branching growth, with stout stems, clothed with glossy, dark green foliage. Dislikes wet weather. M.

Sabrina: Meilland, 1960. Grand Gala × Premier Bal. Crimson on the inside with amber yellow and carmine reverse. The flowers are large, very full and globular, inclined to coarseness, fragrant, and carried erect on tall, upright growth, with glossy, large, dark green leaves, tinted bronze and purple. May need protection from black spot. T.

Sam McGredy: McGredy, 1937. Delightful × Mrs Charles Lamplough. Deep cream and buff, deepening to sunflower yellow at the base. The flower is moderately full, with very large petals, and is carried on sturdy stems, with light green, matt foliage. An exhibition variety, not recommended to the novice or for garden display. Best on maiden plants. L.

Santa Fé: McGredy, 1967. Mischief × Super Star. Rich rosy-salmon, with a paler reverse. The flowers are large, full, inclined to be globular and a little rough early in the season. Growth is vigorous and upright, with matt dark green foliage. M.

Sarah Arnot: Croll, 1956. Ena Harkness × Peace. Warm rose-pink. Full, fragrant flowers, shapely at first, opening rather loosely, on tall, upright growth, with large, semi-glossy, light green foliage. Very free flowering. T.

Scandale: Gaujard, 1958. Peace × Opera. A blend of creamy-white and pale pink, overlaid crimson towards the petal edges. Rounded flowers of medium size with scalloped petals, moderately full, shapely at first, opening loosely. Growth is tall and upright, with glossy, medium green foliage. Very free flowering. Does not mind rain. T.

Serenade: Boerner, Jackson and Perkins, 1950. Sonata × Mev. H. A. Verschuren. Orange-coral with deeper shadings. The medium-sized flowers are moderately full, opening flat. Growth is vigorous, tall and branching with matt, dark green, copper-tinted foliage which needs watching for mildew. T.

Shannon: McGredy, 1965. Queen Elizabeth × McGredy's Yellow. Bright pink, very full, rounded flowers which need fine weather to open properly. No scent. Growth is tall and upright, with large, glossy, medium green foliage, with almost round leaflets. T.

Show Girl: Lammerts, Armstrong Nurseries, 1949. Joanna Hill × Crimson Glory. Deep carmine-pink. Full, pointed blooms with high centres, borne on vigorous, upright growth with semi-glossy, medium green foliage. May need watching for mildew. The colour turns very 'blue' in the older flowers and the petals often crinkle unpleasantly. T.

Signora (Signora Piero Puricelli): Aicardi, 1936. Julien Potin × Sensation. A lovely blend of orange, pink and flame, heavily veined with scarlet. The full, fragrant blooms are delightful at the half-open stage, but appear somewhat loose later, with serrated petals. Growth is vigorous and upright, with long, straight stems, furnished with glossy, bronze-green foliage. An outstanding autumn rose, but the young growth needs watching for mildew. T.

Silva: Meilland, 1964. Peace × Confidence. Pale apricot, flushed salmon-pink, with a pale yellow reverse. The medium-sized flowers are full, slightly fragrant and borne erect on stout brown stems, with dark, glossy bronze-green foliage. Growth is vigorous and upright. Free flowering and a pleasing decorative variety. M.

Silver Lining: Dickson, 1958. Karl Herbst × Eden Rose seedling. Silvery-pink on the inside, with a silver reverse. The shapely flowers, with gracefully reflexing petals, are very fragrant. Growth is vigorous and branching, ideal for bedding, with glossy, dark green, rather small foliage. A rose of refinement, but rather pale for garden display. M.

Soraya: Meilland, 1956. (Peace × Floradora) × Grand'mère Jenny. Vivid orange-red with darker, blackish shadings. Full, medium-sized flowers, fading to mauve in the final stages. Growth is vigorous and upright, with long stems suitable for cutting. The foliage is glossy, dark green tinted red, crimson when young. Requires sunny weather to be seen at its best. May need protection from black spot, and the old flowers must be removed regularly. T.

Souvenir de Jacques Verschuren: Verschuren-Pechtold, 1950. Katherine Pechtold × Orange Delight. Orange, shaded salmon. Full, fragrant flowers of medium size produced in abundance. Growth is vigorous and upright, with semi-glossy, dark green, bronze-tinted foliage. M.

Spek's Yellow (Golden Scepter): Verschuren, 1947. Golden Rapture × unnamed seedling. Deep golden-yellow, held to a late stage. Full, shapely flowers of medium size, opening loosely and carried on tall, vigorous growth, with dark green glossy foliage. In the autumn large trusses are often produced, like a floribunda. Very free flowering, but needs watching for mildew. T.

Stella: Tantau, 1959. Horstmann's Jubiläumsrose × Peace. Cream or pale buff in the centre, flushed pink and deepening to carmine at the edges of the petals. Very full, shapely flowers, carried on vigorous, tall growth, with glossy, medium green foliage, tinted bronze. Does not mind rain. May need protection from rust. T.

Sterling Silver (First Lady): Fisher, 1957. Seedling × Peace. Silvery-lilac, with deeper shadings. Full, very fragrant flowers of medium size, opening quickly. Growth is only moderately vigorous and upright, with glossy, dark green foliage. Good for cutting or for growing under glass. May need protection from black spot. M.

Sultane: Meilland, 1946. J. B. Meilland × Orange Nassau. Scarlet on the inside, with a deep yellow reverse. Full, slightly fragrant flowers, attractive at first, but opening quickly. Growth is moderately vigorous, with glossy, dark green foliage, coppery-red when young. May need protection from black spot. M.

Summer Sunshine (Soleil d'Été): Swim, 1962. Buccaneer × Lemon Chiffon. Rich deep yellow. Full flowers, of medium size which open quickly, with large petals. Growth is vigorous and upright, with dark green, semi-glossy foliage. A striking variety, but the plants do not seem to have a long life in my garden. M.

Super Star (Tropicana): Tantau, 1960. (Seedling × Peace) × (seedling × Alpine Glow). Pure light vermilion of extraordinary brilliance. The flowers are full, shapely, fragrant, and carried erect on tall, vigorous growth, with abundant, matt, medium green foliage. Free flowering and tending to produce flowers in trusses in the autumn. A very healthy and outstanding variety. T.

Sutter's Gold: Swim, 1950. Charlotte Armstrong × Signora. Light orange-yellow, flushed deep pink and heavily veined scarlet. Pointed buds, opening into shapely, very fragrant, full flowers, of medium size, carried on tall, rather spindly growth, with dark green, bronze-shaded foliage. It makes a somewhat gaunt plant, but the wiry stems are excellent for cutting. T.

Symphonie: Meilland, 1950. Peace × (Signora × Mrs John Laing). Silvery-pink, heavily veined deep carmine pink, shading to yellow at the base. The flowers are very large, full, globular and very fragrant. Growth is vigorous and branching, with glossy, leathery foliage, medium green tinted bronze. Free flowering and good in autumn. May need watching for mildew. M.

Tahiti: Meilland, 1947. Peace × Signora. Amber yellow, suffused carmine and shaded peach. The flowers are of medium size, full, with serrated petals, very fragrant and open many at a time on very vigorous growth, tall and branching, with dark, glossy foliage. Does not mind rain and very good in autumn. T.

Tally Ho: Swim, 1948. Charlotte Armstrong × unnamed seedling. Rose-red shading to carmine, with a deeper reddish-carmine on the reverse. The flowers are large and full, shapely at first, very fragrant and borne in profusion on very vigorous, branching growth with semi-glossy, reddish-green foliage. May need careful watching for mildew. T.

Teenager: Croll, 1958. Ena Harkness × Sutter's Gold. Rose-pink, shading to yellow towards the base, with a pale yellow reverse. The medium-sized flowers are moderately full and very fragrant. Growth is very vigorous, thorny, tall and upright, with matt, medium green foliage. Very floriferous. T.

The Doctor: Howard and Smith, 1936. Mrs J. D. Eisele × Los Angeles. Bright pink, without a trace of blue. The large, full but rather loosely-formed flowers have unusually large petals and open quickly. There is a wonderful fragrance. Growth is moderately vigorous and branching, with semi-glossy medium green foliage. It requires light pruning and a liberal diet, and may need protection from black spot. L.

Tiffany: Lindquist, 1957. Charlotte Armstrong × Girona. Soft rosy-salmon, shading to golden-yellow at the base. Large, full, long-petalled flowers, with serrated edges are characteristics of this variety. There is a pronounced fragrance. Growth is very vigorous and upright, carrying the flowers erect on long stems, which are

204

furnished with matt, deep green, large foliage. This is a good variety in fine weather, but it will not tolerate much rain. T.

Town Crier: J. H. Hill Co., 1961. Peace × Yellow Perfection. Straw yellow, deepening to orange-yellow in the heart. The flowers are of medium size, full, rather globular, opening quickly and carried on moderately vigorous, branching growth, with rather small glossy green foliage, tinted bronze when young. Good in autumn. L.

Tradition: Kordes, 1964. Schlösser's Brillant × Don Juan. Rich scarlet-crimson, non-fading rounded flowers, moderately full, scentless, but lasting well in good condition. Moderately vigorous and branching, with matt, medium green foliage, tinted red when young. Quick to repeat and free flowering. M.

Traviata: Meilland, 1962. Baccara × (Independence × Grand'-mère Jenny). Bud very long and pointed, light crimson on margins of petals, merging into white at the base and on the reverse. Moderately full, opening wide quickly. Free flowering on vigorous, rather upright growth, with matt, dark green foliage. T.

Tzigane: Meilland, 1951. Peace × J. B. Meilland. Bright scarlet on inside of petals, with a chrome yellow reverse. Full, shapely, fragrant flowers are displayed flamboyantly on moderately vigorous, upright growth, with glossy, very dark green, copper-tinted foliage. A look-out should be kept for mildew. M.

Ulster Monarch: McGredy, 1951. Sam McGredy × Mrs Sam McGredy seedling. Buff, deepening to light apricot in the heart. The medium-sized flowers are beautifully modelled, full, high pointed and borne on moderately vigorous upright growth, with glossy medium green foliage. An exhibitor's rose, not recommended for garden display. L.

Valerie Boughey: Fryer's Nurseries, 1960. Sport from Tzigane. Coppery-orange-cerise, shading to gold at the base and fading to orange-carmine. The flowers are full, rather globular, fragrant and produced very freely early in the season, repeating quickly. Growth is vigorous and upright, with glossy, copper-beech coloured foliage which needs watching for mildew. Very good in autumn and cheerful throughout the season. M.

Vienna Charm (Wiener Charme): Kordes, 1963. Golden Sun × Chantre. Deep coppery-orange, paler towards the petal edges. The full flowers are of pleasing shape, fragrant and of gorgeous colouring. Growth is vigorous and tall, somewhat spindly, with dark green, glossy foliage. May need protection against black spot. T.

Violinista Costa: Camprubi, 1936. Sensation × Shot Silk. Orange-cerise to carmine. The medium-sized flowers are full, with many short petals forming a rather shapeless but showy flower which opens wide quickly. Very free flowering on spreading, angular growth with many thorns and attractive glossy coppery-green foliage. Makes a fine standard head, but needs watching for mildew. M.

Virgo: Mallerin, 1947. Pole Nord × Neige Parfum. White, sometimes flushed pink in the bud. The flowers are of medium size, tapering, moderately full opening loosely. Very floriferous on vigorous, upright growth, with matt, dark green foliage. Needs watching for mildew and it is impatient of rain. M.

Vivien Leigh: S. McGredy IV, 1963. Queen Elizabeth × Brilliant. Crimson with darker blackish shadings. The flowers are full, of medium size, high centred, opening quickly, only slightly fragrant. Growth is vigorous and tall, with plentiful dark reddish-green foliage, semi-glossy and needing protection from black spot. T.

Wendy Cussons: Gregory, 1959. Independence × Eden Rose. Sparkling cerise. The flowers are full, of immaculate shape and very fragrant. Growth is vigorous, tall and branching, with glossy, dark green foliage, tinted red. Very prolific and does not mind rain. An outstanding variety. Good in autumn. T.

Western Sun: Poulsen, 1965. Spek's Yellow seedling × Golden Sun. Deepest tawny-gold, without shading. The flowers are full, well formed and carried on moderately vigorous growth, with dark, semi-glossy foliage which needs watching for mildew. Free flowering. M.

Westminster: Robinson, 1959. Gay Crusader × Peace. Cherry-red on the inside, with yellow, striped red on the reverse. The large, full blooms are definitely appealing at first, but they open loosely and fade later. Very fragrant. Growth is tall and angular, rather gaunt, with semi-glossy, medium green, bronze-tinted foliage. May need protection from rust. T.

Westward Ho: Allen, 1964. Pink Charming × Karl Herbst. Mahogany-red on the inside, with a silvery reverse—a most unusual colour combination. The full, globular blooms are fragrant and produced freely on vigorous, upright growth, with copper-bronze foliage and wood. A very distinct variety. M.

Whisky Mac: Tantau, 1968. Deep gold, overlaid orange and bronze. The medium-sized blooms are shapely, full and very fragrant. The bushy growth is well furnished with dark green glossy foliage, bronze tinted when young. A free-flowering, unusually fragrant addition to this colour group. M.

White Christmas: Howard and Smith, 1953. Sleigh Bells × seedling. Pure white, deepening to ivory at the base. Large, full, rather globular blooms with some fragrance, borne on moderately vigorous, upright growth, with dark green, matt foliage. Good in dry weather, but will not tolerate much rain. M.

Winefred Clarke: Robinson, 1965. Peace × Lydia. Golden-yellow in the heart, paling to cream in the outer petals. The full, well-formed flowers last well, but need fine weather to be seen at their best. Growth is vigorous and branching, with glossy, medium green foliage. Free flowering and good in autumn. M.

Wisbech Gold: McGredy, 1964. Piccadilly × Golden Sun. Intense golden-yellow, flushed pink at the edges. The globular flowers are full, shapely at first, opening confused, with many open at the same time and lasting well on the plants. Growth is moderately vigorous, bushy and compact, with bright green glossy foliage, but the plants are not very hardy in my garden. Free flowering. May need watching for black spot. L.

Youki San: Meilland, 1965. Lady Sylvia × Message. White, with a greenish tinge. The dainty flowers are moderately full, fragrant and produced in great profusion on moderately vigorous, branching growth, with small, light green foliage. Needs watching for mildew and will not stand much rain. L.

HYBRID TEAS

'At-a-glance' Colour Chart

DEEP YELLOW	SCARLET-CRIMSON	MEDIUM PINK
Belle Blonde	Champs Elysées	City of Hereford
Buccaneer	Crimson Brocade	Gavotte
Dr A. J. Verhage	Ena Harkness	Grace de Monaco
Gold Crown	John S. Armstrong	Guinevere
Isobel Harkness	Klaus Störtebeker	Margaret
King's Ransom	Konrad Adenauer	Mme Caroline Testout
Lydia	Lancastrian	Percy Thrower
Spek's Yellow	Mardi Gras	Picture
Summer Sunshine	Milord	Pink Supreme
Western Sun	New Style	Sarah Arnot
Wisbech Gold	Tradition	Symphonie

ROSES

CORAL-SALMON
ORANGE-SALMON
(with buff reverse)
Colour Wonder
Miss Ireland

COPPERY-SALMON-RED
Hawaii
Mary Wheatcroft
Mrs Sam McGredy
Valerie Boughey

DEEP CRIMSON
Charles Mallerin
Chrysler Imperial
Crimson Glory
Ellen Mary
Josephine Bruce
Mister Lincoln
Mme Louis Laperrière
Papa Meilland
Vivien Leigh

SALMON-PINK AND CORAL-SALMON
Bel Ange
Camelot
Evensong
Femina
Garvey
Invitation
Mischief
Santa Fé

LIGHT YELLOW
Dorothy Peach
Golden Splendour
Grandpa Dickson
McGredy's Yellow
Peace
Town Crier
Winefred Clarke

SALMON-RED
Brandenburg
Montezuma

LIGHT VERMILION
Cherry Brandy
Duke of Windsor
Jolie Madame
Princess
Super Star

GERANIUM-RED AND ORANGE-SCARLET
Allegro
Lucy Cramphorn
Opera
Pharaoh
Soraya

CERISE, CARMINE AND LIGHT RED
Bacchus
Criterion
Dr Albert Schweitzer
Maria Callas
Tally Ho
Violinista Costa
Wendy Cussons

LIGHT PINK
Anne Letts
Blessings
Bonsoir
Carla
First Love
Lady Sylvia
Mme Butterfly
Monique
Silver Lining
Tiffany

MEDIUM YELLOW
Amatsu Otome
Ellinor Le Grice
Ethel Sanday
Gertrude Gregory
Golden Giant
Marcelle Gret
Parasol
Peer Gynt

YELLOW, ORANGE AND PINK BLENDS
Bayadère
Chicago Peace
Elsa Arnot
Gail Borden
Grand'mère Jenny
Helen Traubel
My Choice
President Herbert Hoover
Signora
Silva
Sutter's Gold
Tahiti
Teenager
Whisky Mac

DEEP PINK
Ballet
Eden Rose
June Park
Lady Seton
Paris-Match
Pink Favourite
Pink Peace
Prima Ballerina
Prince of Denmark
Shannon
Show Girl
The Doctor

LILAC-PINK
Lilac Rose

LAVENDER, LILAC AND MAUVE
Blue Moon
Cologne Carnival
Heure Mauve
Intermezzo
Sterling Silver

DARK VERMILION
Baccara
Elida
Fragrant Cloud
Fritz Thiedemann
Numéro Un

Exhibiting roses. *Left:* Six hybrid tea
blooms in an exhibition box
Below left: Three hybrid tea blooms in an
exhibition vase
Below right: Eighteen hybrid tea blooms in
an exhibition bowl

Bantry Bay (Large-flowered Climber)

DESCRIPTIVE LIST OF HYBRID TEA ROSES

DEEP SCARLET AND TURKEY RED

Brilliant
Christian Dior
Dame de Coeur
Ernest H. Morse
Greetings
Karl Herbst
Red Devil

ORANGE, FLAME AND APRICOT

André le Troquer
Apricot Silk
Beauté
Bettina
Diorama
Doreen
Flaming Sunset
Lady Belper
Majorette
Mojave
Pilar Landecho
Serenade
Souvenir de Jacques
    Verschuren
Vienna Charm

WHITE AND CREAM

Bridal Robe
Frau Karl Druschki
McGredy's Ivory
Message
Pascali
Virgo
White Christmas
Youki San

WHITE, CREAM AND PALE PINK BLENDS

Angel Wings
Jean Campbell
La Jolla
Memoriam
Michèle Meilland
Ophelia
President Pats
Royal Highness

IVORY AND CREAM GROUND, WITH CARMINE/RED MARGINS AND SUFFUSIONS

Ideal Home
Perfecta
Rose Gaujard
Scandale
Stella
Traviata

CREAM, BUFF AND APRICOT

(noticeably deeper in the heart)

Anne Watkins
Diamond Jubilee
Fred Gibson
Golden Melody
Gordon Eddie
Polly
Sam McGredy
Ulster Monarch

BICOLOR

Brasilia (light scarlet and
    pale gold)
Caramba (crimson and
    silver)
Eve Allen (cherry-red and
    old-gold)
Francine (crimson and
    silver)
Grand Gala (scarlet and
    silver)
Isabel de Ortiz (deep pink
    and white)
Kronenbourg (crimson
    and old gold)
Lady Eve Price (cerise
    and cream)
Marjorie Le Grice
    (orange-flame and pale
    yellow)
Piccadilly (scarlet and
    yellow)
Regalia (wine-red and
    silver)
Sabrina (crimson and
    amber-yellow)
Sultane (scarlet and deep
    yellow)
Tzigane (scarlet and
    chrome-yellow)
Westminster (cherry-red
    and gold)
Westward Ho
    (mahogany-red and
    silver)

21

Descriptive List of Floribunda Roses

Recommended varieties of floribunda and floribunda hybrid tea type roses and the floribunda dwarfs

The floribunda varieties have increased by leaps and bounds, both in numbers and colour range, during the past 20 years or so. There are now so many of them that, as in the case of the hybrid teas, it is necessary to indicate the habit of growth, using the letters 'T', 'M' or 'L' to denote that a variety is taller than average, of medium growth or lower growing than average, respectively. While this is only an approximation, it will at least prevent serious mistakes being made, such as planting the very tall Queen Elizabeth in front of the low-growing Marlena.

Such comments as I have made on susceptibility to black spot or rust are only likely to be a guide to amateurs living in pure-air districts, where these diseases are usually troublesome. In industrial areas and large towns where air pollution is to be expected, these comments may be ignored as residents in such areas seldom have much of a problem with these diseases.

It is well to bear in mind that a floribunda variety *must* be free flowering, with as short an interval as possible between successive crops. It should have a well-spaced truss of flowers (not overcrowded) and should shed its petals cleanly when the flower has faded—not retain them, to form an unsightly mummified brown mass. The varieties described briefly in this chapter have been selected from a much longer list of those I have grown over the years as being the most likely to give satisfaction, subject to any reservations made in individual cases. The name and date given after the varietal name indicate the raiser and the date of introduction.

DESCRIPTIVE LIST OF FLORIBUNDA ROSES

Africa Star: West, 1965. Parentage unknown. Lilac-mauve, very full flowers, with short petals, giving a 'quartered' appearance. Short, spreading growth with dark, bronze-green foliage. May need protection from black spot. L.

Alain: Meilland, 1946. (Guinée × Wilhelm) × Orange Triumph. Bright scarlet-crimson. Full medium-sized flowers in large trusses on vigorous branching growth, with matt, medium green small leaves, which need watching for mildew. M.

Alamein: McGredy, 1963. Spartan × Queen Elizabeth. Rich scarlet. Large, well formed at first, opening flat, borne in small trusses. Foliage dark green and semi-glossy. Bushy, branching growth. M.

Alison Wheatcroft: Wheatcroft Bros., 1959. A sport from Circus. Apricot-yellow, flushed and edged crimson, but not as full-petalled as the parent. Moderately vigorous, with dark green foliage, tinted bronze. May need protection from black spot. M.

Allgold: Le Grice, 1956. Goldilocks × Ellinor Le Grice. Deep golden-yellow, held to the end, in a medium-sized, moderately full flower up to 3 in. across. Growth is normally rather short and branching, with glossy, bright green foliage, very resistant to disease. Still the best yellow floribunda of bedding habit. L.

Allotria: Tantau, 1958. Red Favourite × Käthe Duvigneau. Orange-scarlet, rosette-shaped, full flower, opening flat. Moderately vigorous, branching growth, with semi-glossy medium green foliage. M.

Ama: Kordes, 1955. Obergärtner Wiebicke × Independence. Bright scarlet flowers in large trusses, opening semi-double and holding their colour well in all weathers. Very free flowering and trouble-free. Tall and branching growth with healthy foliage. T.

Amberlight: Le Grice, 1961. (Seedling × Lavender Pinocchio) × Marcel Bourgouin. Amber shading to brownish-yellow. The flowers are large, moderately full, with frilled petals, very fragrant and carried in a widely-spaced truss on vigorous, branching growth, with dark green, semi-glossy foliage. T.

Ambrosia: Dickson, 1962. Seedling × Shepherd's Delight. Dark, burnt-orange single flowers, shading to amber in the centre and fading with mauve tints in the final stages. Moderately vigorous, branching growth, with dark, matt foliage. L.

211

Angela: Kordes, 1956. Masquerade × Spek's Yellow. Golden-yellow, shaded pink and suffused crimson, the latter spreading as the flower ages. The long, pointed buds open into moderately full but fragrant flowers, mostly produced singly or in small trusses. A tall, upright grower, which needs watching for mildew. T.

Anna Louisa: De Ruiter, 1967. Exquisitely-formed, full hybrid tea type flowers of a delicate shade of pink, deeper in the heart, borne in rather small trusses. Bushy, branching habit of growth, with glossy mid-green foliage. May need protection from black spot. M.

Anna Wheatcroft: Tantau, 1959. Cinnabar × seedling. Light vermilion, without shading. Semi-double flowers opening flat, with conspicuous golden anthers and carried in medium trusses on spreading growth. May need protection from black spot. M.

Ann Elizabeth: Norman, 1962. Clear rose-pink, semi-double flowers, opening from long-pointed buds in rather loose trusses, which are carried on a tall, rather lax plant. Very free flowering. Some support may be needed where light pruning is practised. Best planted at the back of a border. T.

Anne Poulsen (Anne-Mette Poulsen): Poulsen, 1935. Ingar Olsson × red hybrid tea. Bright carmine-red, semi-double flowers, rather globular, in flat trusses. Free flowering on very vigorous, stiff growth, with large, semi-glossy, dark green foliage. May need watching for mildew. T.

Antique: Kordes, 1967. Rich crimson on the inside with a contrasting golden-yellow reverse. The flowers are large, full and shapely at first, rather globular, and carried on vigorous, bushy growth, with dark green, glossy foliage. A striking new colour combination, with a compact bedding habit. M.

Apricot Nectar: Boerner, Jackson and Perkins, 1965. Unnamed seedling × Spartan. Pale apricot, shading to gold at the base. Full flowers, up to 4 in. across, borne on vigorous, tall growth with semi-glossy, medium green foliage. A novel colouring for a floribunda. May need watching for mildew. T.

Arabian Nights: McGredy, 1963. Spartan × Beauté. Rich salmon-red flowers, with large but few petals, opening quickly, but still attractive. Growth is tall and upright, with large, dark green foliage, tinted crimson when young. Useful for cutting. T.

Arthur Bell: McGredy, 1965. Cläre Grammerstorf × Piccadilly. Deep golden-yellow at first, paling to creamy-yellow with age. Shapely, full young flowers, unusually fragrant for a floribunda.

Tall upright growth, with many main stems and densely foliaged. A great improvement on Honeymoon. T.

Ascot: Dickson, 1962. Brownie × seedling. Coral-salmon to salmon-pink, according to the weather. Semi-double, cupped flowers, carried on very short, branching growth, with semi-glossy light green foliage. May need watching for mildew. L.

Athos: Laperrière, 1966. Light vermilion, with paler reverse; full flowers, 3 in. across, borne in rather close trusses with many flowers open together, creating a vivid effect. Bushy, branching habit. Best in sunny weather as the footstalks are somewhat weak. M.

August Seebauer: Kordes, 1950. Break o' Day × Else Poulsen. Deep rose-pink, full flowers, freely produced on tall, branching growth, with abundant, semi-glossy, light green foliage. May need protection against black spot. T.

Baby Sylvia: Fryer's Nurseries, 1959. Lady Sylvia × unnamed seedling. Delicate flesh pink, shaded salmon in the centre. Full, shapely flowers, 3 in. across, in medium clusters. Free flowering on very vigorous, tall growth with matt, medium green foliage. T.

Beaulieu Abbey: Cobley, 1964. Masquerade × Docteur Valois. Creamy-yellow, heavily margined and flushed pink on each petal. Full, well formed at first, opening flat. Moderately vigorous, with dark green, glossy foliage. M.

Blue Diamond: Lens, 1963. Purpurine × (Purpurine × Royal Tan). Large, full flowers of hybrid tea form early in the season, of a pleasing shade of lavender-mauve, with purplish-bronze foliage and wood and a bushy, branching habit. After the first flush the flowers are borne in large trusses. L.

Bobbie Lucas: McGredy, 1967. Elizabeth of Glamis × Margot Fonteyn. Deep salmon-orange. Full, shapely, hybrid tea type flowers produced early in the season on upright, medium growth, with glossy medium green foliage. Repeats quickly and is good in autumn. A very rich colour which is held fairly well. M.

Border Coral: De Ruiter, 1958. Signal Red × Fashion. Rich coral-salmon. Full flowers, 3 in. across, carried in a large truss and produced very freely on vigorous, spreading growth, with large, glossy medium green leaves. Good in autumn. May need protection from black spot. M.

Celebration: Dickson, 1961. Dickson's Flame × Circus. Salmon-pink, with a silvery reverse. Shapely hybrid tea type flowers at first, opening loosely. Moderately vigorous growth, with healthy foliage. The flowers are inclined to mottle with age. M.

Chanelle: McGredy, 1958. Ma Perkins × (Mrs William Sprott × Fashion). Cream and peach-pink shades, suffused buff. The young flowers are like miniature hybrid teas and carried very profusely on strong, branching growth. Normally this variety is very disease resistant and trouble-free. M.

Charleston: Meilland, 1963. Masquerade × (Radar × Caprice). Pointed buds opening into large, moderately full flowers, comprising crimson and yellow in startling contrast. Unlike most of the Masquerade seedlings, the colours remain distinct to a late stage instead of merging into each other. Growth is moderately vigorous, with dark green, glossy foliage which needs protection from black spot. Not recommended for gardens where this disease is troublesome. L.

Charlotte Elizabeth: Norman, 1965. Parentage unknown. Very deep rose-pink, almost carmine. The flowers are full, well formed at first and as large as some hybrid teas. They are carried singly or in small trusses on upright growth, and not as freely as I should like. May need protection from black spot. M.

Charming Maid: Le Grice, 1953. Dainty Maid × Mrs Sam McGredy. Soft salmon-pink, shading to yellow in the centre. The single flowers are 4 in. across, with slightly waved petals and are borne in small clusters on tall growth, with large, glossy, dark green leaves. A very dainty flower, but with rather long flowerless intervals. T.

Charm of Paris: Tantau, 1966. Prima Ballerina × Montezuma. Large, full flowers, well formed, in a light salmon-pink shade and very fragrant. Growth is branching and ideal for bedding, with healthy green foliage. Very close to the hybrid teas. At its best in dry weather. M.

Circus: Swim, 1955. Fandango × Pinocchio. Yellow, with pink and salmon suffusions, spreading as the flower ages. Full flowers, of regular form, in fairly large trusses. Branching growth, ideal for bedding, with dark green foliage. May need protection from black spot. M.

City of Belfast: S. McGredy IV, 1968. Evelyn Fison × (Korona × Circus). Rich scarlet, full-petalled flowers, $2\frac{1}{2}$-3 in. across, with slightly frilled petals, borne in medium-sized trusses. Growth is compact, moderately vigorous and branching, with glossy medium green foliage, reddish when young. Excellent for bedding and for small gardens. L.

City of Leeds: McGredy, 1966. Evelyn Fison × (Spartan × Red Favourite). Rich salmon, moderately full flowers succeeding shapely buds and carried very freely on upright growth, with dark green foliage. The flowers spot rather easily in bad weather. M.

Cognac: Tantau, 1956. Alpine Glow × Mrs Pierre S. du Pont. Apricot in the heart, paling towards the edges. Full, globular flowers in medium clusters, borne on bushy growth with small, dark green glossy leaves, which need watching for black spot. The first in its colour group. Free flowering. M.

Colour Carnival: Le Grice, 1962. Pale yellow, heavily flushed and edged bright pink. The flowers are very full, globular and carried in medium trusses on a compact, bushy plant, with light green, matt foliage, which needs protection from black spot. L.

Columbine: Poulsen, 1956. Danish Gold × Frensham. Creamy-yellow, delicately edged and flushed pink on each petal. The flowers are exquisitely formed, fragrant and carried in a widely spaced cluster. Growth is very vigorous, with glossy, dark green foliage. I have not found it to be sufficiently free flowering. T.

Concerto: Meilland, 1953. Alain × Orange Triumph. Bright scarlet, semi-double flowers, rather small according to present standards. Very free flowering on branching growth, with glossy green foliage. M.

Copper Delight: Le Grice, 1956. Goldilocks × Ellinor Le Grice. Deep orange-yellow, semi-double flowers in well-spaced, wide trusses, and very fragrant. Branching habit with glossy, dark green, copper-tinted foliage. May need protection from black spot. M.

Coventrian: H. Robinson, 1962. Highlight × unnamed seedling. Rich cerise and quite unfading. The flowers are large, very full, well formed like a hybrid tea and carried in medium clusters on short, bushy growth, with dark, purplish-green foliage. Growth is not really strong enough for display, and it needs protection from black spot. L.

Daily Sketch: McGredy, 1960. Ma Perkins × Grand Gala. Pink and silver bicolor, with the pink intensifying to red and spreading as the flower ages. Shapely and full, opening loosely. Very fragrant. Very vigorous, tall and branching, with glossy, bronze-tinted foliage. May be grown as a hedge. T.

Dainty Maid: Le Grice, 1938. D. T. Poulsen seedling. Pale pink

215

inside, with a carmine-pink reverse. The flowers are semi-double, opening wide with golden stamens and are carried upright in wide trusses on tall growth. One of the best of the earlier introductions. T.

Dearest: Dickson, 1960. Spartan seedling. Soft rosy-salmon, full-petalled flowers in large trusses. There is a characteristic clove scent, like that of the parent. Vigorous and branching, with dark green, glossy foliage. The flowers are impatient of rain. T.

Decapo: De Ruiter, 1960. Fashion × a floribunda seedling. Large, full flowers, with short petals in a pleasing orange-salmon shade. Very free flowering on a strong, bushy plant. I prefer it to Fashion, as it seems less prone to disease. M.

Diamant: Kordes, 1962. Korona × Spartan. Deep vermilion to salmon-red. Large, full, well-formed flowers, carried on vigorous, upright growth, with medium, glossy foliage. The trusses are small but vivid. T.

Dickson's Flame: Dickson, 1958. Independence seedling × Nymph. Vermilion-red, non-fading, moderately full flowers in small trusses, displayed on a spreading, short plant, producing new growth at an acute angle. Small, glossy leaves. Pruning to inward-pointing eyes is recommended to build up the plant. L.

Dimples: Le Grice, 1967. Creamy-white, deepening to lemon in the centre. Full, fragrant flowers, produced in small trusses on branching growth. Does not mind rain but may need watching for black spot and mildew. Very free flowering. M.

Dominator: De Ruiter, 1960. New Yorker × Sweet Repose. Deep cerise or carmine-pink. The semi-double flowers open wide quickly and are carried on tall growth. The colour is rather hard, but held to the end. T.

Elizabeth of Glamis: McGredy, 1964. Spartan × Highlight. A soft salmon shade, richer in the heart. The long buds open into hybrid tea type flowers, moderately full, with long petals, but opening loosely. Fragrant. Free flowering and quick to repeat on upright, vigorous growth. Delightful when half open, but the colour fades in the later stages. The plants have a rather weak constitution in my garden. M.

Elysium: Kordes, 1961. Light salmon, paling to almost pearly tints. Large, full, well-formed flowers, slightly fragrant, carried on tall, erect growth, with glossy, deep green foliage. Impatient of rain and the colour tends to be insipid. T.

Escapade: Harkness, 1967. Pink Parfait × Baby Faurax. Lilac-rose, paling to white in the centre; semi-double flowers, 4 in. across,

Faults in exhibition roses. *Top left:* An overblown bloom. *Top right:* A quartered
bloom. *Bottom left:* A split bloom. *Bottom right:* An overdressed bloom

Left: Handel (Large-flowered Climber)
Below: Pink Perpetue (Large-flowered Climber)

Opposite: Golden Showers (Large-flowered Climber)

Left: A weeping standard, when of the quality of the specimen portrayed, makes a superb lawn feature

Below: When roses are grown against house walls in the vicinity of windows, fragrance is something to keep in mind. On warm, sunny days this attribute is much appreciated

fragrant, carried in well-spaced trusses. Growth is vigorous and bushy, with glossy, light green foliage. A newcomer of charming simplicity. M.

Europeana: De Ruiter, 1963. Ruth Leuwerik × Rosemary Rose. Dark crimson, rosette-shaped flowers, full, produced in large trusses on vigorous, branching growth. The heavy trusses may need tying, especially after rain. Large, abundant foliage, purplish-crimson when young and highly coloured to a late stage. Somewhat prone to mildew. M.

Evelyn Fison: McGredy, 1962. Moulin Rouge × Korona. Bright orange-scarlet, non-fading, full-petalled flowers, carried freely in medium trusses in all weathers. Growth is vigorous and branching. A showy variety. M.

Fairlight: Robinson, 1965. Joybells × seedling. Rich coppery-salmon, conspicuously veined scarlet, shaded yellow at the base. Full, hybrid tea type flowers borne in medium trusses, displayed well above the foliage. Fragrant and free flowering. Growth is bushy, with stems and young leaves coppery-red, maturing dark green. A pleasing and distinct floribunda. M.

Farandole: Meilland, 1959. (Goldilocks × Moulin Rouge) × (Goldilocks × Fashion). Vermilion. The flowers are of medium size, full and borne in large clusters on vigorous, branching growth, with dark, leathery foliage. Free flowering. M.

Fashion: Boerner, Jackson and Perkins, 1947. Pinocchio × Crimson Glory. Rich orange-salmon, moderately full, cupped flowers in small trusses on bushy, branching growth, clothed with small, matt, bronze-green foliage. There is a marked susceptibility to rust and black spot in pure-air districts, but it does well in industrial areas. The first of the orange-salmon group. L.

Faust: Kordes, 1956. Masquerade × Spek's Yellow. Golden-yellow, shaded pink. Full flowers of hybrid tea shape, slightly fragrant, in large, heavy trusses on tall, upright growth, with glossy, abundant foliage. Very strong and hardy. May need watching for mildew. T.

Fervid: Le Grice, 1960. Pimpernel × Korona. Vivid scarlet single flowers with slightly frilled petals, carried in medium trusses on tall, upright growth. May need protection from black spot. T.

Fidélio: Meilland, 1964. Radar × Caprice. Long-pointed buds opening into hybrid tea type flowers, high centred, but opening wide, in a vivid orange-scarlet, slightly deeper on the reverse. They are borne singly and in small trusses on vigorous, upright growth, with dark green, bronze-tinted foliage which needs protection from black spot. M.

Firecracker: Boerner, Jackson and Perkins, 1955. Pinocchio seedling × Numa Fay seedling. Bright carmine, shading to yellow at the base. The flowers are semi-double, $3\frac{1}{2}$ in. across and borne very freely on vigorous branching growth. The foliage is semi-glossy, medium green and fairly healthy. M.

Fireworks (Feuerwerk): Tantau, 1962. Light orange-vermilion. The scentless semi-double flowers open flat and are displayed in wide trusses on tall growths. Excellent for the back of a border. T.

Flamenco: McGredy, 1960. Tantau's Triumph × Spartan. Rich salmon-red on the inside, paler on the reverse. The flowers are moderately full, shapely at first, opening flat. Growth is vigorous and upright with large, semi-glossy, medium green foliage. Very free flowering and quick to repeat. M.

Frensham: Norman, 1946. Seedling × Crimson Glory. Deep scarlet-crimson, shapely hybrid tea type buds, opening semi-double in well-spaced trusses. Strong, tall growth with abundant, glossy green foliage. Does not mind rain and makes a good hedge if it can be kept free of mildew. For many years the most popular floribunda, but now increasingly prone to mildew. T.

Fresco: De Ruiter, 1968. Metropole × Orange Sensation. Rich tangerine orange on the inside of the petals, with a contrasting golden yellow reverse. The flowers are full, shapely at first, opening to a rounded form, about $3\frac{1}{2}$ in. across and borne both singly and in small trusses on strong, bushy growth. The foliage is plentiful, carried well up to the flowers and to the base of the plant, dark green, glossy and bronze tinted when young. A very promising novelty, strikingly effective in the garden, quick to repeat and does not mind rain. May need protection from black spot. M.

Geisha Girl: McGredy, 1964. Gold Cup × McGredy's Yellow. Golden-yellow at first, fading to creamy-yellow. The flowers are shapely at first, moderately full, borne on tall, branching growth, with ample matt, medium green large leaves. T.

Golden Fleece: Boerner, Jackson and Perkins, 1956. Diamond Jubilee × Yellow Sweetheart. Light straw yellow, deeper in the heart. The flowers are large, $4\frac{1}{2}$ in. across, full, fragrant, and carried very freely on vigorous branching growth. The foliage is matt, dark green and plentiful. May need watching for mildew. M.

Golden Jewel: Tantau, 1959. Goldilocks × Masquerade seedling. Golden-yellow, very full but short-petalled fragrant flowers, which retain their colour fairly well. Compact, bushy growth, with small, medium green foliage. M.

Golden Slippers: Von Abrams, 1961. Goldilocks × unnamed seedling. Orange-flame inside, with a reverse of pale gold. Small hybrid tea shaped flowers, delightful at first, moderately full, opening loosely and fading quickly; fragrant. Bushy growth with glossy green foliage, bronze tinted. Very healthy, free flowering and excellent for small beds. Good in cool weather. L.

Golden Treasure: Tantau, 1965. Intense golden-yellow, moderately full, hybrid tea type flowers produced singly and in small trusses. At the half-open stage these are particularly pleasing, with long petals, but when fully expanded they are rather thin. The colour is held well. Growth is somewhat upright, with glossy rich green foliage. A promising newcomer. M.

Goldgleam: Le Grice, 1966. Gleaming × Allgold. Bright canary yellow, slightly lighter than Allgold. Moderately full flowers, 3½ in. across, borne very freely and continuously throughout the season on vigorous, branching growth, clothed with glossy, bright green foliage, bronze tinted when young. Does not mind rain. A very promising new yellow which retains its colour intensity until petal fall. M.

Goldilocks: Boerner, Jackson and Perkins, 1945. Seedling × Doubloons. Rich yellow at first, fading rapidly to cream. Very full flowers, with many small petals, produced freely on moderately vigorous, branching growth. Glossy, dark green foliage which needs protection from black spot. L.

Gold Marie: Kordes, 1958. Masquerade × Goldenes Mainz. Golden-yellow, stained crimson in the bud and young flower. Full, globular form; fragrant. Vigorous and spreading growth with glossy, dark green, bronze-tinted foliage. Needs watching for mildew and there is a tendency for wood to die back in the winter. T.

Happy Event: Dickson, 1964. (Masquerade × Karl Herbst) × Rose Gaujard. Cherry-red on a yellow groundwork, fading with age to carmine and pale yellow. The flowers are quite large, 4 in. across, and are borne on moderately vigorous, branching growth, with dark green, glossy foliage. Does not mind rain. M.

Herself: G. W. C. Vincent, 1966. Sweet Repose × Moulin Rouge. Delicate pastel pink shades in a semi-double, short-petalled flower.

Growth is moderately vigorous and upright, with rather small, semi-glossy foliage, which needs protection from black spot. L.

Highlight: Robinson, 1956. Seedling × Independence. Orange-scarlet, moderately full flowers in large trusses, on very strong upright growth, with large, semi-glossy leaves. The trusses are well displayed above the leaves and are a particularly vivid colour, but a tendency to 'blue' in the final stages is inherited from the pollen parent. T.

Honeymoon (Honigmond): Kordes, 1960. Cläre Grammerstorf × Spek's Yellow. Canary yellow, fading to creamy-yellow. Very double, small-petalled flowers of rosette shape, borne in small clusters. Vigorous, upright growth with abundant, bright green, glossy foliage. Does not repeat quickly after the first flush. T.

Iceberg (Schneewittchen): Kordes, 1958. Robin Hood × Virgo. The buds are tinted pink, opening into moderately full pure white blooms with nicely pointed centres, and carried in medium to large trusses. Growth is vigorous and tall, but rather slender, with glossy, long-pointed foliage. A very free-flowering and deservedly popular variety, but it needs watching for black spot and mildew. T.

Ice White: McGredy, 1966. Mme Léon Cuny × (Orange Sweet-heart × Tantau's Triumph). White, deepening to creamy-white in the centre of the moderately full flower, which is shapely in the early stages. Growth is vigorous and branching, with glossy dark green foliage. M.

Independence (Geranium, Kordes' Sondermeldung, Reina Elisenda): Kordes, 1950. Crimson Glory × Baby Château. Sealing-wax red with blackish shadings. The scentless flowers are large, full and well formed and carried in small trusses if not disbudded. Very free flowering on strong, branching growth, with beautiful disease-resistant, glossy foliage, crimson in the early stages. Very striking in hot weather, but 'blues' badly in the final stages. The parent of many modern varieties of brilliant colouring and the first of its type. M.

Irish Mist: McGredy, 1967. Orangeade × Mischief. Orange-salmon. The hybrid tea type flowers are well formed, moderately full and carried on vigorous, branching growth, with dark green, semi-glossy foliage. The petals have characteristic serrated edges. M.

Ivory Fashion: Boerner, Jackson and Perkins, 1957. Sonata × Fashion. Ivory white, sometimes shading to pale buff in the heart. The flower is large, moderately full and well formed at first, opening flat. Growth is moderately vigorous with matt green foliage. Needs watching for black spot and is best in dry weather. M.

Jane Lazenby: McGredy, 1958. Alain × Mme Henri Guillot. Orange-carmine, shading to yellow at the base. The flowers are moderately full, fragrant and open quickly on vigorous, tall growth, inclined to be spreading. Dark green, glossy foliage. T.

Jan Spek: McGredy, 1966. Cläre Grammerstorf × Faust. The rosette-shaped full flowers open a bright yellow, which fades to creamy-yellow. Growth is short and bushy, well furnished with healthy, bright green, semi-glossy foliage. A free-flowering variety suitable for edgings to beds and borders. L.

Jiminy Cricket: Boerner, 1954. Goldilocks × Geranium Red. Rich tangerine-red, shading to yellow at the base. The flowers are moderately full and cupped, fragrant and fade to orange-pink with age. The growth is vigorous, upright and branching, with small, glossy, dark green, copper-tinted foliage. Free flowering. Best in cool weather. M.

John Church: McGredy, 1964. Ma Perkins × Red Favourite. Rich orange-salmon. The hybrid tea type flowers are full and shapely with pointed centres, and are carried in small clusters on vigorous, upright growth, with semi-glossy, rather small foliage. M.

Joybells: Robinson, 1961. Unnamed seedling × Fashion. Rich pink, large, full flowers, with short petals giving an 'old-world' effect. Fragrant. Strong branching growth resembling the hybrid teas, with many thorns and large, glossy, medium green leaves. M.

Joyfulness (Frohsinn): Tantau, 1961. Horstmann's Jubiläumsrose × Circus. Long-pointed buds opening to hybrid tea shaped flowers, apricot flushed and shaded salmon-pink, moderately full, in small trusses. The richest colour soon fades. Upright growth with dark, glossy, bronze-tinted foliage. Needs watching for black spot. M.

Jubilant: Dickson, 1967. Dearest × Circus. Peach-pink paling to silvery-pink towards the edges of the petals. The flowers are moderately full, opening flat quickly, and are borne freely in medium trusses. Growth is vigorous and upright, with abundant, glossy, medium green foliage. M.

Karen Poulsen: Poulsen, 1935. Kirsten Poulsen × Vesuvius. Rich scarlet, single flowers carried in large trusses. Growth is moderately vigorous, often producing one strong growth giving an unbalanced effect. Semi-glossy, medium green foliage. Does not mind rain. M.

King Arthur: Harkness, 1967. Pink Parfait × Highlight. Rich salmon-pink, full flowers, about 4 in. across, carried in small trusses on medium, branching growth, with large matt foliage. Colour tends to mottle in the later stages. M.

Korona: Kordes, 1954. Bright orange-scarlet, fading to deep salmon-pink; moderately full flowers, but rather formless, produced very freely in medium trusses. Growth is tall and upright, with large, dark, glossy foliage. May need protection from black spot. T.

Lilac Charm: Le Grice, 1961. Lavender Pinocchio seedling. Single flowers, about 3 in. across in pale lilac, with contrasting red anthers and golden stamens. Fragrant. Very free flowering in small trusses on short, branching growths, with very dark green matt foliage. A delightful rose, but may need protection from black spot. L.

Lilli Marlene: Kordes, 1959. (Our Princess × Rudolph Timm) × Ama. Deep scarlet with crimson shadings. The flowers are rounded, semi-double and carried upright in a well-spaced truss well above the foliage. Compact even growth, with medium green, semi-glossy foliage. Makes a very effective bed. M.

Love Token: Gregory, 1964. Rosy-coral. The rounded flowers are full, carried in a well-spaced truss and open freely in all weathers. Growth is vigorous and spreading, with large, dark green foliage, purplish when young. M.

Lucky Charm: Robinson, 1961. Large, moderately full, globular, golden-yellow flowers, edged and flushed flame-red, with a delightful fragrance. Growth is tall, strong and branching, with abundant, glossy, bronze-tinted foliage. T.

Mandy: Robinson, 1963. Pinocchio × Sweet Repose. Creamy-yellow, heavily suffused peach-pink. Charming full flowers, like miniature hybrid teas of regular form, full-petalled, in medium trusses. Strong, erect growth with dark green copper-tinted foliage. A very pretty decorative variety. T.

Manx Queen (Isle of Man): Dickson, 1963. Shepherd's Delight × Circus. A colourful blend of gold, orange and pink shades. Moderately full flowers in a well-spaced truss, carried on bushy, branching growth with dark green foliage. A free-flowering bedding variety. L.

Ma Perkins: Boerner, Jackson and Perkins, 1952. Red Radiance × Fashion. Medium rose-pink, paling towards the petal edges. Moderately full, cupped flowers produced freely on vigorous, tall growth, with semi-glossy, dark green foliage. T.

Märchenland: Tantau, 1951. Swantje × Hamburg. Pale pink, deeper on the reverse. The flowers are moderately full, produced with the greatest freedom and have some fragrance. The growth is vigorous and upright, amply furnished with glossy, dark green, bronze-tinted foliage. T.

Marlena: Kordes, 1964. Scarlet, shaded crimson. Small, scentless, cupped flowers, moderately full, on low branching growth, with very small dark green foliage. Free flowering and excellent for edgings. L.

Masquerade: Boerner, Jackson and Perkins, 1950. Goldilocks × Holiday. Yellow, with a pink flush gradually spreading and intensifying to a dull red as the flower ages. Semi-double flowers, borne in large trusses on vigorous, branching growth. Sets seed pods very freely and these should not be allowed to develop. T.

Matterhorn: D. L. Armstrong and Swim, 1965. Buccaneer × Cherry Glow. White, deepening to ivory in the heart. Pointed flowers of hybrid tea shape, full, opening quickly and carried on very tall, upright growth, with medium green foliage. May need watching for mildew. Best in dry weather. T.

Merlin: Harkness, 1967. Pink Parfait × Circus. Rich pink, shading off to yellow in the centre and changing to a uniform light reddish-pink as the flower ages. The buds and half-open flowers are very attractive, of hybrid tea shape, opening to semi-double, and carried on long footstalks. Very free flowering on compact plants, with small, glossy, deep green leaves. M.

Meteor: Kordes, 1958. Feurio × Gertrud Westphal. Bright orange-scarlet, full flowers, on short, branching growth. No scent. A useful, free-flowering rose for planting in front of taller varieties in this colour group. L.

Miracle: G. Verbeek, 1958. Unnamed seedling × Fashion. Orange-salmon, full, shapely young flowers, opening quickly. Growth is very vigorous and tall, clothed with glossy, medium green foliage. T.

Molly McGredy: McGredy, 1969. Paddy McGredy × (Mme Léon Cuny × Columbine). Cherry red on the inside, with a silver reverse. The flowers are of medium size, full and borne freely in small to medium-sized trusses. Growth is upright but bushy, well furnished with glossy, dark green foliage. The best new seedling of 1968.

Moonraker: Harkness, 1967. Pink Parfait × Highlight. Cream, deepening to buff in the heart. The flowers are large, of hybrid tea type but opening flat, full, up to $4\frac{1}{2}$ in. across and slightly fragrant. Growth is vigorous, tall and branching, with matt, light green foliage which needs watching for mildew. T.

223

Moulin Rouge: Meilland, 1952. Alain × Orange Triumph. Deep glowing scarlet. Rather small, moderately full flowers in medium trusses. Growth is vigorous and branching, with glossy, light green foliage. M.

My Girl: De Ruiter, 1964. Decapo × floribunda seedling. Deep salmon-orange camellia-shaped full flowers in small, rather lax trusses. Moderately vigorous growth with dark, coppery foliage which needs protection from black spot. Rather weak stems detract from the display value of this variety. M.

Ohlala: Tantau, 1957. Fanal × Crimson Glory. Crimson, paling towards the centre. The flowers are semi-double, at their best when open wide and 3½ in. across, borne in large trusses on very vigorous, tall, branching growth, with abundant, large, medium green foliage. This is a healthy, easily-grown variety which is exceptionally free flowering. T.

Orangeade: McGredy, 1959. Orange Sweetheart × Independence. Brilliant orange-vermilion, semi-double flowers, 3 in. across, in medium trusses. Growth is vigorous and branching, with dark green, bronze-tinted foliage which needs protection from black spot. M.

Orange Sensation: De Ruiter, 1960. Light vermilion, shaded orange. Moderately full, fragrant flowers displayed in medium trusses on branching, rather compact growth, with light green, matt foliage. A free-flowering variety which does not mind rain but needs watching for mildew and black spot. M.

Orange Silk: McGredy, with sole rights to C. Gregory and Son Ltd., 1968. Orangeade × (Ma Perkins × Independence). Orange-vermilion. The flowers are of hybrid tea form at first, full, opening loosely, in medium trusses. Growth is vigorous and branching, with dark green glossy foliage. Free flowering and quick to repeat. M.

Orange Triumph: Kordes, 1937. Eva × Solarium. Orange-scarlet, full, pompon-like small flowers in large trusses borne freely on very vigorous growth, well furnished with dark, bronze-tinted foliage. A very healthy variety and a parent of some popular modern floribundas. T.

Overture: Le Grice, 1961. Deep, purplish-lilac-mauve. The hybrid tea shaped flowers are large and full for a floribunda, borne singly and in small clusters on very short, sturdy growth, with dark green, purplish-tinted foliage, red when young. Not vigorous enough for garden display, but useful for a small bed or edging. L.

Paddy McGredy: McGredy, 1962. Spartan × Tzigane. Deep

Top left: When planting a standard rose place the stake in position first
Top right: An efficient way of securing standard roses is with sacking wound in figure-of-eight fashion round the stem and the stake. *Bottom left:* The completed tie. *Bottom right:* The variety Peace as a half-standard, budded on a seedling briar. The latter was grown on as a single stem in the author's garden

carmine-pink, with a paler reverse. Full, well-shaped flowers, as large as some hybrid teas, in large trusses, which tend to be top-heavy. Moderately vigorous, branching, compact growth, with small, dark green foliage. Needs protection from black spot and rust in pure air districts. L.

Paprika: Tantau, 1958. Märchenland × Red Favourite. Vivid turkey red, lighter towards the centre. Semi-double flowers, $3\frac{1}{2}$ in. across, borne in large trusses on strong branching growth. The foliage is dark green, varnished and abundant, and most attractive. A striking variety. M.

Pernille Poulsen: Poulsen, 1965. Ma Perkins × Columbine. Salmon-pink, fading with age. Large, fragrant, moderately full, loosely-built flowers, carried well above the foliage on compact, branching growth. Large, semi-glossy foliage. L.

Pink Parfait: Swim, 1962. First Love × Pinocchio. Light pink, shading to pale yellow at the base. Moderately full and nicely pointed form at the half-expanded stage. Free flowering. Vigorous, branching, almost thornless growth, with semi-glossy foliage. M.

Plentiful: Le Grice, 1961. Deep pink, with a paler reverse. Very full, 'quartered' flowers with short petals, giving an 'old-fashioned' appearance. Short, branching growth with glossy, medium green foliage. A useful variety of neat habit and quick to repeat. L.

Posy: Le Grice, 1951. Rosenelfe × Dusky Maiden. Mauve-pink, deeper on the reverse. The flowers are full, with many but short petals, freely produced in clusters on short growth, with dark green foliage. A very compact variety, suitable for small beds or edgings. L.

Princess Michiko: Dickson, 1966. Spartan × Circus. Bright tangerine-orange, fading to a dull red with age, semi-double. Colour somewhat variable according to weather conditions, sometimes assuming a salmon tint. Vigorous, upright growth, with dark green, rather sparse copper-tinted foliage. May need protection against black spot and rust. M.

Queen Elizabeth: Lammerts, 1955. Charlotte Armstrong × Floradora. Clear pink, full and well-formed hybrid tea type flowers on long footstalks, produced both singly and in trusses. Very vigorous, tall, upright growth with almost thornless wood. Large, abundant foliage. Will make a hedge 6 ft. tall. There is a tendency to produce blind shoots early in the season. T.

Red Dandy: Norman, 1960. Ena Harkness × Karl Herbst. Rich scarlet-crimson flowers, $3\frac{1}{2}$ in. across, full and shapely, resembling small blooms of Ena Harkness. Tall, strong growth, carrying the trusses erect. Reasonably free flowering, considering the quality of the blooms. Matt, medium green foliage. Very close to the hybrid teas. T.

Red Favourite (Schweizer Gruss): Tantau, 1951. Karl Weinhausen × Cinnabar. Deep crimson, semi-double flowers, rather smaller than average. Moderately vigorous, branching growth with glossy, medium green foliage. Does not mind rain. L.

Redgold: Dickson, 1967. [(Karl Herbst × Masquerade) × Faust] × Piccadilly. Golden-yellow, edged and flushed cherry-red. Moderately full flowers, borne in small trusses on moderately vigorous, upright growth, with glossy, dark green foliage. Most attractive when first open but the richest colours fade quickly. M.

Rodeo: Kordes, 1960. Obergärtner Wiebicke × Spartan. Scarlet-crimson. Full, but loosely-formed flowers of cupped type borne in medium clusters on short, bushy growth, with light green, semi-glossy foliage. The main virtue is the compact growth, combined with freedom of flowering. L.

Rosemary Rose: De Ruiter, 1955. Gruss an Teplitz × floribunda seedling. Bright carmine. The flowers are rosette shaped, very full and 3 in. across, borne in clusters. Growth is vigorous and branching, with matt, medium green foliage, tinted purplish-red, which needs watching for mildew. A distinct variety with an old-fashioned charm. M.

Rose of Tralee: McGredy, 1964. Leverkusen × Korona. Rich pink, flushed salmon. The moderately full flowers are rather formless, but borne in great profusion on moderately vigorous, bushy growth, with matt, medium green foliage. Good in autumn. M.

Rumba: Poulsen, 1959. (Poulsen's Bedder × Floradora) × Masquerade. Golden-yellow shaded pink and edged coppery-red, fading with age. Small, full, rosette-shaped flowers resembling those of the polyantha pompons. Moderately vigorous, upright growth, with glossy dark green foliage. The faded flowers must be removed as they do not shed their petals. M.

Ruth Hewitt: Norman, 1963. Unnamed seedling × Queen Elizabeth. White, guard petals stained deep pink. Pointed, full hybrid tea type flowers, opening rather loosely in a heavy truss. Dark green, glossy foliage provides an effective background. Vigorous branching growth. The flowers easily spoil in rain but can be very lovely in dry weather. M.

Ruth Leuwerik: De Ruiter, 1960. Käthe Duvigneau × Rosemary Rose. Bright turkey red. The full flowers are produced very freely on bushy branching growth, densely clothed with glossy, dark green, bronze-tinted foliage. Needs watching for mildew and black spot. M.

Safari: Tantau, 1967. Soft yellow, lightly flushed delicate pink at the edges as the flowers age. Moderately full, fragrant blooms in small trusses on short growths, with the foliage carried well up the stems. Repeats quickly and shows promise as a healthy, prolific variety of compact habit. Very good in autumn. L.

Sangria: Meilland, 1966. Scarlet-crimson. The moderately full flowers have wavy petals and are borne in moderate trusses on strong, branching growth, with abundant medium green foliage. May need watching for black spot. T.

Sarabande: Meilland, 1957. Cocorico × Moulin Rouge. Bright scarlet, single flowers in medium trusses, carried freely on branching, compact growth. L.

Saratoga: Boerner, Jackson and Perkins, 1963. White Bouquet × Princess White. Creamy-white buds, opening into pure white, full flowers, 4 in. across, borne very freely in clusters and carrying a distinct fragrance. Vigorous, branching growth, with glossy, dark green healthy foliage. M.

Scania: De Ruiter, 1965. Cocorico × seedling. Deep velvety blood-red. The flowers are large, well formed, like small hybrid teas, nicely pointed but opening out wide later. They are carried upright, singly and in small clusters, on moderately vigorous growth, with matt, reddish-green foliage, which needs watching for black spot. The rich colour is held to the end. M.

Scarlet Queen Elizabeth: Dickson, 1963. Korona seedling × Queen Elizabeth. Orange-scarlet, rather globular flowers, moderately full, displayed on tall upright growth. It should be noted that this is a seedling and not a sport from Queen Elizabeth. The shape of the flower is quite different and, to me, not as pleasing. T.

Scented Air: Dickson, 1965. Spartan seedling × Queen Elizabeth. Deep salmon-pink, moderately full, fragrant flowers, 3½ in. across, shapely at first but opening quickly. Tall, bushy growth with glossy, dark green foliage. Free flowering and repeats quickly. T.

Sea Pearl: Dickson, 1964. Perfecta × Montezuma. A refined blend of pale orange and pearly-pink, with a pale yellow reverse. The flowers are of hybrid tea shape at first, moderately full, opening wide, on tall, upright growth with pleasing glistening dark green foliage. T.

227

She: Dickson, 1962. (Independence × Fashion) × Brownie. Deep rose-opal to salmon, paling to lemon yellow at the base. The moderately full flowers are cupped, attractive at first, fading with age. Growth is vigorous and branching, with semi-glossy, dark green, healthy foliage. A free-flowering variety of unusual colouring. M.

Shepherdess: Mattock, 1967. Allgold × Peace. Yellow ground, flushed and edged reddish-salmon on each petal. Hybrid tea type flowers, shapely at first, opening semi-double, carried singly and in trusses. Vigorous branching growth, with glossy, dark, bronze-tinted foliage. M.

Shepherd's Delight: Dickson, 1958. Masquerade seedling × Joanna Hill. A combination of flame, orange and yellow shades. The flowers are semi-double, carried erect on tall growth with large, semi-glossy foliage. Very free flowering. Too tall a grower for bedding, but excellent for the back of a border. T.

Siesta: Meilland, 1965. Deep coral-flame, shading to gold at the base. Rather cupped form with short petals, moderately full and carrying many flowers open at the same time. Growth is bushy and branching and excellent for bedding, with healthy semi-glossy foliage, carried down to the base. Good in all weathers. M.

Sir Lancelot: Harkness, 1967. Vera Dalton × Woburn Abbey. Apricot-yellow, deeper in the heart and paling with age. The shapely buds develop into semi-double flowers, opening to $3\frac{1}{2}$ in. across. Growth is moderately vigorous and branching, with matt, light green foliage, rather on the small side. Best in fine weather and needs watching for black spot. M.

Sombrero: McGredy, 1962. Masquerade × Rubaiyat. Cream, flushed and margined rosy-red. The flowers are large, full, shapely at first, opening loosely. Growth is vigorous, with light green, semi-glossy foliage, which may need protection from black spot. M.

Spartan: Boerner, Jackson and Perkins, 1954. Geranium Red × Fashion. Rich salmon to salmon-red, very full flowers, $3\frac{1}{2}$ in. across, with a distinct clove scent. Very free flowering in medium trusses, but the blooms ball in wet weather. Vigorous, upright growth with bronze-tinted foliage. May need protection against rust. T.

Summer Song: Dickson, 1962. Seedling × Masquerade. Yellow and orange blend, with semi-double, fragrant flowers borne on short stems on a compact, branching plant. Glossy, bronze-tinted foliage which may require protection from mildew. L.

Sundance: Poulsen, 1954. Seedling × Eugène Fürst. Light yellow, flushed and shaded pink. The flowers are semi-double, about $2\frac{1}{2}$ in. across, with petals opening wide almost immediately. Growth is vigorous and upright, with matt, light green foliage which needs watching for mildew. A delicate blend of soft pastel shades, perhaps overshadowed by more striking introductions of intensified colouring. T.

Sweet Repose (The Optimist): De Ruiter, 1956. Geheimrat Duisberg × a polyantha. A refined blend of cream, amber and pink shades, deepening with age as the pink turns to a dull red. The flowers are full, well formed, fragrant and carried in large trusses on vigorous, tall branching growth. The abundant foliage is dark green, tinted bronze. T.

Tamango: Meilland, 1967. Bright crimson. The large, full flowers are not of particularly shapely form, but give a cheerful display over a long period and last well on the plants. Growth is vigorous and branching, breaking freely from the base, with large, medium green glossy foliage carried to soil level. Very free flowering, but may need protection from black spot. M.

Tambourine: Dickson, 1959. Karl Herbst seedling. Cherry-red with an orange-yellow reverse to the petals. The fragrant flowers are moderately full, globular, opening to $3\frac{1}{2}$ in. and are carried in large trusses on very vigorous upright growths, furnished with glossy, healthy foliage. May be used as an internal hedge. T.

Telstar: Gandy, 1963. Rosemary Gandy × Masquerade. Orange and yellow, flushed scarlet as the flower ages. Semi-double, opening flat very quickly. Free flowering. The growth is vigorous and branching, with semi-glossy dark green foliage. M.

Tiki: McGredy, 1964. Mme Léon Cuny × Spartan. Delicate shell pink, with pearly-cream tints. The flowers are $3\frac{1}{2}$ in. across, full, well-formed, and contrast pleasingly with the dark glossy foliage. Free-flowering. Best in cool weather. M.

Tivoli: Poulsen, 1955. Poulsen's Supreme × (Souvenir de Claudius Denoyel × Hvissinge-Rose). Rich pink, shading to yellow in the heart. Moderately full flowers, shapely at first, fragrant and produced freely on very vigorous growth, with glossy, dark green foliage. T.

Tombola: De Ruiter, 1967. Amor × (Ena Harkness × Peace). Deep salmon-orange, suffused carmine-pink and shading off to gold at the base. The large hybrid tea type flowers are full, well formed and fragrant, opening confused. Growth is stout, vigorous and upright, with large, glossy dark green leaves. A very pleasing variety at its best, with rather a long interval between crops. M.

Toni Lander: Poulsen, 1959. Independence × Circus. Rich coppery-salmon-red, flushed scarlet. The flowers are moderately full, cupped and carried erect in large trusses. Growth is strong and upright, with glossy, copper-tinted foliage. An eye-catching variety which may need protection from black spot and rust. M.

Travesti: De Ruiter, 1965. Orange Sensation × Circus. Yellow and orange, overlaid with cherry red, with a yellow reverse. The young flowers are smaller than average, tightly whorled and particularly attractive, opening semi-double and fading in the later stages. Growth is bushy and branching, making a uniform plant for bedding, with small, dark green, semi-glossy leaves. L.

Vagabonde: Lens, 1962. Mannequin × Fashion. Light orange-salmon. The medium-sized flowers have high-pointed centres with elegant petals, full and dainty, borne in small clusters on vigorous, bushy growth, with abundant dark green, glossy foliage. Free flowering and good in autumn. M.

Variety Club: McGredy, 1965. Columbine × Circus. A confection of pink, cream and yellow, varying in intensity with the weather. The flowers are full, like miniature hybrid teas and are borne freely in medium trusses on vigorous branching growth, with pleasing glossy foliage. A colourful variety. M.

Vera Dalton: Norman, 1961. (Paul's Scarlet Climber × Paul's Scarlet Climber) × (Mary × Queen Elizabeth). Soft pink, which never 'blues' with age. Full, hybrid tea type flowers are produced very lavishly on vigorous, tall, branching growth. The foliage is semi-glossy, dark green and may need protection from black spot. A good rose, with some mottling of the petals in the later stages. T.

Vesper: Le Grice, 1967. Coppery-orange. The full flowers are of medium size, slightly fragrant and produced in small trusses early and in large trusses later in the season. A branching grower, with abundant, healthy bronze-green foliage. Very good in the autumn and a most appealing colour. M.

Vilia: H. Robinson, 1960. Bright coral-pink, shaded salmon. The small, single flowers are displayed in large trusses and are fragrant, with the appeal of the wild rose. Growth is vigorous and upright, clothed with dark green, glossy foliage. Good in autumn. M.

Violet Carson: McGredy, 1963. Mme Léon Cuny × Spartan. Soft peach-pink, with a silvery reverse to each petal. The flowers are full, of hybrid tea form and carried in medium trusses on sturdy, branching growth, with dark green, crimson-tinted foliage. A rose of refinement. M.

Vogue: Boerner, Jackson and Perkins, 1949. Pinocchio × Crimson Glory. Rich carmine-pink, deeper on the reverse. The flowers are high centred, very well formed, exceptionally fragrant for a floribunda, and carried in medium clusters on vigorous, upright, bushy growth, with semi-glossy, medium green foliage. Needs watching for mildew. M.

Woburn Abbey: Sidey and Cobley, 1962. Masquerade × Fashion. Groundwork orange, shaded yellow and salmon-orange. Moderately full, cupped flowers, rather formless but fragrant. Vigorous growth, with dark green foliage, which may need watching for mildew. M.

Yellowhammer (Yellow Dazzler): McGredy, 1954. Poulsen's Yellow × unnamed seedling. Rich golden-yellow without shading, and held to the end. The small flowers are full, perfectly formed, fragrant and excellent for buttonholes. Growth is moderately vigorous and branching, with glossy, dark green, bronze-tinted foliage, needing protection against black spot. Best in fine weather. M.

Yvonne Rabier: Turbat, 1910. *R. wichuraiana* × a polyantha. White, small, full flowers of rosette shape, with small petals. Fragrant. Very free flowering in medium trusses. Vigorous, with small, glossy, dark green foliage. M.

Zambra: Meilland, 1961. (Goldilocks × Fashion) × (Goldilocks × Fashion). Rich orange, shaded yellow, with yellow reverse. Semi-double flowers, somewhat below average size, displayed in medium trusses on short, branching growth. The glossy, medium green foliage may need protection from black spot. L.

Zingaro: Sanday, 1964. Masquerade × Independence seedling. Bright crimson, fading to dull red with age. Medium-sized, semi-double flowers topping short growth, clothed with ample, reddish green, semi-glossy foliage. Useful for small beds or for narrow borders. L.

THE FLORIBUNDA DWARFS

These are sometimes referred to as polyantha compacta roses. They are really closer to the old polyantha pompon group, now largely superseded by the modern floribundas, than to the floribundas themselves, but have the advantage of not suffering from mildew like most of the polyantha pompons. Of sturdy, but spreading habit, they make dense little bushes, seldom exceeding 12 in. in height and often much less. The inflorescence has been compared not inaptly with that of the phlox, with dense heads, packed tightly with small flowers of single, semi-double or double form.

Although they have a great capacity for flowering and the heads of bloom remain presentable for an appreciable period, the colour range is limited to shades of red and pink, and they have no scent. Because of this, it may well be that some of the very compact-growing floribundas, like Marlena, will displace them. It is felt, though, that there may still be a limited demand for these quite distinct little plants, which help to bridge the gap between the miniatures on the one hand, and the floribundas on the other. They are absolutely hardy and require little pruning beyond the removal of the old flower heads and any exhausted or dead growths.

Bashful: De Ruiter, 1955. Bright reddish-pink, with a distinct white eye. Small, single flowers in very large trusses. L.

Doc: De Ruiter, 1954. Robin Hood × a polyantha seedling. Bright rose-pink, moderately full flowers, with very small petals, resembling the well-known rambler Dorothy Perkins, on an extremely short, bushy plant. Very free-flowering. L.

Dopey: De Ruiter, 1954. Crimson-scarlet, semi-double flowers, in large trusses. L.

Grumpy: De Ruiter, 1956. Medium pink, full flowers. Very bushy and compact. L.

Happy: De Ruiter, 1954. Robin Hood × Katharina Zeimet seedling. Medium red – sometimes described as 'currant-red' – semi-double flowers. Growth is slightly stronger than most in the group. L.

Jean Mermoz: Chenault, 1937. *R. wichuraiana* × a hybrid tea. Pale pink, with deeper shadings; full flowers with very small petals, borne in clusters. Growth is dwarf and branching up to about 15 in., with glossy dark foliage. L.

Sleepy: De Ruiter, 1955. (Orange Triumph × Golden Rapture) × a polyantha seedling. Reddish-pink, full flowers. L.

Sneezy: De Ruiter, 1955. Pink, single flowers, in very large, crowded trusses. L.

The Fairy: Bentall, 1932. Sport from Lady Godiva. Light pink, full flowers with tiny petals, carried in clusters. Small glossy foliage. Very profuse flowering. L.

FLORIBUNDAS
'At-a-glance' Colour Chart

ORANGE-SALMON

Ascot
Bobbie Lucas
Decapo
Elizabeth of Glamis
Fashion
Irish Mist
John Church
Miracle
My Girl
Orange Silk
Tombola
Vagabonde

ORANGE-SCARLET

Allotria
Evelyn Fison
Fervid
Fidélio
Highlight
Independence
Korona
Meteor
Orange Triumph
Sarabande
Scarlet Queen Elizabeth

**SALMON-PINK AND
CORAL-SALMON**

Celebration
Charming Maid
Charm of Paris
Dearest
King Arthur
Love Token
Pernille Poulsen
Rose of Tralee
Scented Air
She
Vilia

**CERISE, CARMINE
AND LIGHT RED**

Anne Poulsen
Coventrian
Dominator
Firecracker
Jane Lazenby
Paddy McGredy
Rosemary Rose
Vogue

LIGHT PINK

Anna Louisa
Baby Sylvia
Dainty Maid
Elysium
Herself
Jubilant
Märchenland
Pink Parfait
Tiki
Violet Carson

DEEP YELLOW

Allgold
Arthur Bell
Golden Treasure
Gold Marie
Yellowhammer

**LIGHT AND ORANGE-
VERMILION**

Anna Wheatcroft
Athos
Farandole
Fireworks
Orangeade
Orange Sensation
Siesta

**DEEP SCARLET AND
TURKEY RED**

Alamein
Ama
City of Belfast
Concerto
Karen Poulsen
Moulin Rouge
Paprika
Ruth Leuwerik

**ORANGE, FLAME AND
APRICOT**

Apricot Nectar
Cognac
Copper Delight
Golden Slippers
Joyfulness
Manx Queen
Shepherd's Delight
Sir Lancelot
Summer Song
Vesper
Woburn Abbey
Zambra

SALMON-RED

Arabian Nights
Border Coral
City of Leeds
Diamant
Dickson's Flame
Flamenco
Spartan

DEEP PINK

August Seebauer
Charlotte Elizabeth
Plentiful

233

ROSES

SCARLET/CRIMSON

Alain
Frensham
Lilli Marlene
Marlena
Ohlala
Red Dandy
Rodeo
Sangria
Tamango
Zingaro

MEDIUM PINK

Ann Elizabeth
Joybells
Ma Perkins
Queen Elizabeth
Tivoli
Vera Dalton

LIGHT YELLOW

Geisha Girl
Golden Fleece
Goldilocks
Honeymoon
Safari

YELLOW, ORANGE AND PINK BLENDS

Alison Wheatcroft
Angela
Beaulieu Abbey
Charleston
Circus
Colour Carnival
Lucky Charm
Masquerade
Redgold
Rumba
Telstar
Travesti

MEDIUM YELLOW

Faust
Golden Jewel
Goldgleam
Jan Spek

BURNT ORANGE

Ambrosia
Princess Michiko

AMBER AND BROWNISH-YELLOW

Amberlight

COPPERY-SALMON-RED AND TANGERINE-RED

Fairlight
Jiminy Cricket
Toni Lander

DEEP CRIMSON

Europeana
Red Favourite
Scania

PALE BUFF SHADED PEACH

Chanelle
Mandy

WHITE AND CREAM

Dimples
Iceberg
Ice White
Ivory Fashion
Matterhorn
Moonraker
Ruth Hewitt
Saratoga
Yvonne Rabier

LAVENDER, LILAC AND MAUVE

Africa Star
Blue Diamond
Lilac Charm
Overture

LILAC-PINK

Escapade
Posy

CREAM, EDGED OR SUFFUSED PINK

Columbine
Sea Pearl
Shepherdess
Sombrero
Sundance
Sweet Repose

RICH PINK AND CREAM BLENDS

Happy Event
Merlin
Variety Club

BICOLORS

Antique (crimson and golden-yellow)
Daily Sketch (pink and silver)
Fresco (tangerine-orange and golden-yellow)
Molly McGredy (cherry-red and silver)
Tambourine (cherry-red and orange-yellow)

234

22

Descriptive List of Rambling, Climbing and Pillar Roses

Rambling, climbing and pillar roses, sub-divided into groups according to type of growth and recurrence – Recommended varieties and their descriptions

Many amateurs are hazy about the distinction between rambling, climbing and pillar roses, and are inclined to use these terms as though they are interchangeable. Although there are a number of border-line varieties, most roses of rampant growth fall into one or other of the three groups mentioned, which are characterised mainly by different habits of growth and flowering. As a broad generalisation it can be said that the more rampant the growth, the shorter the flowering period tends to be. This seems to stem from the needs of the rampant growers, immediately after once flowering, to devote their energies to the production of new canes from the base on which the following season's one crop of flowers will be borne. In all fairness, though, it should be mentioned that this one crop is exceptionally lavish and provides a glorious display of colour for perhaps three weeks in the year, or maybe a little longer with some varieties, or in the cooler districts.

Rambling Roses

The rambling types (mostly Wichuraiana ramblers) fit in with this description. They are mainly hybrids of *R. wichuraiana,* a prostrate-growing species of Japanese origin, the small glossy foliage of the parent having been inherited by most of the garden hybrids. Those most typical have flexible canes up to 10 or 12 ft. long, with the trusses of small flowers borne on numerous laterals along much of the length of the canes. Many of the earliest introductions of this type have rosette-shaped (or in a few cases, single) flowers, borne in large trusses, and the growth is liable to develop mildew when

235

there is not a free circulation of air. Varieties of this type include:

F	Albéric Barbier	F	François Juranville
	American Pillar		Lady Godiva
	Crimson Shower	F	Sanders' White
	Dorothy Perkins		Veilchenblau
	Excelsa		

F = Fragrant

Some other ramblers have larger or more shapely flowers, borne on a stiffer type of growth, and because of this they lack the grace and elegance of the typical Wichuraiana ramblers. On the other hand, the flowers of many of them are fragrant and more impressive individually. Typical varieties are:

F	Albertine	F	Easlea's Golden Rambler
	Chaplin's Pink Climber	F	Emily Gray
	Crimson Conquest		Paul's Scarlet Climber
F	Dr W. Van Fleet		

F = Fragrant

All ramblers are best trained in the open garden on arches, pergolas and rustic fences, keeping them away from walls and close-boarded fences. They may also be used to good effect as ground cover, especially for trailing down steep banks.

Climbing Roses

Climbing roses, in the main, bear most of their flowers on laterals or sub-laterals from the main canes, which are retained as long as they continue to grow vigorously. They include the climbing sports of bush hybrid teas and of some floribundas, although with the exception of Cl. Masquerade and Cl. Fashion, the climbing floribundas are usually of more restrained growth and therefore more suitable for pillars of moderate height. The older climbers are diverse in character, ranging from the huge growth of Mermaid, when once established in a congenial position, to the fairly compact habit of some of the climbing sports of hybrid teas, such as Cl. Mme Henri Guillot and Cl. Mme Edouard Herriot. It is a moot point whether such modern varieties as Danse du Feu, Cl. Fashion and Parkdirektor Riggers should be treated as climbers or as pillar roses. In my experience they produce too many stout canes to be conveniently trained on single upright pillars, so I have treated them as climbers, although they can be grown very successfully on tripods.

Climbing sports of bush hybrid teas are normally more suitable for training on walls and close-boarded fences, to which their canes should be tied in horizontally to encourage flowering. Some typical climbing roses are:

	Allen Chandler	F	Cl. Shot Silk
	Cl. Caprice		Cl. Spek's Yellow
F	Cl. Crimson Glory	F	Cl. Sutter's Gold
F	Cl. Ena Harkness		Danse du Feu
F	Cl. Etoile de Hollande		Dortmund
F	Cl. Fashion	F	Guinée
F	Cl. Golden Dawn	F	Kathleen Harrop
F	Cl. Mme Butterfly	F	Maigold
	Cl. Mme Caroline Testout		Meg
	Cl. Mme Edouard Herriot		Mermaid
	Cl. Mme Henri Guillot	F	Mme Gregoire Staechelin
	Cl. Masquerade		Parkdirektor Riggers
F	Cl. Mrs Herbert Stevens	F	Paul's Lemon Pillar
	Cl. Mrs Pierre S. du Pont		Soldier Boy
	Cl. Mrs Sam McGredy	F	Zéphirine Drouhin

F=Fragrant

Pillar Roses

Pillar roses include most of the modern, recurrent-flowering climbers of restrained growth—say up to 10 ft. or so, although some of them will grow larger over the years on a good soil. They are especially suitable for the smaller garden or gardens where labour is at a premium, as they require the minimum amount of training, tying up and pruning. They carry flowers for more days in the season than the ramblers and nearly all the climbers, and are undoubtedly a great advance on the older groups. The following varieties are examples of pillar roses:

F	Aloha		Handel
	Altissimo		Hamburger Phoenix
	Autumn Sunlight		Joseph's Coat
	Bantry Bay	F	New Dawn
	Casino		Parade
	Cl. Goldilocks		Pink Perpetue
F	Copenhagen	F	Royal Gold
	Etude	F	Schoolgirl
	Galway Bay	F	Sympathie
F	Golden Showers		

F=Fragrant

Note: Many of the climbing roses listed earlier may also be grown successfully on pillars, preferably in tripod fashion, to enable the canes to be trained spirally to combat bareness at the base.

Figure 30. A tripod offers more scope for displaying pillar roses than a single upright pillar. A method of facilitating training by nailing lengths of rustic timber on a single upright pillar is shown on the right

Repeat Flowering

Differing opinions are expressed from time to time about the reliability of repeat flowering of the individual varieties. Some variations may be expected from season to season, according to climatic conditions and probably, for the same reasons, between different areas. Different methods of training may also account for variations in patterns of behaviour. Quite apart from the weather, though, the prompt removal of spent flower heads will do much to encourage a further crop. Some varieties, such as Meg, Soldier Boy and Cl. Masquerade yield large quantities of seed pods, and if these are allowed to mature the production of a second floral display will be impeded, if not prevented, as the objects of flower production, from the plant's point of view, will have been achieved. It is difficult to over-emphasise the importance of removing all seed pods in the early stages if–as is likely–recurrent flowering is the objective. Even so, some of the climbing sports of hybrid teas are rather sparing in the production of their flowers even in the early summer flush, and I have included only those which I have found to be reasonably free flowering from personal experience.

DESCRIPTIVE LIST OF RAMBLING, CLIMBING AND PILLAR ROSES

The varieties described are recurrent or intermittent flowering except where marked S, indicating that the variety carries a heavy flush of bloom for a few weeks in summer, although further flowers may be produced later under favourable conditions.

Abbreviations used:

Cl. Flori.—Climbing Floribunda
Cl. H.T. —Climbing Hybrid Tea type
L.F.C. —Large-flowered Climber
Ramb. —Rambler
S —summer flowering

A —suitable for arches
P suitable for pillars or tripods
Sc—suitable for screens
W—suitable for walls or close-boarded fences

(S) **Albéric Barbier:** Ramb. Barbier, 1900. *R. wichuraiana* × Shirley Hibberd. Yellow buds opening to creamy-white, small-petalled, fragrant, very double flowers in large trusses. Rampant growth, with glossy, dark green foliage. A. Sc.

(S) **Albertine:** Ramb. Barbier, 1921. *R. wichuraiana* × Mrs A. R. Waddell. Salmon-red buds, opening to coppery-pink, very fragrant flowers, moderately full, opening quickly. Growth is very vigorous, stiff and thorny, with matt dark green foliage, reddish when young. Needs watching for mildew. A. Sc.

Allen Chandler: L. F. C. Prince, 1923. Hugh Dickson × unnamed seedling. Rich scarlet, semi-double, large flowers in small trusses, slightly fragrant. Vigorous growth, with healthy, semi-glossy foliage. P.

Aloha: L. F. C. Boerner, Jackson and Perkins, 1955. Mercedes Gallart × New Dawn. Deep rose, shaded salmon, large, very full flowers in small trusses; fragrant. Moderately vigorous, short growth, with abundant, glossy and disease-resistant foliage. P. or large bush.

Altissimo: L. F. C. Delbard-Chabert, 1967. Deep scarlet, shaded crimson, single flowers, 4 in. across, in small trusses. Vigorous growth, with matt foliage. May need protection from black spot. P.

(S) **American Pillar:** Ramb. Dr W. Van Fleet, 1902. (*R. wichuraiana* × *R. setigera*) × a red hybrid perpetual. Rose-pink with a white eye, single, small flowers in large trusses. Rampant growth, with glossy, dark green foliage. Needs watching for mildew. A. Sc.

Autumn Sunlight: L. F. C. Gregory, 1966. Danse du Feu × Cl. Goldilocks. Clear vermilion, full-petalled flowers, rather rounded, in small trusses. Healthy, medium green, semi-glossy foliage borne on vigorous growth. A lovely colour. P.

Bantry Bay: L. F. C. McGredy, 1967. New Dawn × Korona. Medium rose-pink, with a tinge of salmon, deeper in the heart. Shapely in the bud, opening semi-double to 3 in., with the flowers widely spaced in the truss. Vigorous growth with semi-glossy, medium green, healthy foliage. A promising novelty. W. or P.

(S) **Caprice, Climbing:** Cl. H.T. Sport from Caprice (Lady Eve Price). Cerise, reverse of petals cream; moderately full, fragrant flowers, loosely formed. Vigorous growth, with abundant, glossy, dark green foliage, reddish when young. Very free flowering. W. or P.

Casino: L. F. C. McGredy, 1963. Coral Dawn × Buccaneer. Soft yellow, fairly full, shapely flowers, opening loosely in small trusses. Vigorous growth, with glossy, bright green foliage. May need protection from black spot. W. or P.

(S) **Chaplin's Pink Climber:** Ramb. Chaplin, 1928. Paul's Scarlet Climber × American Pillar. Bright pink, semi-double flowers with golden stamens; medium trusses. Very vigorous growth, with glossy, leathery dark green foliage. No flowers after main flush. A. Sc.

Copenhagen: L. F. C. Poulsen, 1964. Seedling × Ena Harkness. Rich scarlet, large, moderately full, fragrant flowers in small trusses. Vigorous growth, with glossy, abundant, medium green foliage. P.

(S) **Crimson Conquest:** Cl. H.T. Chaplin, 1931. Sport from Red Letter Day. Deep scarlet with white base, single, small, in small trusses. Vigorous growth, with glossy, medium green foliage. A. Sc.

(S) **Crimson Glory, Climbing:** Cl. H.T. Miller, 1941. Sport from Crimson Glory. Rich deep crimson, large, full flowers, very fragrant. Vigorous, with semi-glossy, reddish-green foliage. Needs watching for mildew. W. or P.

Left: The large-flowered
recurrent climber Schoolgirl,
which has fragrant orange-
apricot blooms
Below: The popular and very
fragrant Wichuraiana rambler
Albertine. The buds of this
variety are salmon-red,
opening to coppery-pink

Fred Loads (Flori. shrub)

(S) **Crimson Shower:** Ramb. Norman, 1951. Excelsa seedling. Crimson, semi-double, small flowers, rosette type; late flowering in large trusses over a longer period than most in its group. Vigorous growth, with glossy, light green, small leaves. A. Sc.

Danse du Feu: L. F. C. Mallerin, 1954. Paul's Scarlet Climber × *R. multiflora* seedling. Orange-scarlet, moderately full flowers, shapely at first, opening flat; medium trusses. Growth vigorous, with many main growths and glossy, medium green foliage, bronze when young. Colour 'blues' in later stages. W. P. or large bush.

(S) **Dorothy Perkins:** Ramb. Jackson and Perkins, 1901. *R. wichuraiana* × Mme Gabriel Luizet. Bright rose-pink flowers, double, small and rosette shaped in large trusses. Rampant growth with glossy, light green, small foliage. Needs watching for mildew. A. Sc.

Dortmund: L. F. C. Kordes, 1955. Seedling × *R. kordesii*. Bright red with white eye, large, single flowers in large trusses. Vigorous and branching growth, with glossy, healthy foliage. A much improved and recurrent-flowering American Pillar, of more restrained and healthier growth. P.

(S) **Dr W. Van Fleet:** Ramb. Van Fleet, 1910. (*R. wichuraiana* × Safrano) × Souvenir du Président Carnot. Pale flesh pink. Shapely flowers in large trusses on very vigorous growth. Fragrant. Glossy, dark green and abundant foliage. A. Sc.

(S) **Easlea's Golden Rambler** (Golden Rambler): Ramb. Easlea, 1932. Yellow, splashed red on outside petals. Large, full, fragrant flowers in medium trusses. Vigorous stiff growth with plentiful, glossy, dark green foliage. A. Sc. P.

(S) **Emily Gray:** Ramb. Williams, 1916. Jersey Beauty × Comtesse du Cayla. Rich golden-buff, deeper in the heart. Pointed buds, opening flat, semi-double, in small trusses, fragrant. Very vigorous growth, with glossy, dark green foliage, bronze when young, and purplish-crimson wood. Best with very light pruning. A. Sc.

Ena Harkness, Climbing: Cl. H.T. Murrell, 1954. Sport from Ena Harkness. Bright crimson-scarlet, full, shapely, very fragrant blooms, freely produced. Upright, vigorous growth, with semi-glossy, medium green foliage. W. or P.

(S) **Etoile de Hollande, Climbing:** Cl. H.T. Leenders, 1931. Sport from Etoile de Hollande. Deep, velvety crimson, moderately full flowers, loosely formed; very fragrant and free flowering. Very vigorous growth, with abundant semi-glossy, dark green foliage. W.

Etude: L. F. C. Gregory, 1968. Danse du Feu × New Dawn.

Deep salmon-pink, rounded semi-double flowers, in small to medium trusses. Vigorous growth, with glossy, medium green small foliage. An attractive pillar rose. P.

(S) **Excelsa** (Red Dorothy Perkins): Ramb. Walsh, 1909. Bright rosy-crimson, rosette-shaped, small flowers in large trusses in July. Rampant growth with glossy, medium green, small foliage. Needs watching for mildew. A. Sc.

(S) **Fashion, Climbing:** Cl. Flori. Boerner, 1951. Sport from Fashion. Rich orange-salmon, moderately full, fragrant flowers in small trusses; very free flowering in early summer. Vigorous growth to 8 ft. with many main canes. Matt, bronze-tinted foliage, which may need protection from disease. W. P.

(S) **François Juranville:** Ramb. Barbier, 1906. *R. wichuraiana* × Mme Laurette Messimy. Deep pink, shaded fawn and yellow. Very full, small-petalled, flat flowers in medium trusses, with a sweet-briar fragrance. Rampant pliable canes, with glossy, dark green, small foliage, reddish-bronze when young. One of the best of its type. Early flowering. A Sc.

Galway Bay: L. F. C. McGredy, 1966. Heidelberg × Queen Elizabeth. Medium pink, becoming deeper towards the petal edges. The large but semi-double flowers are borne in small trusses over a prolonged period, with healthy, medium green foliage support. The colour of the flowers is held well to the end. P.

(S) **Golden Dawn, Climbing:** Cl. H.T. Le Grice, 1947. Sport from Golden Dawn. Primrose yellow, tinted pink on outer petals; large and very full; very fragrant. Vigorous to about 8 ft., with semi-glossy, medium green, large foliage. Very free flowering in June, but few flowers later. W. P.

Golden Showers: L. F. C. Germain, 1957. Charlotte Armstrong × Capt. Thomas. Golden-yellow, pointed buds, opening to large, semi-double flowers, paling with age; fragrant; very free and recurrent; moderately vigorous and upright growth, with glossy, bronze-tinted foliage. May need protection from black spot. P. or large shrub to 6 ft. or more.

(S) **Goldilocks, Climbing:** Cl. Flori. Boerner, 1954. Sport from Goldilocks. Golden-yellow at first, paling to cream. Very full flowers, with small petals, borne in medium trusses. Moderately vigorous, with glossy, dark green foliage. May need protection from black spot. P.

Guinée: L. F. C. Mallerin, 1938. Souvenir de Claudius Denoyel ×

Ami Quinard. Deep scarlet, with blackish shadings; full, very fragrant. Moderately vigorous growth, with semi-glossy, medium green foliage. W. P.

Hamburger Phoenix: L. F. C. Kordes, 1955. *R. kordesii* × seedling. Crimson, semi-double, large, no scent. Very free and recurrent. Vigorous to 9 ft., with glossy medium green foliage. P.

Handel: L. F. C. McGredy, 1965. Columbine × Heidelberg. Cream, heavily edged and flushed deep pink; moderately full, opening to 3½ in. Vigorous growth, with semi-glossy, dark green, bronze-tinted foliage. Needs watching for mildew. P.

Joseph's Coat: L. F. C. Armstrong, 1963. Buccaneer × Circus. Golden-yellow, heavily flushed and overlaid cherry red and orange-flame. Moderately full flowers in medium trusses. Moderately vigorous growth, with semi-glossy medium green foliage. P. or large specimen bush.

Kathleen Harrop: Bourbon climber. Dickson, 1919. Sport from Zéphirine Drouhin. Shell-pink, semi-double flowers in small clusters, with pointed buds; very fragrant; vigorous, thornless growth, with pointed, matt foliage. Needs watching for mildew. Sc. P. or hedge.

(S) **Lady Godiva:** Ramb. Paul, 1908. Flesh pink, double sport from Dorothy Perkins (see p. 241). Otherwise identical. A. Sc.

Maigold: L. F. C. Kordes, 1953. Poulsen's Pink × Frühlingstag. Bronze-yellow, moderately full flowers in medium clusters; very fragrant; free flowering. Very vigorous to 10 ft. or more, with semi-glossy, medium green foliage, not subject to disease. An excellent early-flowering climber, with some recurrence. W. or P.

(S) **Masquerade, Climbing:** Cl. Flori. Dillon, 1958. Sport from Masquerade. Yellow, flushed pink, deepening to dull red with age; semi-double flowers in large trusses. Very free flowering in June, with some blooms later. Vigorous, with glossy, dark green foliage. Seed pods must not be allowed to form. A. P.

Meg: L. F. C. Gosset, 1954. Probably from Paul's Lemon Pillar × Mme Butterfly. Delicate pink, shading to apricot-yellow. Large, single flowers in small clusters. An early flush, with some flowers later if the pear-shaped seed pods are removed early. Vigorous growth, with large, dark green, glossy leaves. Sc. P.

Mermaid: Bracteata climber. Paul, 1917. *R. bracteata* × a tea rose. Primrose yellow, single flowers, 4 in. across, with amber stamens, carried in small clusters. Very free and recurrent. Very vigorous when established, but resents transplanting. Brittle, thorny wood, with bronze-green, oval, glossy foliage. Needs protection in severe frosts and should not be pruned. W. Sc.

(S) Mme Butterfly, Climbing: Cl. H.T. Smith, 1926. Sport from Mme Butterfly. Flesh pink, tinted salmon, shading to apricot-yellow. Full, very fragrant, free flowering in June. Moderately vigorous, with small, matt, medium green leaves. W.

Mme Caroline Testout, Climbing: Cl. H.T. Chauvry, 1902. Sport from Mme Caroline Testout. Warm pink, paling towards the edges of the petals. Very full and globular. Little fragrance. Free flowering in June, in clusters, with reliable autumn crop. Growth vigorous and very thorny, with matt, medium green foliage. May need watching for mildew. W. or P.

(S) Mme Edouard Herriot, Climbing: (Cl. Daily Mail.) Cl. H.T. Ketten, 1921. Sport from Mme Edouard Herriot. Flame and terra-cotta, fading to shrimp pink. Moderately full, with weak neck. Moderately vigorous, with bright green glossy foliage. May need protection from black spot. W. or P.

(S) Mme Gregoire Staechelin: L. F. C. Dot, 1927. Frau Karl Druschki × Château de Clos Vougeot. Coral-pink, splashed and overlaid crimson; large, loosely-formed very fragrant flowers, freely borne in early summer. Very vigorous, with large, semi-glossy foliage. W. or P.

(S) Mme Henri Guillot, Climbing: Cl. H.T. Meilland, 1942. Sport from Mme Henri Guillot. Coral-red to orange-carmine. Large, moderately full, opening quickly in small clusters. Moderately vigorous, with glossy, large, bright green foliage. May need protection from black spot. W. or P.

(S) Mrs Herbert Stevens, Climbing: Cl. H.T. Pernet-Ducher, 1922. Sport from Mrs Herbert Stevens. Long pointed bud, white, sometimes flushed peach-pink on outside petals, opening moderately full and shapely. Fragrant. Free flowering on wiry stems. Moderately vigorous, with matt, small, light green foliage. W. or P.

(S) Mrs Pierre S. du Pont, Climbing: Cl. H.T. Hillock, 1933. Sport from Mrs Pierre S. du Pont. Deep reddish-gold flowers of medium size, double, well formed, paling with age. Moderately vigorous growth, with rather small, dark green glossy foliage. Free flowering. May need protection from black spot. W. or P.

(S) Mrs Sam McGredy, Climbing: Cl. H.T. Buisman, 1937. Sport from Mrs Sam McGredy. Coppery-salmon-red, fading to coppery-salmon-pink. Flowers large, full and well formed, produced freely. Growth vigorous, with crimson wood and young foliage, maturing glossy dark green. May need protection from black spot. A very beautiful variety. W. or P.

New Dawn: Ramb. Dreer, 1930. Sport from Dr W. Van Fleet. Pale flesh pink, deeper in the heart. Moderately full and very fragrant, borne in medium trusses. Moderately vigorous, with small, glossy, medium green leaves. One of the earliest and most recurrent varieties – every basal growth seems to produce terminal flower buds. P. or hedge.

Parade: L. F. C. Boerner, Jackson and Perkins, 1957. New Dawn seedling × Cl. World's Fair. Carmine-red, full, slightly fragrant, produced in medium clusters. Vigorous, dense growth, with glossy, dark green, disease-resistant foliage, tinted red when young. An excellent recurrent climber. P.

Parkdirektor Riggers: L. F. C. Kordes, 1957. *R. kordesii* × Our Princess. Blood-red, semi-double flowers, 3 in. across, in medium trusses. Growth vigorous, with abundant, glossy, dark green foliage, not subject to disease. No scent. Very free and recurrent, if the seed pods are removed. Sc. P.

(S) **Paul's Lemon Pillar:** L. F. C. Paul, 1915. Frau Karl Druschki × Maréchal Niel. Pale lemon in heart, paling to white towards edges of petals. Very large, full and shapely. Fragrant. Vigorous growth, with large, semi-glossy, medium green foliage. No flowers after the June flush. W. or P.

(S) **Paul's Scarlet Climber:** Ramb. Paul, 1915. Paul's Carmine Pillar × Soleil d'Or. Deep scarlet, semi-double, rounded flowers in small clusters. No scent. Growth vigorous and upright, with matt, medium green, small foliage. May need watching for mildew. A. Sc. P.

Pink Perpetue: L. F. C. Gregory, 1965. Danse du Feu × New Dawn. Clear pink on inside with carmine-pink on reverse. Moderately full flowers in medium clusters. Vigorous growth, with healthy, glossy, dark green foliage. An excellent recurrent pillar rose. P.

(S) *R. helenae:* species. 1907. Introduced from Central China. Creamy-white, fragrant, single flowers carried erect in large corymbs, forming dense rounded heads and followed by small, oval, scarlet heps which make a pleasing display in the autumn. Growth is rampant and armed with hooked prickles, eminently suitable for scrambling up old fruit trees or over hedges. The large, dark green leaves form a suitable background for the flowers. 15-20 ft. Sc.

Royal Gold: L. F. C. Morey, 1957. Cl. Goldilocks × Lydia. Intense, deep yellow. Large, full, fragrant flowers. Moderately vigorous, with medium green semi-glossy foliage. Needs watching for black spot. Wood tends to die back in severe winters. W. or P.

(S) Sanders' White: Ramb. Sanders, 1915. Parentage unknown. White, full, small-petalled, rosette-shaped flowers in medium trusses; fragrant. Growth very vigorous, with glistening, bright green, small foliage. A. Sc. or ground cover.

Schoolgirl: L. F. C. McGredy, 1964. Coral Dawn × Belle Blonde. Orange-apricot, full, shapely fragrant flowers, in small clusters. Vigorous growth, with glossy, dark green foliage. P.

(S) Shot Silk, Climbing: Cl. H.T. Prince, 1937. Sport from Shot Silk. Orange-salmon, flushed carmine, with golden base. Full, globular, very fragrant flowers borne in small clusters. Vigorous growth, with glossy, medium green foliage. One of the best of its type. W.

(S) Soldier Boy: L. F. C. Le Grice, 1955. Unnamed seedling × Guinée. Bright scarlet-crimson, single, in small clusters. Vigorous, with semi-glossy, medium green foliage. Mainly June flowering, but some later flowers appear if seed pods are removed. P.

(S) Spek's Yellow, Climbing: (Cl. Golden Scepter.) Cl. H.T. Walters, 1956. Sport from Spek's Yellow. Rich golden-yellow, without shading. Moderately full flowers in small clusters. Vigorous growth, with glossy, deep green foliage. Needs watching for black spot. W. or P.

(S) Sutter's Gold, Climbing: Cl. H.T. Weeks, 1953. Sport from Sutter's Gold. Light orange-yellow, shaded pink and veined red. Very fragrant. Very free flowering in early summer. Vigorous growth, with glossy bronze-green foliage, but rather sparse. W. or P.

Sympathie: L. F. C. Kordes, 1966. Scarlet, without shading. The flowers are of hybrid tea form, moderately full, medium sized and pleasantly fragrant. They are carried in medium clusters, open well in the rain and there is good repeat flowering. The foliage is glossy, dark green and healthy. P.

(S) Veilchenblau: Ramb. Schmidt, 1909. Crimson Rambler seedling. Violet-mauve, with white centre; semi-double, small flowers borne in large trusses. Fragrant. Very vigorous growth, with glossy, light green foliage. A. Sc. P.

Zéphirine Drouhin: Bourbon climber. Bizot, 1868. Parentage unknown. Bright carmine-pink, semi-double flowers, opening from pointed buds in clusters. Very fragrant. Free flowering and excellent in autumn. Vigorous, thornless growth with matt, pointed, light green foliage, tinted red. Needs watching for mildew. Still worth a place on its merits. Sc. P. or hedge.

RAMBLING, CLIMBING AND PILLAR ROSES
'At-a-glance' Colour Chart .

ORANGE-SALMON
Cl. Fashion

DEEP SCARLET
Allen Chandler
Copenhagen
Crimson Conquest
Parkdirektor Riggers
Paul's Scarlet Climber
Sympathie

LIGHT PINK
Dr W. Van Fleet
Kathleen Harrop
Lady Godiva
New Dawn

DEEP YELLOW
Emily Gray
Maigold
Cl. Mrs Pierre S. du Pont
Royal Gold
Cl. Sutter's Gold

**YELLOW, ORANGE
AND PINK BLENDS**
François Juranville
Cl. Masquerade
Meg
Cl. Mme Butterfly
Cl. Shot Silk

ORANGE-VERMILION
Autumn Sunlight

SCARLET-CRIMSON
Altissimo
Dortmund (white eye)
Cl. Ena Harkness
Excelsa
Hamburger Phoenix
Soldier Boy

DEEP PINK
Aloha
Chaplin's Pink Climber
Pink Perpetue
Zéphirine Drouhin

WHITE
(including cream and lemon shadings)
Albéric Barbier
Cl. Mrs Herbert Stevens
Paul's Lemon Pillar
R. helenae
Sanders' White

**ORANGE, FLAME,
APRICOT**
Joseph's Coat
Cl. Mme Edouard Herriot
Schoolgirl

DEEP CRIMSON
Cl. Crimson Glory
Crimson Shower
Cl. Etoile de Hollande
Guinée

MEDIUM PINK
American Pillar (white eye)
Bantry Bay
Dorothy Perkins
Galway Bay
Cl. Mme Caroline Testout
Mme Gregoire Staechelin

LIGHT YELLOW
Casino
Cl. Golden Dawn
Cl. Goldilocks
Mermaid

**CERISE AND CREAM
BICOLORS**
Cl. Caprice

LAVENDER-MAUVE
Veilchenblau

MEDIUM YELLOW
Easlea's Golden Rambler
Golden Showers
Cl. Spek's Yellow

ROSES

CARMINE

Parade

**DEEP PINK AND
CREAM BLEND**

Handel

SALMON-PINK

Albertine
Etude

**COPPERY-SALMON-
RED**

Cl. Mrs Sam McGredy

ORANGE-SCARLET

Danse du Feu

CORAL-RED

Cl. Mme Henri Guillot

Left: The blood red Kordesii climber Parkdirektor Riggers –a very free-flowering and disease-resistant variety

Below: One of the best-known roses –the bright carmine-pink Bourbon climber Zéphirine Drouhin, sometimes called the thornless rose

Left: Chinatown (Flori. shrub)
Below: Penelope (Hybrid Musk shrub)

Opposite page: The miniature roses Baby Masquerade *(top,)* Little Flirt *(centre)* and New Penny *(bottom)*

Left: The semi-double floribunda-shrub rose Dorothy Wheatcroft which has bright orange-red flowers borne in very large trusses

Below left: The rose-pink Rugosa shrub variety Pink Grootendorst

Below right: The young red wood of *Rosa sericea pteracantha* is embellished with enormous, broad, translucent ruby-red thorns

23

Descriptive List of Shrub and Hedging Roses

Shrub and hedging roses, and recommended varieties—External and internal hedges—Staggered planting in two rows—Achieving symmetry

There is no clear line of demarcation between the climbers on the one hand, and shrub and hedging roses on the other hand. All roses are shrubs, but the term is used here in a more restricted sense, to embrace those types of robust growth, too large for formal bedding but not as rampant as the true climbers and ramblers. These form a mixed bag, which ranges over the old garden roses (many of which, though, are summer flowering only) the modern recurrent-flowering shrub roses of assorted pedigree, the floribunda shrub roses, the hybrid musks, hybrid Rugosas, Chinensis shrubs, Bourbons, Gallicas and many other groups. Some of the most vigorous hybrid teas and floribundas also will make large specimen shrubs, or may be used as internal hedges when lightly pruned.

I feel bound to say that I have not attempted to deal fully with the old garden roses. These are sufficiently diverse and numerous to justify a separate work. They do not usually look their best when interplanted indiscriminately with modern hybrids, and as this is a book devoted primarily to modern roses, I have contented myself by mentioning here just a few of those old garden roses which bloom more than once in each season, and some others which concentrate most of their flowers into an early summer display. These will provide gardeners who have small gardens with a nucleus which they may expand over the years, if the idea of exploring the resources of these representatives of more leisurely times should appeal to them.

General Care

As shrub roses and hedges may be expected to occupy the same position for many years, it is important to dig the site thoroughly

249

and to incorporate plenty of manure or compost, chopped turf and meat and bone meal before planting. For quick results it is usual to plant a hedge in a double row, with the plants in the two rows staggered. Distance between plants in the rows could be as much as 3 ft. for the stronger, branching varieties, down to as little as 18 in. for some of the floribundas of upright habit, such as Queen Elizabeth. Pruning will be more severe when hedging roses are planted fairly closely, to avoid overcrowding. Pruning will also aim at providing some uniformity of outline in a hedge of assorted varieties, even though rose hedges are essentially informal in character compared with clipped evergreens and similar hedges. In pruning specimen shrubs, symmetry should be aimed at, and bareness at the base avoided by cutting back some of the main growths to within a foot or so of the ground from time to time.

External hedges need to justify themselves by being utilitarian as well as ornamental. This means that an external rose hedge should be sufficiently prickly or dense growing to discourage intruders, whether these are animals or small boys. The ornamental aspect is taken care of, not only during the flowering periods, but also by the nature of the foliage and its colour changes, especially in the autumn, and by the brilliant heps which many of the single-flowered varieties ripen in abundance.

Lastly, the reader is warned against the cheap offers of 'rose-like' hedging plants which appear periodically in the press. (Reference has been made to cheap offers already in Chapter 4.) These are not shrub and hedging roses within the scope of the present chapter, but merely rootstocks of various types; they are no more suitable for garden hedges than the native English Briar (*R. canina*) of the countryside.

A SELECTION OF SHRUBS AND HEDGING ROSES

SECTION I: In this section have been grouped all those varieties which are recurrent or intermittent flowering. Varieties marked 'E' are particularly suitable for external hedges.

Ballerina: Hybrid Musk shrub. Bentall, 1937. Delicate apple blossom pink with a white eye. The small, single flowers are displayed in large clusters, are fragrant and carried on vigorous growth. The foliage is glossy, light green and abundant. 3-4 ft.

250

Berlin: Kordes, 1949. Eva × Peace. Orange-scarlet, with golden stamens. The single blooms are produced very freely. Light green foliage.

(E) **Blanc Double de Coubert:** Rugosa shrub. Cochet-Cochet, 1892. Sport from *R. rugosa alba*. Pure white, with papery textured petals, opening flat. The very fragrant flowers are borne prolifically on a dense bush from 5-6 ft. high, with healthy, light green, deeply-veined foliage.

Bonn: Kordes, 1949. Hamburg × Independence. Moderately full flowers, 3 in. across in a rich orange-scarlet shade. Free flowering. Foliage light green, large and glossy. Forms a large bush.

Boule de Neige: Bourbon shrub. Lacharme, 1867. Blanche Lafitte × Sappho. Creamy-white. Very full, rounded flowers with a delicious fragrance. Dark green foliage.

Buff Beauty: Hybrid Musk shrub. 1939. Buff or apricot-yellow, paling slightly with age. Fully double, sweetly scented and very prolific, especially late in the season.

Chinatown: Floribunda shrub. Poulsen, 1963. Columbine × Cläre Grammerstorf. Yellow, often tinted pink. Flowers 4 in. across, fragrant. Growth very vigorous and tall, clothed with glossy, bright green, large leaves.

Cocktail: Meilland, 1957. (Independence × Orange Triumph) × Phyllis Bide. Crimson, with a primrose centre which fades to white and then becomes tinted pink. Single flowers, approximately 2 in. across in medium clusters, borne very freely and repeating quickly. Growth reaches 4-5 ft., but may die back in winter in exposed gardens. The foliage is semi-glossy, small, medium green, tinted bronze, and may need protection from black spot.

Cornelia: Hybrid Musk shrub. Pemberton, 1925. Coral-pink, shaded apricot. Small, rosette-like flowers with a musk fragrance. Glossy, small, dark green leaves, on graceful stems. May need support.

Dorothy Wheatcroft: Floribunda shrub. Tantau, 1960. Bright orange-red, semi-double flowers in huge trusses. Very vigorous, tall and branching, with glossy foliage.

Elmshorn: Kordes, 1950. Hamburg × Verdun. Light red or deep carmine-pink, thinly-double flowers in clusters, very freely produced. Makes a bush about 5 ft. high, with abundant reddish-green foliage. Needs watching for mildew.

Felicia: Hybrid Musk shrub. Pemberton, 1928. Trier × Ophelia. Salmon-pink, shaded yellow. Perfectly formed buds, opening loosely. Very fragrant. Stiff, upright growth for its type, with matt, medium green foliage. An excellent autumn rose.

(E) **Frau Dagmar Hastrup:** Rugosa shrub. Hastrup, 1914. Rose-pink, large single flowers, freely and continuously produced, followed by large crimson heps. A compact bush up to 5 ft., densely foliaged.

F. J. Grootendorst: Rugosa shrub. De Goey, 1918. *R. rugosa typica* × Baby Rambler. Light crimson small flowers, with fringed petals, like a pink. Very free and continuous flowering. Leaves light green, small and deeply veined. Bushy, prickly growth.

Fred Loads: Floribunda shrub. Holmes, 1967. Orange Sensation × Dorothy Wheatcroft. Vermilion-orange single flowers of startling brilliance, 4 in. across and fragrant, carried in trusses on tall, upright growth. The foliage is large, semi-glossy and light green.

Golden Wings: Shepherd, 1956. Soeur Thérèse × (*R. spinosissima altaica* × Ormiston Roy). Single, yellow, fragrant flowers, deeper in the centre, with reddish stamens, borne singly and in clusters. Growth is moderately vigorous and branching, up to 4 ft., with matt, light green foliage. Very free flowering.

Gruss an Teplitz: Chinensis shrub. Geschwind, 1897. (Sir Joseph Paxton × Fellemberg) × (Papa Gontier × Gloire des Rosomanes). Deep scarlet with crimson crayonnings; full, rounded, richly fragrant flowers. Vigorous growth to 6 ft. with dark green foliage, red when young.

Heidelberg: Floribunda shrub. Kordes, 1958. Minna Kordes × Floradora. Bright crimson-scarlet, rather paler on the reverse. Large, full flowers, carried freely in clusters, shapely at first, opening loosely. Growth is vigorous to 6 ft. with abundant, glossy, medium green foliage, tinted bronze.

Honorine de Brabant: Bourbon shrub. Pale lilac-pink, spotted and striped mauve and crimson. The flowers are loosely formed, cupped and quartered; they carry a refreshing fruity scent, and are borne recurrently on a strong bush, up to 6 ft. with abundant light green foliage.

Hugh Dickson: Hybrid tea type. Hugh Dickson, 1904. Lord Bacon × Gruss an Teplitz. Deep scarlet-crimson. The very large, full, globular blooms are exceptionally fragrant and carried singly and in small clusters on very vigorous, tall growth, with abundant matt, reddish-green foliage, which may need watching for mildew. It is best either pegged down or grown as a climber, taking care to tie the long growths either arched over or spirally, to force the lower eyes into growth. Up to 8 ft.

Kassel: Kordes, 1958. Hamburg × Scarlet Else. Deep scarlet, large semi-double flowers in small trusses. Dark semi-glossy foliage carried on arching branches.

Lady Sonia: Mattock, 1960. Grandmaster × Doreen. Rich golden-yellow, paling with age. Large flowers of moderate petallage, freely borne on upright growths, with ample dark green glossy foliage.

Louise Odier: Bourbon shrub. Margottin, 1851. Soft pink, fragrant flowers of pleasing camellia shape. Vigorous bush to 6 ft., but may need support.

Lübeck (Hansestadt Lübeck): Floribunda shrub. Kordes, 1962. Orange-scarlet at first, deepening to dark scarlet with age. The flowers are large, full, rather shapeless, and carried in large heads at the top of vigorous, tall growth, with dark, glossy foliage. 5 6 ft.

Mme Ernst Calvat: Bourbon shrub. Schwarz, 1888. Pink sport from Mme Isaac Pereire in a more attractive shade than the parent. Sweetly scented. Very vigorous to 6 ft., but needs some support.

Mme Pierre Oger: Bourbon shrub. Oger, 1878. Sport from La Reine Victoria. Creamy-white, shaded pink. Fragrant. Slender, erect bush up to 6 ft.

Moonlight: Hybrid Musk shrub. Pemberton, 1913. Trier × Sulphurea. Small, semi-double flowers in clusters, pale lemon shading to white, with musk fragrance. Small, glossy, dark green leaves, reddish-bronze when young, clothing dark brown wood.

(E) **Nevada:** Dot, 1927. Parentage uncertain, but thought to be La Giralda × R. *moyesii* form or seedling. Pale creamy-white, tinted pink, almost single flowers carried all along the length of the arching branches. Light green matt foliage. Flowers again after the early summer display, especially in a warm summer. Very vigorous to 7 ft.

Nymphenburg: Kordes, 1954. Sangerhausen × Sunmist. Pale salmon-pink, shading to yellow at the base. Flowers large, fairly full and borne intermittently in small clusters. Sharp fruity scent.

Pax: Hybrid Musk shrub. Pemberton, 1918. Trier × Sunburst. Flowers large and shapely at first, white, with golden anthers, opening semi-double; fragrant. Foliage dark green, borne on brown stems.

Penelope: Hybrid Musk shrub. Pemberton, 1924. Ophelia ×

seedling. Creamy-salmon-pink, fading to off-white with age. The semi-double fragrant flowers are borne in clusters, with large heads of bloom in the autumn. Vigorous, with bronze-tinted semi-glossy foliage.

Pink Grootendorst: Rugosa shrub. Grootendorst, 1923. A rose-pink sport from F. J. Grootendorst (see page 252), more attractive in colour, but otherwise similar.

Prosperity: Hybrid Musk shrub. Pemberton, 1919. Marie Jeanne × Perle des Jardins. White, tinted pink on petal edges. The many small petals form a round, pompon-like flower, borne in clusters, with some fragrance. Vigorous to 6 ft., with glossy, dark green foliage, tinted bronze when young.

Reine des Violettes (Queen of the Violets): Hybrid tea type. Millet-Malet, 1860. Pius IX seedling. Deep purple in the half-open stage, paling to violet or mauve in the expanded flower, with a slightly paler reverse. Very full petalled with quartered form, button eye and exceptionally fragrant. Will make a bush 5-6 ft. high on a good soil, with stems clothed with greyish green, matt leaves.

Roger Lambelin: Hybrid tea type. Schwarz, 1890. Fisher Holmes sport. Deep crimson to maroon, heavily margined and streaked with white. The flower is large, full, with fringed, irregular petals and fragrant. Vigorous to 4 ft. but needs generous treatment. May need watching for mildew.

(E) *R. rugosa typica:* 1796. Introduced from Japan. Bright carmine-pink or magenta single flowers, large and fragrant, produced freely and recurrently in clusters, followed by large, brilliant red, round heps, resembling small tomatoes. The later flowers are borne concurrently with the heps of the earlier flowers on very bushy branching growth, armed with numerous fine bristles placed closely. The foliage is dense, rich green and wrinkled (rugose). The bush is very healthy and flourishes on poor sandy soils, reaching 5-6 ft. The white form, *R. rugosa alba,* and the wine red *R. rugosa atropurpurea* are often preferred to the type as having more pleasing colouring in the flowers, which thus associate better with the bright red round heps. The foliage changes to vivid gold and russet shades in autumn.

(E) **Sarah Van Fleet:** Rugosa shrub. Van Fleet, 1926. Bright rose-pink, large, semi-double, very fragrant flowers, produced freely in clusters. Foliage is large, glossy, medium green and bronze tinted when young. It makes a dense bush up to 6 ft. high.

Schneezwerg: Rugosa shrub. Lambert, 1912. A white polyantha ×
R. rugosa. Pure white, rosette-shaped, semi-double flowers, freely
borne over a long period. Foliage small, glossy, mid-green. Small
orange-red heps are noticeable at the same time as the later flowers.

Solus: Watkins, 1967. Kathleen Ferrier × Dickson's Flame.
Orange-scarlet, semi-double flowers, 3½ in. across, losing some
brilliance with age and carried in small clusters on tall upright
growth, with ample dark green, glossy foliage.

Souvenir de la Malmaison: Bourbon shrub. Béluze, 1843. Mme
Desprez × a tea rose. Blush-white. Large fragrant flowers, borne
freely and recurrently on bushy growth.

Sparrieshoop: Kordes, 1953. (Baby Château × Else Poulsen) ×
Magnifica. Large single, rosy-salmon-pink flowers with yellow
stamens, fading paler. Fragrant. Vigorous growth to 6 ft., with
plentiful, large, glossy, medium green foliage, coppery-bronze in
the early stages.

Uncle Walter: Hybrid tea shrub. McGredy, 1963. Brilliant ×
Heidelberg. Scarlet, shaded crimson. The flowers are carried in
clusters, but larger and better quality flowers will be produced by
disbudding. Glossy, dark green foliage, crimson when young.

Vanity: Hybrid Musk shrub. Pemberton, 1920. Château de Clos
Vougeot × seedling. Deep rose-pink, single, fragrant flowers, 3 in.
across, carried on strong growths, but with rather poor foliage
support. Very prolific in autumn.

Variegata di Bologna: Bourbon shrub. Bonfiglioli, 1909. White
or blush-white, with contrasting crimson-purple stripes. The
flowers are full, globular, quartered and very fragrant, and are
borne very freely in early summer with some recurrence. Very
vigorous growth to 6 ft. or more and best trained on some form of
support. Needs protection from black spot.

Will Scarlet: Hilling, 1952. Sport from Wilhelm. Scarlet buds,
opening into semi-double scarlet flowers, paler in the centre. Dark
green, bronze-tinted foliage. Makes a fine display on a 5 ft. plant,
followed by orange-red heps.

SECTION II: All varieties in this section are mainly early-summer
flowering, although some flowers may be produced in smaller
quantities later in the season.

Canary Bird (probably derived from *R. xanthina spontanea*):
Introduced from N. China and Korea. Rich yellow, single flowers,

opening to $2\frac{1}{2}$ in. across and borne along the length of arching stems with brown wood. Very free flowering in May, followed by small, dark maroon heps. It will make a decorative shrub up to 6 ft. high and nearly as much across in time, with bright green, small and fern-like foliage. The wood tends to die back in severe winters.

Charles de Mills (Bizarre Triomphant): Gallica shrub. Purplish-crimson to maroon. Very large, full, quartered, fragrant blooms, borne on vigorous growth, up to 4 or 5 ft.

Commandant Beaurepaire: Bourbon shrub. Moreau-Robert, 1874. Bright rose-pink, mauve, purple and maroon may all be found at some stage in the large, moderately full, cupped and extremely fragrant flowers. These are borne very freely around midsummer, against a background of light green, pointed, smooth foliage. Very few flowers appear after the main display. About 5 ft.

(E) **Conrad Ferdinand Meyer:** Rugosa shrub. Muller, 1899. (Gloire de Dijon × Duc de Rohan) × *R. rugosa germanica*. Silvery-pink, very large and exceptionally full-petalled flowers with strong fragrance, borne in May and June and usually again in the autumn. Very vigorous, making a rather gaunt specimen up to 8 ft. with very thorny stems.

Constance Spry: Austin, 1961. Belle Isis × Dainty Maid. Clear rose-pink. The fragrant flowers, borne all along the growths, are large, cup shaped and full. The attractive pointed foliage is dark green, and copper tinted when young. 6 ft.

Du Maître D'Ecole: Gallica shrub. Soft old rose, shaded mauve and fading to lilac-pink. The flowers are large, full, quartered, with button eyes, opening flat, and very fragrant. Growth is sturdy and vigorous, with large leaves. 3 ft.

Fantin-Latour: Centifolia shrub. Blush-pink. The large, full, flat flowers are borne in the greatest profusion on a sturdy, bushy plant, with dark, large foliage. Fragrant. Makes a good shrub up to 5 ft.

Fritz Nobis: Hybrid Rubiginosa. Kordes, 1940. Joanna Hill × *R. rubiginosa magnifica*. Flesh-pink, shaded salmon. Large, well formed at first, opening semi-double, very fragrant, followed by reddish heps. Growth is bushy and branching up to 6 ft., with glossy, medium-green foliage.

(E) **Frühlingsgold:** Hybrid Spinosissima. Kordes, 1937. Joanna Hill × *R. spinosissima hispida*. Large, semi-single flowers, clear yellow, fading paler, carried on long arching branches. Very fragrant. Light green matt foliage and prickly wood.

Canary Bird (Shrub)

Above left: Rosa sweginzowii macrocarpa has large, flask-shaped bright red heps
Above right: Rosa rugosa alba, a variety with large, showy, bright red heps
Left: Rosa helenae, a distinctive species with small, oval, scarlet heps

(E) **Frühlingsmorgen:** Hybrid Spinosissima. Kordes, 1941. (E. G. Hill × Cathrine Kordes) × *R. spinosissima altaica*. Single flowers, deep pink with yellow centre and maroon stamens. Foliage matt, medium green and small. Usually carries some flowers after the early summer flush.

Gloire des Mousseux: Centifolia Moss shrub. Laffay, 1852. Bright pink, fading somewhat with age. The flowers are large, quartered, with button eyes, and light green mossing. Abundant light green foliage, clothing a sturdy bush up to 4 ft.

Lavender Lassie: Kordes, 1959. Lilac-pink, rosette-like flowers with many but small petals, carrying a musk fragrance. Growth is moderately vigorous, with glossy, light green foliage. There are some later blooms.

Max Graf: Bowditch, 1919. *R. rugosa × R. wichuraiana*. Bright pink, nearly single flowers, paling to white in the centre, with yellow stamens and a fruity scent. Very vigorous trailing branches, with dense, glossy, dark green foliage, acting as a ground cover and excellent for clothing steep banks or for the front of shrub borders.

Mme Hardy: Damascena shrub. Hardy, 1832. White. The flowers are full, quartered, flat, with a button eye and green pointel, and carry an exquisite fragrance. Vigorous growth, to 5 ft., with abundant dark green foliage.

Mme Plantier: Alba shrub. Plantier, 1835. Probably a hybrid between *R. alba* and *R. moschata* seedlings. White, tinted cream. The flowers are full, of pompon shape, with button eye and green pointel. It makes an arching bush of 5-6 ft., with dense growth and small, light green foliage, but will climb much higher on rich soils.

Nuits de Young (Old Black): Centifolia Moss shrub. Laffay, 1852. Deep maroon-purple, with golden stamens. The flowers are small, well mossed and carried freely on a slender bush, 4-5 ft. tall, with small, dark green foliage.

Rosa damascena versicolor (York and Lancaster): Damascena shrub. Prior to 1700. The semi-double flowers are sometimes pink, sometimes blush-white, sometimes half pink and sometimes with different coloured individual petals, but seldom, if ever, striped with crimson. Of sentimental interest because of its link with the Wars of the Roses, but growth is not very vigorous and it requires generous treatment. Up to 4 ft.

R. gallica versicolor (Rosa Mundi): Gallica shrub. Crimson, semi-double flowers, splashed and striped with blush-pink and white.

A sport from *R. gallica officinalis,* to which it is similar except in colouring, and to which it sometimes reverts. It makes a compact and dense bush up to 4 ft., and is exceptionally profuse during the early summer display.

R. hugonis: Introduced from Central China, 1899. Pale yellow, cupped, single flowers, borne along the length of the branches in May, with tiny, fern-like foliage, and followed by small, dark maroon-coloured heps. Will make a graceful shrub to 6 ft., but sometimes dies back in severe weather.

R. moyesii: Introduced from Western China, 1894. Blood-red, single flowers borne in small clusters, followed by highly decorative, large, bottle-shaped heps. Growth is tall, with thorny stems and small, dark green foliage. Up to 10 ft.

R. primula (the Incense rose): Introduced from Turkestan, 1910. Primrose yellow, single, fragrant flowers are borne very freely in May, followed by small reddish heps. The young growth is reddish-brown, with small, dark green, narrow leaves which diffuse an aromatic fragrance of myrrh. Upright, prickly growth up to 6 ft. or more under favourable conditions.

R. pteragonis cantabrigiensis: Hurst, 1931. *R. hugonis* × *R sericea.* Yellow, semi-single, fragrant and very free flowering in early summer, followed by small, orange-red heps. The fern-like foliage is very graceful and carried on hairy growths on an upright bush up to 7 ft. high.

R. rubrifolia (*R. ferruginea*): Introduced from Central Europe, prior to 1830. Clear pink, single flowers, paling to white in the centre. These are followed by brownish-red heps, but the main attraction is the decorative growth, which is almost thornless, purplish-copper when young, with grey and mauve tinted foliage, with a coppery sheen. Vigorous, open habit to 6 ft.

R. sericea pteracantha (*R. omeiensis pteracantha*): Introduced from Western China, 1890. Small, four-petalled white flowers in early summer are succeeded by conspicuous, pear-shaped, orange-red heps. The leaves are small, giving a fern-like effect, but the main attraction is the young red wood, which is embellished with enormous, broad, translucent ruby-red thorns, becoming darker on maturity. It makes a very vigorous, dense shrub, 10 ft. or more high, depending on pruning. May be hard pruned to produce plenty of decorative young shoots.

R. sweginzowii macrocarpa: A hybrid of the species which was introduced from N.W. China. The single flowers are a bright pink, carried both singly and in small clusters, followed by large, flask-shaped bright red heps which ripen early in the season. Growth is strong and bushy, up to 12 ft. and armed with large prickles. Of bushier habit of growth than the better known *R. moyesii* and *R. moyesii rosea* and therefore a more suitable specimen for the garden, but more prickly.

R. willmottiae: Introduced from Western China, 1904. Rich mauve-pink, single flowers, borne very profusely on wiry, twiggy growth in early summer, followed by small pear-shaped orange-red heps. It forms a dense bush up to 6 ft. or more and as much across, with very decorative small, fern-like, glaucous leaves with 7 to 9 tiny leaflets, providing a light and dainty effect, and therefore popular for use in floral arrangements.

Scarlet Fire (Scharlachglut): Kordes, 1952. Poinsettia × *R. gallica* Grandiflora. Bright scarlet, single flowers, with golden stamens, borne freely in clusters along arching branches, and followed by large, pear-shaped red heps. Growth is vigorous and spreading, up to 6 ft. and as much across, with dull green, matt foliage.

Tour de Malakoff: Centifolia shrub. Soupert et Notting, 1856. Cerise-magenta at first, veined and shaded purple, fading to lavender-grey in the final stages. The flowers are very fragrant, large and full, but loosely formed. They are carried on vigorous but rather pendulous growth up to 6 ft. which needs some support.

William Lobb (Duchesse d'Istrie, Old Velvet Moss): Centifolia Moss shrub. Laffay, 1855. The colour varies from crimson-purple through purple-magenta to mauve and lilac-grey. Large, full, loosely-formed flowers with green moss, moderately fragrant and borne in large clusters on very vigorous growth up to 6 ft. or more, with prickly stems. Rather an ungainly shrub, best planted with others of more graceful habit.

SHRUB AND HEDGING ROSES

'At-a-glance' Colour Chart

VERMILION-ORANGE

Fred Loads

BLOOD RED

R. *moyesii*

DEEP CRIMSON TO MAROON AND PURPLE

Charles de Mills
Nuits de Young
William Lobb

DEEP PINK

Frühlingsmorgen
(with yellow centre)
R. *rugosa typica*
Vanity

WHITE, INCLUDING CREAM, BLUSH AND LEMON SHADINGS

Blanc Double de Coubert
Boule de Neige
Mme Hardy
Mme Pierre Oger
Mme Plantier
Moonlight
Nevada
Pax
Prosperity
R. *rugosa alba*
R. *sericea pteracantha*
Schneezwerg
Souvenir de la Malmaison

MEDIUM YELLOW

Canary Bird
Golden Wings
Lady Sonia

ORANGE-SCARLET

Berlin
Bonn
Dorothy Wheatcroft
Lübeck
Solus

CRIMSON AND MAROON, MARGINED AND STREAKED WHITE

Roger Lambelin

MEDIUM PINK

Conrad Ferdinand Meyer
Constance Spry
Gloire des Mousseux
Louise Odier
Max Graf
Mme Ernst Calvat
Pink Grootendorst
R. *rubrifolia*
R. *sweginzowii macrocarpa*
Sarah Van Fleet

LIGHT YELLOW

Frühlingsgold
R. *hugonis*
R. *primula*
R. *pteragonis*
  cantabrigiensis

STRIPED VARIETIES

R. *gallica versicolor*
(crimson, pink and
white stripes)
Variegata di Bologna
(white with crimson-
purple stripes)

SCARLET

Kassel
Scarlet Fire
Will Scarlet

SCARLET-CRIMSON

Gruss an Teplitz
Heidelberg
Hugh Dickson
Uncle Walter

CARMINE AND LIGHT RED

Elmshorn
F. J. Grootendorst
R. *rugosa atropurpurea*

LIGHT PINK

Ballerina
Fantin-Latour
Frau Dagmar Hastrup
Fritz Nobis
Sparrieshoop

LIGHT PINK AND YELLOW BLENDS

Felicia
Nymphenburg
Penelope

LILAC PINK

Lavender Lassie
R. *willmottiae*

PINK, MAUVE AND PURPLE SHADINGS

Commandant Beaurepaire
Du Maître d'École
Honorine de Brabant
Tour de Malakoff
Reine des Violettes

DESCRIPTIVE LIST OF SHRUB AND HEDGING ROSES

PINK AND WHITE
(not striped)

R. damascena versicolor

DEEP YELLOW
Chinatown

**CRIMSON WITH
PRIMROSE CENTRE**
Cocktail

BUFF AND APRICOT
Buff Beauty

CORAL-SALMON
Cornelia

24

Descriptive List of Miniature Roses

Their uses – Minimum requirements in window boxes and troughs – Propagation by cuttings and budding – Recommended varieties, sub-divided according to height

The cult of miniature roses is a somewhat specialised hobby within a hobby. Vast numbers of amateur rose growers do not bother with the miniatures but, on the other hand, many amateurs without the facilities for growing hybrid teas and floribundas manage to grow miniature roses in table gardens, tubs, old stone sinks, window boxes, pots or in tiny gardens made by taking up a few flagstones in a paved courtyard. Some people plant them in rock gardens too, and this is a good idea if deep pockets of rich soil are provided for them. It should always be borne in mind that, despite their Lilliputian stature, they are true roses, with all the rose's liking for a moist but well-drained root run and full sunshine for at least several hours every day.

The miniature roses are mainly descended from *R. chinensis minima,* the dwarf form of the China rose, or *R. roulettii.* Much patient breeding went into the development of the earlier, very dwarf forms; de Vink of Holland and Pedro Dot of Spain did a great deal of pioneer work in widening the colour range, which up to quite recent years was largely confined to shades of pink, red and white. Today, all the rose colour groups are represented, and if in the process of crossing with other groups, some of the newer introductions have grown to a somewhat larger size, they are still miniature, in that they rarely exceed 15 in. high. One of the attractions of this delightful group is that all parts of the plant are scaled down in proportion – stems, leaves, buds, flowers and individual petals.

Anybody who has been enchanted by the perfectly planned gardens of miniature roses at Chelsea Flower Show every year will need no convincing that the ideal method of growing them is by themselves in a separate little garden of their own. While there is nothing against planting them as edgings to beds of hybrid tea and floribunda roses, they do tend to become smothered and insignificant unless two or three rows of them are massed together, and unless the larger-flowered, more recent introductions are used. There is no reason at all, though, why such varieties as Coralin, Baby Masquerade, Baby Gold Star, Rosina, Little Flirt and Easter Morning should not make a very attractive edging to orthodox rose beds and borders.

A false impression of the value of miniature roses in pots is sometimes given. While these may be taken indoors when in flower, they are not house plants and their stay should be of short duration, as the dry atmosphere in heated rooms does not suit them, and causes leaf dropping. They should be taken outside again as soon as the flowers have faded and the pots sunk up to their rims in soil and topdressed with moist peat, when further flowers may be produced. While they are among the most recurrent flowering of all groups when planted in the open, if they are confined to stone troughs, window boxes and tubs, they require a depth of at least 15-18 in. of good soil, and adequate provision for drainage if they are to flourish for any length of time. The soil must never be allowed to become dry, and it is an excellent plan to mulch the surface with a layer of moist granulated peat. They will need spraying against greenfly, and some of the yellow and orange varieties will need protection from black spot.

They will do very well with the same soil preparation as hybrid teas and if they are purchased in pots they may be planted any time in open weather. If they are planted more than 12 in. apart there may be too much soil visible, and for the very dwarf varieties 8 in. apart may be sufficient on some soils. Propagation may be either by cuttings or budding, or they may be raised from seed. The advantage of propagation by cuttings is that the dwarf character of the variety is retained, whereas when rootstocks are used, being more vigorous, they tend to produce larger plants after a few years and these may have less appeal than those raised from cuttings. Vegetative propagation, whether by cuttings or by budding on to rootstocks does, of course, ensure that the new plants retain the characteristics of the parent, subject to the point already made about rootstocks. Seedlings, on the other hand, will show variations in colour, petallage and growth.

Propagation From Cuttings

New season's shoots about 3 in. long are removed in September and cut across just below a leaf bud. To assist rooting, the base should be dipped in a hormone rooting powder, suitable for half-ripe wood cuttings, first wetting the lower part of the cutting to assist adhesion of the powder. The cuttings are then inserted round the side of a pot in a mixture of coarse sand and loam in equal parts. They should be kept in a close atmosphere and sprayed through a fine nozzle at least once a day, whether in a greenhouse or a cold frame. When rooted they may be transferred to individual pots, using John Innes Potting Compost No. 2. Alternatively the cuttings may be inserted in a V-shaped trench in a sheltered part of the garden, using gritty soil. Longer cuttings may be used than those for insertion in pots, but not more than one third of their length should be above soil level. It is essential that the soil be kept moist. Cloches may be placed over the cuttings as a protection during the winter.

Propagation by Budding and Raising From Seed

This follows the general procedure already detailed in Chapter 11.

SOME RECOMMENDED VARIETIES

Very Dwarf

Colibri: Orange-yellow, flushed pink
Dwarfking: Medium red
Mon Petit: Light crimson
Perla de Alcanada: Carmine
Perla de Montserrat: Light pink, deeper shadings
Pour Toi: Cream, shaded greenish-white
Presumida: Orange-yellow in centre, shading to cream
Robin: Cherry red
Simple Simon: Deep pink
Sweet Fairy: Lilac-pink
Tinker Bell: Bright rose-pink
Yellow Doll: Clear yellow, shading to cream

Slightly Taller

Baby Gold Star: Deep yellow
Baby Masquerade: Yellow, pink and red
Cinderella: Blush pink to white
Coralin: Salmon-red
Easter Morning: Pale yellow buds opening cream
Eleanor: Coral-pink
Granadina: Crimson shaded scarlet
Little Flirt: Flame, pale yellow reverse
New Penny: Salmon-pink to coral
Red Imp (Maid Marion): Deep crimson
Rosina (Josephine Wheatcroft): Rich yellow
Scarlet Gem: Bright orange-scarlet

Part Three

Rose Awards

Display Gardens

Roses for Various Purposes

Recommended Suppliers

Glossary

25

Rose Awards in Britain and
Other Countries

*The significance of the various awards to new roses – The Royal National Rose
Society's awards – All-America Rose Selections – Continental awards – The need
for new varieties – Deterioration after vegetative propagation for some years –
New colour groups Some weaknesses justifying attention by rose breeders
Plant Breeders' Rights to encourage breeders*

Awards to new roses in this country are made only after exhaustive
and impartial trials by The Royal National Rose Society extending
over two or three years in their own Trial Ground, where the seedlings are inspected by the individual judges from June to September.
Before a seedling can become eligible to receive an award it must
have been planted in the Trial Ground for at least two seasons. If a
majority of the 20 judges consider it worthy, based on periodic
inspections during the flowering season, it may be awarded a Trial
Ground Certificate (T.G.C.) at the end of the second year. This does
not indicate that the variety is necessarily outstanding; rather is it
evidence that it will do well under ordinary conditions of cultivation,
such as may be provided in the average amateur's garden.

Of the relatively few seedlings which reach Certificate of Merit
(C. of M.) standard, the outstanding ones are often given this higher
award after only two seasons, whereas the rest do not receive the
award until the end of the third season. Here again, a clear majority
of the judges has to consider a seedling worthy of this higher award,
which is an indication that it is of more than average merit. A
few varieties may be considered worthy of a Gold Medal award
(G.M.), for which they have to be absolutely outstanding. Not
more than two or three out of 500 or more eligible seedlings are
normally considered worthy of this coveted award in any one year,
and in some years, e.g. 1966, no variety may reach this high standard.

Of the varieties receiving the Gold Medal award in any year, one is selected as the most meritorious and is awarded the President's International Trophy as the best new seedling of the year, irrespective of classification. The most fragrant seedling, of at least Certificate of Merit standard, in each year receives the Henry Edland Memorial Medal, which was awarded for the first time in 1966.

As a rough idea of the proportion of new seedlings considered to be worthy of awards, it can be said that with something like 500 eligible seedlings in their second and third seasons of trial, usually not more than between 20 and 30 basic awards (i.e. G.M., C. of M. and T.G.C.) are made in any one year. This represents only from 4 to 6 per cent of these eligible seedlings. Of these successful seedlings perhaps two, or maybe three, will be considered worthy of a Gold Medal award, and five or six will be of Certificate of Merit standard, the remainder receiving Trial Ground Certificates. There is no restriction on the number of awards made, though, provided that the necessary standard has been reached, and the New Seedling Judging Committee may recommend more or fewer awards according to the circumstances of a particular year. While it is evident from these figures that a high standard is required of a successful seedling, taking account of such qualities as vigour and habit of growth, freedom from disease, colour, form, freedom of flowering, fragrance and general effect, it is equally evident that some breeders are not as selective as they might be in submitting their seedlings for trial.

Foreign Trials

In the United States of America there are 22 test gardens in different areas, in which new seedlings are tested for two years under variable climatic conditions under the auspices of The All America Rose Selections Organisation. After the trial period the A.A.R.S. committee holds a ballot to decide which varieties, if any, are worthy of the award. A two-thirds majority is required. While many excellent roses have won the A.A.R.S., it does not follow that one which does very well in America will be outstanding in Great Britain, as the climatic conditions are so different. By and large, the amateur in this country would be well advised to attach more importance to the R.N.R.S. awards than to those made in America or even on the Continent. The main weakness of many American and Continental introductions when grown here is their intolerance to rain, and a variety which will not open in wet weather can only be regarded as of doubtful value in this country. New rose seedling trials are held at Bagatelle (Paris), Rome, Geneva, Madrid, The Hague, Orléans and other centres, usually offering a Gold Medal award to the best hybrid tea and the best floribunda respectively, and certificates to the runners-up in each group.

Deterioration of Stocks

It may be asked why such a spate of new seedlings is necessary when there are already many excellent varieties in some of the colour groups, offering a quite bewildering choice to the beginner. The trouble is that most varieties tend to deteriorate sooner or later, and to understand this problem it is necessary to realise that every plant of a particular variety has been propagated from a portion of the original seedling–only by such vegetative propagation can stocks of the variety be maintained true to the original character. Thus, every plant of Peace–and there must be millions over the world–has been produced directly or indirectly from a part of the original plant. Because of the enormous demand for plants of a top award winner, there may be a tendency to use every possible bud for propagation, including quite a number below standard. In this way, over a period there may be inferior strains of a variety distributed, and unless great care is taken by the nurserymen in selecting only the strongest buds for propagation, from stems which have borne perfect and typical flowers, deterioration may become marked, and a variety may even drop out of cultivation in extreme cases. The interval between the introduction of a novelty and deterioration setting in to a marked degree does not conform to any particular pattern. Some of the earliest hybrid teas, such as Mme Caroline Testout (1890), still have a strong constitution; on the other hand, some post-war introductions have virtually disappeared within as little as 10 years after their introduction.

There is thus a basic need for new seedlings to replace established favourites which may already have started their decline. Apart from this there are the new colour groups which still offer scope for improvement in both colour range and stability. In all colour groups, whether novel or not, there is always room for high-quality new seedlings which may offer certain improvements–whether in colour stability, resistance to rain or sun, fragrance, repeat flowering, disease resistance, foliage, strength of stem or hardiness.

New Varieties Wanted

Many gaps will have to be filled before it can be said with complete justification that we have too many varieties. Who would not welcome a really rich deep velvety crimson hybrid tea which neither mildews, spots nor burns, and will open freely in wet weather? Or a white hybrid tea with similar qualities? Or first-class pure orange or lavender-mauve floribundas which are not martyrs to black spot? It is a sobering thought that some 30 years after the introduction of the first yellow floribunda, just before the Second War, varieties in a really rich yellow shade, held to a late stage, with a compact bedding habit and ample healthy foliage, as well as freedom and continuity of flowering, are still in very short supply. Apart from Allgold, which has reigned supreme for 12 years, and its recent offspring Goldgleam, a shade lighter, and possibly Golden Treasure, there is little to indicate much progress towards overcoming rapid colour fading and addiction to black spot.

Another weakness among modern hybrid tea roses, which probably stems from using Peace so much in post-war breeding programmes, is the number of varieties which make very large and tall plants, but with insufficient flowers open at any one time. In other words, there is a low ratio of flowers to wood. Because of the size of the flowers and the length and strength of the stems, the interval between crops is necessarily longer than average, and it may well be that in cold districts one crop less will be obtained in each season than from shorter-growing and quicker-maturing varieties. There is the further point, too, that growth of the strength of Peace, Eden Rose and the like can be a positive embarrassment in a small garden.

Plant Breeders' Rights

The introduction in this country of Plant Breeders' Rights, whereby the rose breeder may protect his new variety on proof that it is distinct from any other variety, stable and uniform, and has not been commercialised already, should encourage our breeders to make long-term plans, knowing that any real advance they may achieve will be rewarded by protection against infringement for a reasonable period. Previously the breeder of a new rose of outstanding merit could only hope to enjoy exclusive rights during the two years or so that it took his rivals to work up stocks from purchased budwood—

so rapidly could stocks be built up under glass. It is to be hoped that the protection now afforded by legislation–and so long overdue–will lead to the introduction of novelties of superior qualities, with benefits to their raisers and to amateur rose growers alike.

It may be of interest that The Royal National Rose Society is co-operating with the Plant Variety Rights Office by accommodating varieties on trial for protection rights and by planting a 'museum' collection of four plants of each variety which has been granted rights. These plants are available for comparison in the event of a case of infringement of rights arising, and must therefore remain in the collection until such time as the raiser wishes to relinquish his rights.

The President's International Trophy

The President's International Trophy is awarded by The Royal National Rose Society for the best new seedling of the year. Details are given below of the winners since it was first awarded.

1952	Moulin Rouge (flori.)	1961	Mischief (H.T.)
1953	Concerto (flori.)	1962	No Award
1954	Spartan (flori.)	1963	Elizabeth of Glamis (flori.)
1955	Queen Elizabeth (flori. H.T. type)	1964	Fragrant Cloud (H.T.)
1956	Faust (flori.)	1965	Grandpa Dickson (H.T.)
1957	Perfecta (H.T.)	1966	No Award
1958	Dickson's Flame (flori.)	1967	City of Belfast (flori.)
1959	Wendy Cussons (H.T.)	1968	Molly McGredy (flori. H.T.
1960	Super Star (H.T.)		type)

N.B. This award is made to the best of the Gold Medal award-winning seedlings, irrespective of the class to which it belongs.

26

Notable Rose Display Gardens

Apart from the pleasure to be derived from visiting rose display gardens and feasting one's eyes on the colour, as well as savouring the fragrance of roses *en masse*, such visits are instructive. The observant amateur will take note of the varieties which are most continuously in flower, those which stand up to rain or hot sun reasonably well or, on the other hand, those which fail to open or fade objectionably in strong sunshine. Inspecting the varieties growing as cut-backs in permanent beds will give him a much better idea of their potentialities than seeing them growing as maiden plants in the nursery rows. Such important points as susceptibility to disease and freedom of flowering in the autumn may also be observed with advantage.

Queen Mary's Garden, Regent's Park
Probably the most outstanding rose display garden in this country is in Queen Mary's Garden in the Inner Circle, Regent's Park, London, N.W.1. Here there are over 40,000 plants of all types, arranged both in large formal beds of one variety, and in mixed borders. The main planting is a circular garden, enclosed with tall pillars connected with ropes, on which climbers and ramblers in variety provide an artistic and colourful background to the formal beds. There are numerous beds, too, near the waterside on a lower level and other mass plantings skirting the walks towards Bedford College and in front of the Tea House and the fountain. Additionally, there is a smaller secluded garden behind St John's Lodge, comprising three separate small gardens planted with formal rose beds and approached across a lawn flanked by colourful herbaceous borders. No rose enthusiast should miss the opportunity of visiting Queen Mary's Garden, so beautifully laid out and carefully tended and conveniently close to the centre of London.

Top and bottom: Nurserymen's exhibits of miniature roses. These delightful little flowers are becoming increasingly popular

Above: Rose suckers, with a shoot of a cultivated rose in the centre. A Laxa sucker is shown on the left and a Rugosa sucker on the right. *Below:* Other rose suckers compared with a cultivated rose. A Briar sucker *(R. canina)* is shown on the left and a Multiflora sucker *(R. multiflora)* on the right

Kew Collection

A little farther out there is an interesting collection of roses at the
Royal Botanic Gardens, Kew, although these are planted on a
smaller scale. The natural soil at Kew is poor and gravelly, so that
considerable trouble has to be taken in preparing new beds by
replacing the soil with more suitable imported material. There are
some 5,500 plants in formal beds adjacent to the Palm House,
comprising both old and modern varieties. It is interesting to find a
flourishing bed of the old favourite Mme Caroline Testout, over
60 years old and growing on its own roots. In the southern half of
the gardens there is a most impressive collection of the rose species,
planted in 21 large beds, and elsewhere there is a fine pergola,
planted with a selection of climbing roses and an outstanding hedge
of the hybrid musk Penelope.

The Royal National Rose Society's Gardens

In Hertfordshire there are the Rose Display Gardens of The Royal
National Rose Society, at their headquarters at Chiswell Green
Lane, about four miles from St Albans station, and off the main
Watford Road (A412). These are not public gardens, but may be
visited by members of the Society and their friends from mid-June
to the end of September. The Display Gardens comprise something
like six acres, with more than 450 named varieties, immaculately
tended and planted in beds cut in lawns and in borders. Some idea
of the range of varieties displayed in the various main groups may
be gained from the following analysis:

	No. of varieties
Hybrid teas	102
Floribundas, including floribunda H.T. type	137
Old Garden Roses	28
Species and their near hybrids	34
Hybrid Musks	8
Hybrid Rugosas	8
Modern shrub roses	28
Wichuraiana ramblers	11
Climbers	28
Climbing hybrid tea sports	10
Modern recurrent climbers, including Kordesii	26
Miniatures	22
	442

As might be expected these gardens are an object lesson in how roses should be grown for display. Apart from the comprehensive range of modern hybrid teas and floribundas in bush form, visitors should make a point of seeing the collection of standards and weeping standards which includes many varieties not often seen in this form, as well as an interesting collection of miniature roses. They should not miss, too, the border of modern shrub, species and old garden roses, some of which are also featured at the front of the house. Quite apart from this lay-out, part of the land is set aside as the Trial Ground for new seedling roses, of which there are some 700 distinct varieties, mostly six plants of each, under trial at any one time. Most of these are identified only by a number while undergoing their trials.

As a service to members of The Royal National Rose Society, arrangements have been made with local authorities in various parts of the country for them to plant each year in one of their public parks or gardens, display beds containing new roses which have been awarded the Society's Trial Ground Certificate or a higher award. This arrangement enables members in the area, many of whom may not be able to make the journey to the Trial Ground at St Albans, to see for themselves the award-winning varieties growing under their own local conditions. Display beds of these new varieties are established in the following gardens which are open daily:

South Wales: Roath Park, Cardiff

Yorkshire: The Northern Horticultural Society's Gardens, Harlow Car, Harrogate

Scotland: Saughton Park, Edinburgh

Lancashire: Botanic Gardens, Southport

Somerset: Vivary Park, Taunton

It is intended to provide similar displays for members in other parts of the country.

Specialist Rose Nurseries

Apart from the foregoing, some of the larger specialist rose nurseries have planted their own display gardens, as an adjunct to their nurseries, with ample parking facilities for any members of the public who may wish to look over the gardens at their leisure. Three of the largest of these gardens are mentioned very briefly below:

C. Gregory & Son Ltd., Toton Lane, Stapleford, Nottinghamshire. The rose gardens cover about six acres of lawns in which approximately 200 beds are cut, holding from 75 to 150 plants in each. A field of 10 acres has been allocated as a car park.

R. Harkness & Co. Ltd., The Rose Gardens, Hitchin, Herts. The display garden covers about 10 acres, comprising some 350 beds, plus borders. There are about 30,000 plants in 735 named varieties, including many of the older shrub roses, climbers and species, as well as the popular modern bedding types and miniatures.

S. McGredy & Son Ltd., Derriaghy, Nr. Belfast, alongside the Belfast-Lisburn trunk road. The garden comprises upwards of 20,000 plants in beds containing up to 150 plants each. There are also many climbers and standard roses.

Rose Gardens in Other Countries

For the convenience of those readers who may have visits to other countries in prospect and might wish to take the opportunity of viewing some foreign rose gardens, the following brief references may be helpful:

Denmark: Valbyparken, Copenhagen. There are something like 20,000 plants displayed in large beds, representing nearly 300 varieties.

France: (*a*) Bagatelle, Bois de Boulogne, Paris. About 7,000 rose plants, including some 130 beds for five plants of each new variety submitted in 'le Concours', together with large beds of older varieties, mainly floribundas.

(*b*) La Roseraie de l'Haÿ les Roses, just over three miles south of Paris. Of historical interest, consisting mainly of older varieties and those demonstrating the history and development of the rose. There is also a fine collection of the rose species.

(*c*) Parc de la Tête d'Or, Lyon, covering about 14 acres and embracing over 100,000 plants—possibly the largest rose garden in Europe.

Holland: Westbroekpark, The Hague. About 32,000 plants in nearly 400 varieties, planted in separate beds of 80 plants each.

Italy: Municipal Rose Garden, Via di Valle Murcia (on the Aventine Hill), Rome. About 1,000 varieties in groups of 5 plants of each, and many climbers and rose species.

Spain: Rosaleda del Parque del Oeste, Madrid. There are 267 beds varying in size but averaging 100 plants of each variety.

Switzerland: Parc de la Grange, Geneva. About 12,000 plants accommodated on three terraces in about 150 varieties.

U.S.A. (*a*) The Park of Roses, Columbus, Ohio. This covers about 13 acres, with 55,000 rose plants in over 400 varieties.

(*b*) The Hershey Rose Garden, Hershey, Pennsylvania. There are in all about 42,000 plants comprising a representative collection of modern and older varieties, climbers and species.

(*c*) The Newark Rose Garden (Jackson & Perkins), Newark, New York, extending over 17 acres and embracing more than 36,000 plants.

Selections of Roses for Various Purposes

HYBRID TEA ROSES MOST SUITABLE FOR BEGINNERS

Reliable varieties of proved vigour and hardiness most likely to succeed in unfavourable soils and in industrial areas without expert attention:

Bayadère	Kronenbourg	Piccadilly
Brandenburg	Lady Eve Price	Pilar Landecho
Buccaneer	Lady Sylvia	Pink Favourite
Chicago Peace	Lancastrian	Polly
Dame de Coeur	Lilac Rose	President Herbert Hoover
Eden Rose	Lucy Cramphorn	Prima Ballerina
Ena Harkness	Margaret	Rose Gaujard
Fragrant Cloud	Milord	Sarah Arnot
Frau Karl Druschki	Mischief	Signora
Gail Borden	Mme Butterfly	Spek's Yellow
Gold Crown	Mme Caroline Testout	Super Star
Grand Gala	Mojave	Sutter's Gold
Grand'mère Jenny	Montezuma	Tahiti
Grandpa Dickson	My Choice	Tally Ho
Helen Traubel	Ophelia	Teenager
Josephine Bruce	Parasol	Vivien Leigh
Karl Herbst	Peace	Wendy Cussons

TALL-GROWING HYBRID TEA ROSES

Roses vary in absolute height according to methods of pruning and cultivation, but the following varieties tend to be taller than the average:

Allegro	Christian Dior	Grand'mère Jenny
Angel Wings	Dame de Coeur	Greetings
Apricot Silk	Eden Rose	Helen Traubel
Bacchus	Evensong	John S. Armstrong
Brandenburg	Frau Karl Druschki	Karl Herbst
Buccaneer	Grand Gala	Klaus Störtebeker
Camelot	Gold Crown	Kronenbourg
Chicago Peace	Golden Giant	Lady Seton

277

ROSES

Lilac Rose	Pink Peace	Signora
Lucy Cramphorn	President Herbert Hoover	Spek's Yellow
Margaret	Prima Ballerina	Super Star
Mojave	Red Devil	Sutter's Gold
Montezuma	Rose Gaujard	Tahiti
Ophelia	Sabrina	Tally Ho
Peace	Sarah Arnot	Tiffany
Pilar Landecho	Scandale	Vivien Leigh
Pink Favourite		

COMPACT-GROWING HYBRID TEA ROSES

The following varieties tend to grow below the average height:

Bridal Robe	Fritz Thiedemann	Princess
Champs Elysées	Heure Mauve	Regalia
Colour Wonder	Intermezzo	The Doctor
Doreen	Lady Belper	Ulster Monarch
Dr A. J. Verhage	Lydia	Wisbech Gold
Elsa Arnot	Mme Louis Laperrière	Youki San
Flaming Sunset	Picture	

SOME HYBRID TEA ROSES NOT NORMALLY BADLY AFFECTED BY RAIN

Allegro	Diorama	Josephine Bruce
Amatsu Otome	Doreen	Kronenbourg
Anne Watkins	Ellinor Le Grice	Lady Belper
Apricot Silk	Ena Harkness	Lady Eve Price
Bel Ange	Ernest H. Morse	Lady Seton
Beauté	Eve Allen	Lady Sylvia
Bettina	Evensong	La Jolla
Blue Moon	Flaming Sunset	Lancastrian
Brandenburg	Francine	Lilac Rose
Buccaneer	Gail Borden	Lydia
Camelot	Garvey	Marcelle Gret
Caramba	Gertrude Gregory	Mardi Gras
Champs Elysées	Golden Giant	Mary Wheatcroft
Cherry Brandy	Golden Melody	McGredy's Yellow
Chicago Peace	Grand'mère Jenny	Mischief
Crimson Brocade	Grandpa Dickson	Miss Ireland
Colour Wonder	Helen Traubel	Mme Butterfly
Diamond Jubilee	John S. Armstrong	Mme Louis Laperrière

278

Mojave	Prima Ballerina	Souvenir de Jacques
Monique	Prince of Denmark	Verschuren
Mrs Sam McGredy	Rose Gaujard	Summer Sunshine
Ophelia	Sarah Arnot	Super Star
Parasol	Scandale	Sutter's Gold
Peace	Serenade	Tally-Ho
Piccadilly	Signora	Tradition
Picture	Silva	Traviata
Pink Peace	Silver Lining	Valerie Boughey
Pink Supreme	Spek's Yellow	Violinista Costa
Polly	Stella	Wendy Cussons
President Herbert Hoover		Westward Ho

ROSES SUITABLE FOR EXHIBITION

Some hybrid tea varieties capable of producing large specimen blooms, given good cultivation, disbudding and feeding:

Ballet	Josephine Bruce	Perfecta
Brilliant	June Park	Pink Favourite
Caramba	Karl Herbst	Princess
Chicago Peace	Kronenbourg	Red Devil
Christian Dior	Lady Belper	Rose Gaujard
Dorothy Peach	Margaret	Royal Highness
Eden Rose	McGredy's Ivory	Sam McGredy
Ena Harkness	McGredy's Yellow	Silver Lining
Fragrant Cloud	Memoriam	Stella
Gail Borden	Montezuma	Super Star
Gavotte	My Choice	Ulster Monarch
Grandpa Dickson	Paris-Match	Wendy Cussons
Isabel de Ortiz	Peace	

HYBRID TEA ROSES PARTICULARLY SUITABLE FOR FLORAL ARRANGEMENTS

These carry medium-sized, shapely flowers on firm, fairly thorn-free stems and last reasonably well in water:

Allegro	Brandenburg	Lady Belper
Angel Wings	Dr A. J. Verhage	Lady Sylvia
Apricot Silk	Elida	Mme Butterfly
Baccara	Femina	Message
Beauté	First Love	Michèle Meilland
Bel Ange	Golden Melody	Mischief
Bettina	Grand'mère Jenny	Miss Ireland
Blue Moon	Jean Campbell	Mojave

279

Ophelia	Signora	Sterling Silver
Pascali	Soraya	Super Star
Picture	Souvenir de Jacques	Sutter's Gold
Polly	Verschuren	Virgo
Persident Herbert Hoover	Spek's Yellow	Youki San
Prima Ballerina		

TALL-GROWING FLORIBUNDA ROSES

Angela	Faust	Orange Triumph
Ann Elizabeth	Fervid	Queen Elizabeth
Arabian Nights	Fireworks	Red Dandy
Arthur Bell	Frensham	Scarlet Queen Elizabeth
Baby Sylvia	Geisha Girl	Scented Air
Chanelle	Highlight	Shepherd's Delight
Charming Maid	Honeymoon	Spartan
Columbine	Iceberg	Sweet Repose
Daily Sketch	Korona	Tambourine
Dainty Maid	Lucky Charm	Tombola
Dearest	Märchenland	Toni Lander
Diamant	Matterhorn	Vera Dalton
Dominator	Mandy	
Elysium	Miracle	

COMPACT-GROWING FLORIBUNDA ROSES

Africa Star	Fashion	Paddy McGredy
Alison Wheatcroft	Golden Jewel	Pernille Poulsen
Allgold	Golden Slippers	Plentiful
Ambrosia	Goldilocks	Posy
Anna Louisa	Herself	Red Favourite
Anna Wheatcroft	Ivory Fashion	Redgold
Antique	Jan Spek	Rodeo
Ascot	Lilac Charm	Ruth Leuwerik
Bobbie Lucas	Lilli Marlene	Safari
Charm of Paris	Love Token	Sarabande
Circus	Manx Queen	Scania
Cognac	Marlena	Siesta
Colour Carnival	(very dwarf)	Summer Song
Copper Delight	Meteor	Travesti
Coventrian	My Girl	Zambra
Dickson's Flame	Orange Sensation	Zingaro
Dimples	Overture	

(Absolute height is influenced by such factors as pruning methods, cultivation, type of soil and feeding, but the above selections tend to be taller or shorter than average respectively.)

ROSES SUITABLE FOR WALLS WITH A SOUTHERN OR WESTERN ASPECT

Generally such walls should be reserved for the less hardy roses, but naturally the hardier varieties will also succeed against these walls:

Ena Harkness (Cl.)	Mme Edouard Herriot (Cl.)	Royal Gold
Etoile de Hollande (Cl.)	Mme Henri Guillot (Cl.)	Shot Silk (Cl.)
Golden Dawn (Cl.)	Mrs Herbert Stevens (Cl.)	Spek's Yellow (Cl.)
Guinée	Mrs Pierre S. du Pont (Cl.)	Sutter's Gold (Cl.)
Mermaid	Mrs Sam McGredy (Cl.)	

ROSES SUITABLE FOR WALLS WITH AN EASTERN OR NORTHERN ASPECT

These will also do well against walls facing south or west:

Allen Chandler	Hugh Dickson	Maigold
Caprice (Cl.)	Masquerade (Cl.)	Parkdirektor Riggers
Conrad Ferdinand Meyer	Mme Alfred Carrière	Paul's Lemon Pillar
Danse du Feu	Mme Butterfly (Cl.)	Soldier Boy
Gloire de Dijon	Mme Caroline Testout (Cl.)	Zéphirine Drouhin
Gruss an Teplitz		

SOME ROSES SUITABLE FOR EXTERNAL HEDGES

Blanc Double de Coubert	Frau Dagmar Hastrup	Pink Grootendorst
Conrad Ferdinand Meyer	Frühlingsgold	Prosperity
Elmshorn	Frühlingsmorgen	Sarah Van Fleet
Felicia	Nevada	Scarlet Fire
F. J. Grootendorst	Penelope	Schneezwerg
		Vanity

SOME ROSES SUITABLE FOR INTERNAL HEDGES

Ballerina	Cocktail	Gruss an Teplitz
Berlin	Dorothy Wheatcroft	Heidelberg
Bonn	Faust	Joseph's Coat
Chinatown	Fred Loads	Lady Sonia

Lübeck	Queen Elizabeth	Sparrieshoop
Nymphenburg	Shepherd's Delight	Uncle Walter
Orange Triumph	Solus	

Most of the taller-growing floribundas and many of the old garden roses are also excellent for internal hedges.

Other References

For hybrid teas suitable for growing in pots under glass, see list at the end of Chapter 14.

For fragrant hybrid teas and floribundas, see the selections incorporated in Chapter 16.

For roses suitable for growing as standards, see lists in Chapter 17.

For selections of rambling roses and recurrent-flowering pillar roses, see the introduction to Chapter 22.

For miniature roses, see the selections at the end of Chapter 24.

Some Recommended Suppliers of Roses and Rootstocks

*David Austin Roses, Albrighton, Wolverhampton, Staffs.

The Barton Nurseries, 31, Sibsey Road, Boston, Lincs.

Basildon Rose Gardens Ltd., Burnt Mills Road, Basildon, Essex.

Bees Ltd., Sealand Nurseries, Chester.

Blaby Rose Gardens Ltd., Blaby, Leics.

Cant's of Colchester, 25, Old Rose Gardens, Mile End, Colchester, Essex.

Chaplin Bros. (Waltham Cross) Ltd., Pepper Hill, Amwellbury, Near Ware, Herts.

*James Cocker & Sons (Rose Specialists) Ltd., Whitemyres, Lang Stracht, Aberdeen, Scotland.

Geo. de Ruiter (Roses) Ltd., Fosse Way, Widmerpool, Notts.

Alex. Dickson & Sons Ltd., Newtownards, Co. Down, N. Ireland.

C. J. Dillon & Co. Ltd., Springfield Nurseries, Woolsington, Newcastle-upon Tyne.

R. C. Ferguson & Sons, South Nurseries, Dunfermline, Scotland.

Fryer's Nurseries Ltd., Knutsford, Cheshire.

C. Gregory & Son Ltd., The Rose Gardens, Stapleford, Notts.

*R. Harkness & Co. Ltd., The Rose Gardens, Hitchin, Herts.

Harlow Park Nurseries Ltd., London Road, Potter Street, Harlow, Essex.

Elisha J. Hicks (Roses) Ltd., Orchard Road, Hurst, Nr. Reading, Berks.

*Hillier & Sons, Winchester, Hants.

E. B. Le Grice (Roses) Ltd., Yarmouth Road, North Walsham, Norfolk.

Linwood Roses Ltd., Swanland, East Yorks.

William Lowe & Son (Nurseries) Ltd., The Nurseries, Beeston, Notts.

John Mattock Ltd., The Rose Nurseries, Nuneham Courtenay, Oxford.

H. Merryweather & Sons Ltd., The Nurseries, Southwell, Notts.

Henry Morse & Sons, Westfield Nurseries, Eaton, Norwich.

*Edwin Murrell, Portland Nurseries, Shrewsbury, Salop.

Samuel McGredy & Son Ltd., Royal Nurseries, Portadown, N. Ireland.

Proctor's, Rose Specialists, Chesterfield, Derbyshire.

Herbert Robinson, M.B.E., Victoria Nurseries, Coventry Road, Burbage, Hinckley, Leics.

John Sanday (Roses) Ltd., Almondsbury, Bristol.

*Sunningdale Nurseries, Windlesham, Surrey.

James Townsend & Sons, Lower Broadheath, Worcester.

Stephen Treseder & Son Ltd., Ely Nurseries, Ely, Cardiff, Glam.

Warley Rose Gardens Ltd., Warley Street, Great Warley, Brentwood, Essex.

John Waterer, Sons & Crisp Ltd., The Floral Mile, Twyford, Berks.

Waterhouse Nurseries Ltd., Radway Green, Nr. Crewe, Cheshire.

Watkins Roses Ltd., Kenilworth Road, Hampton-in-Arden, Solihull, Warwicks.

Wheatcroft Bros. Ltd., Ruddington, Notts.

Harry Wheatcroft & Sons Ltd., Edwalton, Notts.

H. Williamson (Hereford) Ltd., Wyevale Nurseries, King's Acre, Hereford.

*These also supply a wide range of old garden roses and shrub roses.

Note: There are also numerous reliable rose specialists operating almost entirely within a localised area, who transact little or no mail order trade.

Suppliers of Rose Rootstocks for Budding

W. T. Anderson, Abingdon-on-Thames, Berks.

The Barton Nurseries, 31, Sibsey Road, Boston, Lincs.

Sidney Smith Ltd., Barton Seagrave, Kettering, 7.

D. Stewart, Arreton Nurseries, Bashley, New Milton, Hants.

Glossary

ANTHER : The apex of the stamen, containing the pollen grains.

BALLING : The clinging together of the outside petals in wet weather, thus preventing the flower from opening.

BICOLOR : A flower in which the inner face of the petal is distinctly different in colour from the outside, or reverse.

BLEEDING : Loss of sap from pruning cuts, due to late pruning after the sap has risen.

BLOWN BLOOM : One that has opened wide, revealing the stamens.

BLUEING : Fading to mauve or 'blue' shades, usually in red and deep pink varieties.

BOX : A conventional method of showing roses in water tubes fixed in a box of regulation dimensions.

BRITISH STANDARD : A standard laid down by the British Standards Institution for minimum dimensions of maiden rose plants (British Standard 3936: Part 2: 1966).

BUD : The term applied to a dormant shoot bud as well as to a flower bud.

BUDDING : The normal method of propagating garden varieties of roses by bark or shield grafting.

BUDDING POINT : The swollen part of the rose plant from which the top growth emerges, where the bud was inserted beneath the bark of the stock.

BURNING : The scorching or bleaching of petals in hot sunshine, usually following a shower.

BUTTON EYE : The folding over of the centre petals in some old garden roses to form a characteristic 'button'.

CALYX : The collective term for the five sepals, the function of which is to protect the flower bud until it opens.

CAMBIUM LAYER : The thin layer of tissue between the bark and the wood which is the part uniting the stock with the scion in successful budding.

CLIMBING SPORT : A mutation of rampant growth from a bush variety, bearing identical flowers to the parent.

CLUSTER : Collective term applied to a number of flowers growing together in the same head and connected by footstalks to a common stem.

CONFUSED CENTRE : Where the centre of a flower has disarranged or unsymmetrical petals.

CUT-BACK : A plant at least in its second season of growth after budding.

DEAD-HEADING : The removal of spent blooms during the growing season.

285

DECADENT WOOD: Ageing wood which has started to decline in vigour.

DE-SHOOTING: The removal of shoots while they are still soft, to prevent over-crowding.

DRESSING (BLOOMS): The manipulation of the petals of a show bloom to improve its appearance.

EMASCULATION: The removal of the anthers of the flower to be used as the seed parent to prevent self-pollination.

EYE: In pruning this means a dormant shoot bud. Otherwise the term is used to refer to the centre of a single or semi-double flower which is distinctly different in colour from the petals.

FLOATERS: Seeds which float when placed in water, usually indicating that they are infertile.

FOLIAR FEEDING: The method of feeding by spraying the foliage and stems with nutrient solutions.

FOOTSTALK (PEDICEL): The short stalk connecting the flower with the main stem.

FULL (BLOOM): A bloom having from 26 to 40 petals.

GRANDIFLORA: A term applied in the United States of America to certain floribunda hybrid tea type varieties, but botanically incorrect.

HALF-STANDARD: A rose plant budded more than 2 ft. above the soil on the main stem or laterals of the rootstock.

HEAD: The complete growth of the variety, borne at the top of the main stem of the rootstock, in standard roses.

HEADING BACK: The removal of the entire top growth of the rootstock just above the inserted bud of the variety

HEEL: The portion of the bark of the old wood adhering to the cut end of a shoot of the current season's growth which is going to be used as a cutting.

HEELING IN: The temporary planting of rose plants in a trench pending suitable conditions for permanent planting.

HEP (HIP): The seed pod, receptacle or fruit of a rose.

HYBRID: Offspring of two different species or varieties.

INFLORESCENCE: The arrangement of the flowers in relation to each other.

LATERAL: A side shoot.

LEACH or LEACHING: The percolation or draining away of nutrient solutions through the soil.

MAIDEN GROWTH: The first season's growth from the inserted bud.

MAIDEN PLANT or MAIDEN: A plant comprising one season's growth from the inserted bud.

MAIN STEM: A mature growth bearing laterals or side shoots.

MODERATELY FULL (BLOOM): One having 15 to 25 petals.

MULCH: The application of a loose covering of absorbent material, several inches thick, to the surface of the soil, to conserve moisture.

NECK: The part of the pedicel or footstalk nearest to the flower.

OVER-DRESSED (BLOOM): A bloom the petals of which have been bent back too far, presenting an unnatural appearance.

PEDICEL: see footstalk.

PEGGING DOWN: Bending over main shoots in an arc by securing the tip to a peg driven in the soil.

pH SCALE: A scale indicating degrees of acidity or alkalinity, of which the mid-point 7.0 is neutral, with degrees of acidity below, and alkalinity above, this point.

PITHY: Unripe. Where the soft pith forms the greater part of the cross-section of a shoot.

POLLEN: The male element that fertilises the ovules of a flower, discharged from the anthers as fine yellow grains.

POLLEN PARENT: The male parent which provides the pollen in cross-pollination.

POLLINATE: To apply pollen to the stigma of a flower.

QUARTERED: The division of the centre of a rose bloom into four, by two deep clefts.

RECURRENT (FLOWERING): Producing flowers at intervals or intermittently.

REMONTANT: Repeat or recurrent flowering.

REVERSE (OF PETAL): The under surface of the petal when expanded.

ROOTSTOCK (UNDERSTOCK): The root system of the rose species on which the variety is budded. The term also applies to the entire plant of the rootstock prior to heading back.

ROSE SICK: The term applied to soil which has grown roses for many years without a change of crop.

ROSETTE (FORM): The regular arrangement of the petals in the form of a flat, low-centred flower.

SEED-PARENT: The female parent which is cross-pollinated with the pollen from the male parent.

SEMI-DOUBLE (BLOOM): Having two or three rows of petals.

SEPAL: One of the five green divisions of the calyx.

SHOT (BUD): The term applied to premature growth from the inserted bud during the same season.

SHY (FLOWERING): Sparing of flowers; not free flowering.

SINGLE (FLOWERING): Having only one row of five petals, with sometimes two or three additional petals.

SINKERS: Seeds which sink when tested in water, taken as *prima facie* evidence of fertility.

SNAG: A piece of wood left beyond the eye in pruning.

SPECIES: Used in this context to describe the wild roses, as distinct from cultivated hybrids. In its wider accepted sense, it refers to plants genetically similar.

SPLIT CENTRE: Where the central cone or spiral of a flower is divided into two by a deep cleft.

SPORT: A natural mutation in colour or growth from the original variety.

SPOTTING: Light or dark spots appearing on the petals during wet weather.

SPREADER or SPREADING AGENT: Ingredient, such as liquid soap, added to a spray solution to assist adhesion to the foliage.

STAMEN: The male part of a flower, comprising filament, anther and connective.

STANDARD: A rose plant budded approximately $3\frac{1}{2}$ ft. above the soil on the main stem or laterals of the rootstock.

STIGMA: The swollen apex of the style which receives the pollen from the anther.

STOCK: see rootstock.

STRATIFICATION: Term applied to the after-ripening of rose heps in damp peat for several months before extracting and sowing the seeds.

SUB-LATERAL: A side shoot emerging from a lateral growth.

SUCKER: Growth from the rootstock below the budding point.

SUMMER-FLOWERING: Term applied to varieties having a main flush of flowers in early summer, with few flowers later.

TIE: A length of thick soft wool secured round the petals of a show bloom to retard development.

TIP or TIPPING: To shorten or remove the immature ends of the growths, usually applied to climbing roses.

TOPDRESSING: The application of fertiliser or manure to the surface of the soil.

TRANSPIRATION LOSSES: Moisture vapour lost through the pores of the leaves.

TRUSS: A compact terminal flower cluster, as in a floribunda rose.

UNDERSTOCK: see rootstock.

UNION: The knitting together or fusion of the bud and the rootstock, or the point where this takes place.

VERY FULL (BLOOM): Having more than 40 petals.

VIABLE: Capable of germinating (as applied to seeds).

WEEPING STANDARD: A Wichuraiana rose variety budded 5 ft. or more above the soil on the main stem or laterals of a rootstock.

WIRING: Supporting a weak-necked rose stem with a length of florist's wire so that the bloom is held upright.

Appendix

All Rose Plants Except Standard Roses

Rootstock The rootstock, measured immediately below the union, shall have a minimum diameter of $\frac{5}{8}$ in.

Root system Root growth shall arise within $2\frac{1}{2}$ in. of the base of the union. The root system shall include a minimum of three major roots for each of which the distance from the union to the root tip is at least 10 in.

Shoots Plants shall have a minimum of two shoots arising directly from the union, or one shoot which branches not more than $2\frac{1}{2}$ in. above the union. The sum of the diameters of the shoots arising directly from the union shall exceed the diameter of the rootstock. The diameters shall be measured immediately above the budded union or the point of branching. These shoots shall be hard and ripe and shall not yield to normal pressure of forefinger and thumb at 3 in. above the budded union.

Additional Requirement for Climbing, Rambler and Pillar Roses

These shall have at least two shoots of not less than 2 ft. 6 in. in length, measured from the union.

Standard Roses

Stem The stem, measured 1 in. below the lower union, shall have a minimum diameter of $\frac{7}{16}$ in.

Root system The root system shall include a minimum of three major roots, for each of which the distance from the base of the stem to the root tip is at least 8 in.

Head This shall be at least double-budded. The unions shall be as close together as possible and shall not be more than 4 in. apart. At each of two unions, the sum of the diameters of the shoots arising directly from the unions shall be not less than $\frac{1}{3}$ of the diameter of the stem measured 1 in. below the lower union. These shoots shall be hard and ripe and shall not yield to normal pressure of forefinger and thumb at 3 in. above the union.

Author's Comment

These minimum dimensions are certainly well overdue. Not long ago I was one of a panel of three judges appointed by the Consumers' Association to assess the quality of rose plants purchased from many different sources in connection with one of their enquiries. My colleagues and I were really appalled at the poor quality of a considerable number of the consignments examined. Many of them were 'seconds' or 'thirds', and some we classified as not worth planting. Thinking of these being planted in a novice's garden makes one realise to the full why many become discouraged and maybe decide that their soil will not grow roses. At the other extreme some consignments were really outstanding in every way and could have been planted with the utmost confidence by anybody, whether expert or tyro. An experience such as this, covering the same varieties obtained anonymously from numerous sources, convinces me that the wise amateur should not take any chances on the quality of the plants – he should order from one of the genuine rose specialists. If he is in doubt as to their identity he should glance through the advertisements in *The Rose Annual* of The Royal National Rose Society or select from the list of rose specialists given on p. 283–284.

Acknowledgements

I am much indebted to Mr Norman H. J. Clarke, F.I.R.A., for his designs of garden features and to Miss E. Lambert for her line-drawings. I am also very grateful to all the photographers and organisations who have loaned or given permission for photographs to be used, namely:

S. McGredy and Son Ltd
COLOUR: facing p. 3, p. 49, p. 81 top, between pp. 88 and 89 top right, facing p. 113 top, between pp. 152 and 153 bottom right, p. 177, between pp. 216 and 217 top left.
BLACK AND WHITE: facing p. 240.

The Royal National Rose Society
COLOUR: facing p. 14, between pp. 56 and 57 right, facing p. 64, between pp. 120 and 121 right, between pp. 152 and 153 left and top right, facing p. 160. p. 184, p. 209, p. 241 and p. 273
BLACK AND WHITE: facing p. 216 and 217 top.

Wheatcroft Bros. Ltd
COLOUR: facing p. 32 top and bottom and p. 81 bottom.

C. Gregory and Son Ltd
COLOUR: between pp. 56 and 57 left, between pp. 88 and 89 left, facing p. 113 bottom, p. 128 bottom, p. 192 top and between pp. 248 and 249.

Amateur Gardening
COLOUR: between pp. 120 and 121 left, facing p. 145 top, between pp. 216 and 217 bottom left, and facing p. 224 bottom.
BLACK AND WHITE: facing p. 33, p. 56 bottom, p. 57, p.65, p. 80, p. 88 p. 89, p. 97, p.112, p. 120, p. 121, p. 144, p. 153 top and bottom left, p. 161, p. 176, between pp. 184 and 185, facing p. 208, p. 249 bottom right and left, p. 257.

Mr Harry Smith
COLOUR: between pp. 216 and 217 right, facing p. 224 top, between pp. 248 and 249 bottom left. facing p. 256.
BLACK AND WHITE: facing p. 56 top.

Mr J. E. Downward
COLOUR: facing p. 96, p.128 top.
BLACK AND WHITE: facing p. 15, p. 48, p. 240 bottom, p. 248 top, p. 249 top and p. 272.

Messrs May and Baker Ltd
BLACK AND WHITE: facing p. 129 top.

Mr R. J. Corbin
BLACK AND WHITE: facing p. 176, p. 193, p. 225 top and bottom left.

The Murphy Chemical Co. Ltd
BLACK AND WHITE: facing p. 152 top and centre.

Mr B. Alfieri
BLACK AND WHITE: facing p. 129 bottom and p. 152 bottom.

Mr. E. F. Allen
BLACK AND WHITE: facing p. 153 bottom right.

Miss Elsa Megson
BLACK AND WHITE: facing p. 248 bottom.

Index

ABBREVIATIONS
d = line-drawing on page given
p = photograph facing page given or
between pages given

NOTE
Species are to be found under Rosa
Varieties are to be found under Rose

adaptability, 20-1
aftercare, 90-101
All America Rose Selections Organisation, 268
ancestry, 125
animal manure, 89
aphids, 102-3 129p
Arabis, 62
arbours. 68d
assessment of plants, 40-3
Aubrieta, 62
autumn in rose garden, 164-9
  colour in, 164
  varieties for, 168-9
awards, 267-71
  British, 267-8
  foreign, 268-9

balling, 100, 121p
bank of roses, 33p
basal shoots, 97
bedding plants: use with roses, 61-2
beds: cleaning, 165
  in lawn, 63, 64
  new: preparing, 165
  plans, 65-7d
  width, 63
bees, leaf-cutting, 106, 152p
beginners: suitable H.T. roses for, 277
beliefs, old, 22-5
black spot, 21, 43, 45, 93, 109-10, 153p
  precautions, 83
bloom, see flower
borders, 66d
British Standards Institution, 40
  rulings, 289-90
budding, 118
  method, 121-3, 176p, 184-5p
  rootstocks for, 118-21

buds: tying, 131-2, 132d
bush roses: planting depth, 57d
  pruning, 88p
  in pots, 142d

canker,. 110-11
capsid bugs, 103-4, 152p
Cardiff, 274
caterpillars, 93, 104
Certificate of Merit, 267, 268
chafers, 104-5
chalk: improving soil over, 22, 50
Chamaecyparis lawsoniana hybrids, 62
cheap offers, 38-9
chlorosis, 47, 87, 113
classification, 34-5
clay, 22-3
  treatment, 47-9
Clematis, 63
climatic conditions, 21
climbers, 236-7
  B.S.I. ruling on, 289
  colour chart, 247-8
  descriptive list, 239-48
  fragrant varieties, 154
  Hybrid Teas, 33
  Kordesii, 34, 78
  neglected: treatment, 172
  planting depth, 57
  pruning, 78d
  repeat flowering, 33-4
    pruning, 72-3, 78
  sports of Floribundas, 33
    pruning, 78-9
  sports of Hybrid Teas, 33, 146-7, 237
    pruning, 72-3, 78-9
  supporting, 58
  tying in, 100-1
  Wichuraiana, 32-3

climbers, Wichuraiana *cont.*:
  pruning, 78
colours: in autumn, 164
  charts: Floribundas, 233-4
  H.T.'s, 207-9
  ramblers, etc, 247-8
  shrub and hedging, 260-1
  description, 176-7
  general susceptibilities, 43
  grouping, 59-61
  and hardiness, 75
  range, 17-18
  of species, 15
compact-growing roses:
  Floribundas, 280-1
  H.T.'s, 278
compost: for potting, 141
conifers: use with roses, 62-3 192p
container-grown plants, 38
cuckoo-spit insect, 105, 129p
Cupressocyparis leylandii, 62
cuttings, 115 16, 184 5p, 264

dead-heading, 99, 121p
Denmark: display gardens, 275
de-shooting, 91d, 92, 98 9
designs, 65-8d
despatch of plants, 52-3
deterioration of stocks, 269
De Vink, 262
die-back, 91, 161p
digging: double, 47-9, 48d
disbudding: for exhibition, 92d, 120p, 130
  in first season, 92
  pot plants, 144-5
diseases, 92-3, 153p, 161p, 178
  fungus, 109-13
  virus, 113-14
display gardens: British, 15p, 272-5
  foreign, 275-6
Dot, Pedro, 262
drainage, 46
draughts, 44

earthing up, 167
east-facing wall, 281
Edinburgh, 274
equipment, labour-saving, 147
evolution, 15-18
exhibiting roses, 129-39, 208p
  care of plants, 130
  disbudding for, 92d, 120p, 130
  feeding for, 130-1

flowers: cutting, 133
  faults in, 137-8, 216p
  preparing, 133-5
  grooming before, 131-3
  judging: points looked for, 138-9
  planning, 129
  staging, 136-7
  timing for, 129, 130
  transportation, 136
  varieties suitable, 279
exhibition box, 135d
eyes: dormant, 70d
  pruning cuts made at, 120p

farmyard manure, 89
feeding: in autumn, 165
  exhibition plants, 130-1
  foliar, 87-8
  liquid, 85, 88, 130-1
  method, 84
  mineral sources, 87
  mulching as, 84
  nutrients required, 86
  pot plants, 144
  after pruning, 73
  time for, 83-4
fence: standards against, 158, 158d
fertilisers: for autumn use, 165
  inorganic, 84-5, 87
  liquid, 85
  method of application, 84
  organic, 86-7, 88-9
  time to apply, 83-4
firming, 90
filmy soil, 30-1
floral arrangements: requirements, 28
  varieties suitable for, 279-80
Floribunda-Hybrid Tea type, 18, 30-1
Floribunda roses, 18, 29-30
  advantages, 149
  autumn-flowering, 168-9
  climbing sports, 33
    pruning, 78-9
  colour chart, 233-4
  compact-growing, 280-1
  descriptive list, 210-31
  dwarf, 231-2
  fragrant, 153-4
  half-standards: suitable varieties, 160
  propagation, 116
  pruning, 77
  standard: pruning, 80, 81d
  tall-growing, 280

flowers: balling, 100, 121p
  condition for showing, 137-9
  cross-section, 125d
  cutting, 92, 99-100, 155
  for exhibition, 133
  faded, removal of, 99, 121p
  faults in, 137-8, 216p
  preparation for exhibition, 133-5
  protecting, 131d
  shapes, 177
  of species, 15
  tying buds, 131-2, 132d
  wiring, 133-4, 134d
foliage, see leaves
foliar feeds, 87-8
fossils, 15
fragrance, 177
  roses for, 151-5
France: display gardens, 275
frog-hopper, 105, 129p
frost, 43, 45, 90-1, 95
fungus diseases, 109-13

gales: damage done by, 166
gall wasps, 105-6, 144p
glass, roses under, 28, 140-5
  compost for, 141
  feeding, 144
  flowering, 144-5
  heating, 143
  preparing plants for, 141-2
  pruning, 142-3
  spraying, 144
  suitable plants, 140-1
  varieties for, 145
  ventilation, 143-4
  watering, 143, 144
glossary, 285-8
Gold Medal award, 267-8
gravelly soil, 50-1
greenfly, 102-3, 129p
greenhouse, see glass, roses under
Gregory & Son Ltd, C.: display gardens,
  274-5
groups of roses: outline, 29-34
growth, 177-8
  new, encouraging, 90-1
Guillot, M., 17

Harkness & Co. Ltd, R.: display gardens,
  275
Harrogate, 274
heating under glass, 142

hedges, 27
  colour chart, 260-1
  descriptive list, 250-9
  general care, 249-50
  neglected: treatment 172
  plants for, 40
  pruning, 79
  varieties for, 281-2
heeling in, 53
Henry Edland Memorial Medal, 268
heps, 100, 257p
history, 15-18
Holland: display gardens, 275
honeydew, 103
hop manure, 89
horticultural societies: local, 41
Hybrid Austrian Briars, 17
hybridisation, 124-8
  fertilisation, 127
  natural, 16-17
  parents: choosing, 124
    qualities inherited from, 125
  pollination, 126-7
  preparation of plants for, 124
  seed parent: preparing, 125-6, 126d
  sowing seed, 127
Hybrid Musks, 116, 117
  pruning, 89p
Hybrid Perpetuals, 16, 17
Hybrid Polyanthas, 18, 116
Hybrid Tea roses, 17, 18, 29
  advantages, 149
  autumn flowering, 168
  beginners' choice, 277
  climbing, 33
  climbing sports, 33, 146-7, 237
    pruning, 72-3, 78-9
  colour chart, 207-9
  compact-growing, 278
  descriptive list, 179-207
  floral arrangement: varieties suitable
    for, 279-80
  fragrant varieties, 153
  pruning, 76, 80p
  rain resistant, 278-9
  standard: pruning, 80d, 80
    suitable varieties for, 159
  tall-growing, 277-8

insecticides, systemic, 103
International Rose Conference, 35
iron deficiency, 47, 87, 113
Italy: display gardens, 275

Juniperus communis hibernica, 62

Kew, Royal Botanic Gardens: rose collection, 273
Kordes, Wilhelm, 17

labour saving, 146-50
lawn: beds cut in, 63, 64
layering, 116-17, 193p
lay-out 63-4, 148
leaf-hopper, 106, 144p
leafmould, 89
leaves, 24
  colour in autumn, 164
  fragrant, 152
  scorch, 93, 95
Luton Hoo, Bedfordshire: rose gardens, 48p

McGredy & Son Ltd, S.: display gardens, 275
maggots, rose, 108
manure: animal 89
  organic, 86-7, 88-9
mildew, 43, 45, 93, 111-12, 161p
minerals: deficiencies, 113
  organic and inorganic sources, 87
miniature roses, 27, 31-2, 262-4, 272p
  indoors, 263
  planting, 263
  propagating, 116, 263-4
    cuttings, 264
  pruning, 79
  requirements, 263
  uses, 262
  varieties, 264
Modern Roses 6, 20
moles, 109
mosaic virus, 113-14, 153p
mulches, 84, 167-8

neglected garden: renovating, 170-3
Nepeta faassenii, 62
north-facing wall, 281
nurseries, 283-4
  display gardens at, 274-5
nurserymen: choice of, 37-8

old roses, 155
ordering roses, 36, 37-8

pegging down, 82, 97p
Pernet-Ducher, M., 17

pests, 129p, 144p, 152p
  animal, 108-9
  insect, 92-3, 102-9
*p*H values, 46-7
pig manure, 89
pillar roses, 237-8
  B.S.I. ruling, 289
  colour chart, 247-8
  descriptive list, 239-47
  disadvantages, 148-9
  training, 101d, 238d
  planning, 63-4, 65-8d, 148
Plant Breeders' Rights, 270-1
planting: depth, 56, 57d, 58, 162
  method, 56-8, 65p, 225p
  preparing plants for, 54-5, 57p
  pruning after, 72-3
  soil preparation, 55
  spring, 58-9
  time for, 53
Polyantha Pompons, 17-18, 31
  pruning, 77
pots, roses in, 140-5
  compost for, 141
  feeding, 144
  flowering, 144-5
  heating, 143
  preparing plants for, 141-2
  pruning, 142-3
  spraying, 144
  suitable plants, 140-1
  varieties for, 145
  ventilation, 143-4
  watering, 143, 144
potting, 141
Poulsen, Svend, 18
poultry manure, 89
President's International Trophy, 268
  winners, 271
propagation, 115-23
protection during winter, 166-8, 167d
pruning, 80p, 88p, 89p, 97p, 112p, 120p
  after planting, 72-3
  established roses, 73-4
  feeding after, 73
  labour saving in, 147
  neglected plants, 171
  of particular groups, 75-81
  pot plants, 142-3, 142d
  reasons for, 69-71
  severity, 76
  standards, 80d, 80-1, 162-3
  time for, 74-5

pruning *cont.:* tips, 81-2
  tools for, 71d, 71-2

quality of plants for sale, 39-40
Queen Mary's Rose Garden, 15p, 41,
  156, 272

rabbits, 108-9
rain: varieties suitable for, 21, 278-9
ramblers, 235-6
  B.S.I. ruling, 289
  colour chart, 247-8
  descriptive list, 239-47
  neglected: treatment, 172
  pegging down, 97p
  pruning, 77, 112p
  supporting, 58
  training, 97p
  Wichuraiana, 24, 32, 146
    propagation, 116
Regent's Park: Queen Mary's Rose
  Garden, 15p, 41, 156, 272
renovation, 170-3
re-potting, 145
Robin's Pincushion, 105-6, 144p
role in modern gardens, 26-7
roots: B.S.I. ruling, 289
  trimming, for potting, 141-2
rootstocks: B.S.I. ruling, 289
  propagation, 23
  suppliers, 284
  types, 23, 118-21
Rosa canina, 16, 23, 70, 96
  froebelii: as rootstock, 119-20
    as rootstock, 119, 121, 122-3
    strains, 119
  chinensis, 16, 17
    minima, 27, 31
    semperflorens, 16
  damascena, 16
    bifera, 16
    semperflorens, 16
    versicolor, 257
  ferruginea, see Rosa rubrifolia
  foetida persiana, 17
  gallica, 16
    versicolor, 257-8
  gigantea, 16
  helenae, 245-6
  hugonis, 27, 258
  moschata, 16
  moyesii, 258
  multiflora, 17, 31

japonica (R. polyantha multiflora, R.p.
  Simplex, Simplex), 23, 96
  as rootstock, 120
  rootstocks, 149
  odorata, 16
  omeiensis pteracantha, see Rosa sericea
    pteracantha
  phoenicia, 16
  primula, 258
  pteragonis cantabrigiensis, 258
  rubrifolia, 258
  rugosa, 96
    alba, 254
    atropurpurea, 254
    Hollandica, 120-1
    rootstocks, 96-7, 120-1, 123, 149
    rugosa, 23
    suckers, 25, 96
    typica, 254
  sericea, 15
    pteracantha, 249p, 258
    sweginzowii macrocarpa, 258-9
  wichuraiana, 15, 32, 235
  willmottiae, 259
  xanthina spontanea, 27
Rose Africa Star, 211
  Alain, 211
  Alamein, 211
  Albéric Barbier, 78, 239
  Albertine, 239, 240p
  Alison Wheatcroft, 211
  Allegro, 280
  Allen Chandler, 33, 239
  Allgold, 211, 270
  Allotria, 211
  Aloha, 63, 154, 239
  Altissimo, 240
  Ama, 211
  Amatsu-Otome, 180
  Amberlight, 211
  Ambrosia, 211
  American Pillar, 240
  André le Troquer, 180
  Angela, 212
  Angel Wings, 180-1
  Anna Louise, 212
  Anna Maria de Montravel, 17-18
  Anna Wheatcroft, 212
  Anne Letts, 181
  Ann Elizabeth, 212
  Anne Poulsen, 212
  Anne Watkins, 181
  Antique, 212

Rose *cont.:* Antoine Ducher, 17
Apricot Nectar, 212
Apricot Silk, 181
Arabian Nights, 212
Arthur Bell, 212-13
Ascot, 213
Athos, 213
August Seebauer, 213
Autumn Damask, 16
Autumn Sunlight, 240
Baby Château, 17
Baby Masquerade, 35, 248-9p
Baby Sylvia, 213
Baccara, 181
Bacchus, 181
Ballerina, 250
Ballet, 181
Bantry Bay, 209p, 240
Bashful, 185p, 232
Bayadère, 181
Beaulieu Abbey, 213
Beauté, 181-2
Bel Ange, 182
Belle Blonde, 32p, 182
Berlin, 251
Beryl Formby, *see* Rose Flaming Sunset
Bettina, 81p, 182
Betty Uprichard, 151
Bizarre Triomphant, *see* Rose Charles de Mills
Blanc Double de Coubert, 251
Blessings, 88-9p, 182
Blue Diamond, 213
Blue Girl, *see* Rose Cologne Carnival
Blue Moon, 182
Bobbie Lucas, 213
Bonn, 251
Bonsoir, 182
Border Coral, 213
Boule de Neige, 251
Bourbon, 16
Brandenburg, 182
Brasilia, 182-3
Bridal Robe, 183
Brilliant, 183
Buccaneer, 183
Buff Beauty, 251
Camelot, 183
Canary Bird, 255-6, 256p
Caprice, *see* Rose Lady Eve Price
Caprice, Climbing, 240
-Caramba, 183
Carla, 183

Casino, 78, 240
Cécile Brunner, 18
Celebration, 213-4
Centifolias, 16
Champs Elysées, 183
Chanelle, 214
Chaplin's Pink Climber, 32, 78, 240
Charles de Mills, 256
Charles Mallerin, 183-4
Charleston, 214
Charlotte Elizabeth, 214
Charming Maid, 214
Charm of Paris, 214
Chastity, 33
Cherry Brandy, 184
Chicago Peace, 184
China, 16
China, Old Crimson, 16
Chinatown, 34-5, 248-9p, 251
Christian Dior, 184
Chrysler Imperial, 151, 184
Circus, 128p, 214
City of Belfast, 214-5
City of Hereford, 184
City of Leeds, 215
Cocktail, 251
Cognac, 215
Cologne Carnival, 184
Colour Carnival, 215
Colour Wonder, 184
Columbine, 215
Commandant Beaurepaire, 256
Concerto, 215
Conrad Ferdinand Meyer, 256
Constance Spry, 256
Copenhagen, 240
Copper Delight, 215
Coral Cluster, 77
Cornelia, 82, 118, 152, 251
Coventrian, 215
Crimson Brocade, 184-5
Crimson Conquest, 240
Crimson Glory, 17, 151, 185
Climbing, 240
Crimson Shower, 241
Criterion, 185
Daily Mail, Climbing, *see* Rose Mme Edouard Herriot, Climbing
Daily Sketch, 215
Dainty Maid, 215-6
Damascenas, 16
Damask, 16
Dame de Coeur, 185

Rose *cont.:*
Danse du Feu, 34, 236, 241
Dearest, 151, 216
Decapo, 216
Detroiter, *see* Rose Brilliant
Diamant, 216
Diamond Jubilee, 185
Dickson's Flame, 216
Dimples, 216
Diorama, 185
Doc, 232
Dog, *see Rosa canina*
Dominator, 216
Dopey, 185p, 232
Doreen, 185
Dorothy Peach, 185
Dorothy Perkins, 32, 77, 241
Dorothy Wheatcroft, 34-5, 249p, 251
Dortmund, 241
Dr A. J. Verhage, 186
Dr Albert Schweitzer, 186
Dr W. Van Fleet, 241
Duchesse d'Istrie, *see* Rose William Lobb
Duchess of Portland, 16
Duftwolke, *see* Rose Fragrant Cloud
Duke of Windsor, 96p, 186
Du Maître d'Ecole, 256
Easlea's Golden Rambler, 241
Eblouissant, 31, 77
Eden Rose, 186
Elida, 56-7p, 186
Elizabeth of Glamis, 120-1p, 216
Ellen Mary, 186
Ellinor Le Grice, 186
Elmshorn, 251
Elsa Arnot, 186
Else Poulsen, 18
Elysium, 216
Emily Gray, 241
Ena Harkness, 128, 187
  Climbing, 241
Ernest H. Morse, 187
Escapade, 216-17
Ethel Sanday, 187
Etoile de Hollande, Climbing, 79, 154, 241
Etude, 241-2
Europeana, 217
Eve Allen, 187
Evelyn Fison, 152-3p, 217
Evensong, 187

Excelsa, 77, 242
Fairlight, 217
Fantin-Latour, 256
Farandole, 217
Fashion, 152, 217
  Climbing, 236, 242
Faust, 217
Felicia, 152, 252
Femina, 187
Fervid, 217
Fidélio, 217-18
Firecracker, 218
Fireworks, Feuerwerk, 218
First Lady, *see* Rose Sterling Silver
First Love, 187
F. J. Grootendorst, 252
Flamenco, 218
Flaming Sunset, 187-8
Fragrant Cloud, 188
Francine, 188
François Juranville, 152, 242
Frau Dagmar Hastrup, 252
Frau Karl Druschki, 82, 188
Fred Gibson, 188
Fred Loads, 35, 241p, 252
Frensham, 128, 218
Fresco, 218
Fritz Nobis, 256
Fritz Thiedemann, 188
Frohsinn, *see* Rose Joyfulness
Frühlingsgold, 256
Frühlingsmorgen, 257
Gail Borden, 188
Gallicas, 16
Galway Bay, 242
Garvey, 188
Gavotte, 189
Geisha Girl, 218
Geranium, *see* Rose Independence
Gertrude Gregory, 189
Gloire des Mousseux, 257
Gloria Mundi, 31
Gold Crown, 189
Golden Dawn, 152
  Climbing, 242
Golden Fleece, 218
Golden Giant, 189
Golden Jewel, 219
Golden Melody, 189
Golden Salmon, 31
Golden Scepter, *see* Rose Spek's Yellow
Golden Showers, 78, 216-17p, 242
Golden Slippers, 152-3p, 219

Rose *cont.:*
  Golden Splendour, 189
  Golden Treasure, 219, 270
  Golden Wings, 252
  Goldgleam, 219, 270
  Goldilocks, 219
    Climbing, 242
  Gold Marie, 219
  Gordon Eddie, 189
  Grace de Monaco, 189
  Grand Gala, 190
  Grand'mère Jenny, 190
  Grandpa Dickson, 88-9p, 190
  Greetings, 190
  Grumpy, 232
  Gruss an Berlin, *see* Rose Greetings
  Gruss an Teplitz, 252
  Guinée, 33, 242-3
  Guinevere, 190
  Hamburger Phoenix, 243
  Handel, 216-17p, 243
  Hansestadt Lübeck, *see* Rose Lübeck
  Happy, 232
  Happy Event, 219
  Hawaii, 190
  Heidelberg, 252
  Helen Traubel, 190
  Herself, 219-20
  Heure Mauve, 190
  Highlight, 220
  Honeymoon (Honigmond), 220
  Honorine de Brabant, 252
  Hugh Dickson, 82, 151, 252-3
  Iceberg, 220
  Ice White, 220
  Ideal Home (Idylle) 190-1
  Independence, 17, 220
  Intermezzo, 191
  Invitation, 191
  Irene Churruca, *see* Rose Golden Melody
  Irish Mist, 220
  Isabel de Ortiz, 191
  Isle of Man, *see* Rose Manx Queen
  Isobel Harkness, 191
  Ivory Fashion, 220-1
  Jane Lazenby, 221
  Jan Spek, 221
  Japanese, *see Rosa rugosa*
  Jean Campbell, 191
  Jean Mermoz, 232
  Jiminy Cricket, 221
  John Church, 221

John S. Armstrong, 191
Jolie Madame, 191
Josephine Bruce, 80, 191-2
Joseph's Coat, 243
Joybells, 221
Joyfulness, 128p, 221
Jubilant, 221
June Park, 192
Karen Poulsen, 221
Karl Herbst, 21, 192
Kassel, 253
Kathleen Harrop, 82, 243
King Arthur, 221-2
King's Ransom, 14p, 192
Kirsten Poulsen, 18
Klaus Störtebeker, 192
Kölner Karneval, *see* Rose Cologne Carnival
Königin der Rosen *see* Rose Colour Wonder
Königliche Hoheit, *see* Rose Royal Highness
Konrad Adenauer, 192
Kordesii Climbers, 34, 78
Kordes Perfecta, *see* Rosa Perfecta
Kordes' Sondermeldung, *see* Rose Independence
Korona, 222
Kronenbourg, 81p, 192
Lady Belper, 192
Lady Eve Price, 193
Lady Godiva, 243
Lady Seton, 49p, 193
Lady Sonia, 253
Lady Sylvia, 193
La France, 17
La Jolla, 193
Lancastrian, 193
Lavender Lassie, 224p, 257
Laxa, *see Rosa canina froebelii*
Leverkusen, 48p
Lilac Charm, 222
Lilac Rose, 193
Lilli Marlene, 222
Little Flirt, 248-9p
Louise Odier, 253
Love Token, 222
Lübeck, 253
Lucky Charm, 222
Lucy Cramphorn, 193
Lydia, 193-4
McGredy's Ivory, 194-5
McGredy's Yellow, 195

Rose *cont.:*
Magenta, 152
Maigold, 154, 243
Mainzer Fastnacht, *see* Rose Blue Moon
Majorette, 194
Mandy, 222
Manx Queen, 145p, 222
Ma Perkins, 222
Marcelle Gret, 152, 194
Märchenland, 222-3
Mardi Gras, 194
Margaret, 194
Maria Callas, 194
Marie Pavic, 18
Marjorie Le Grice, 194
Marlena, 223
Marquesa de Urquijo, *see* Rose Pilar
  Landecho
Rose Maryse Kriloff, *see* Rose Lucy
  Cramphorn
Mary Wheatcroft, 194
Masquerade, 223
  Climbing, 238, 243
Matterhorn, 223 ·
Max Graf, 257
Meg, 33, 238, 243
Memoriam, 21, 195
Merlin, 223
Mermaid, 120, 236, 243-4
Message, 195
Meteor, 223
Michèle Meilland, 195
Mignonette, 17
Milord, 195
Miracle, 223
Mischief, 113p, 195
Miss France, 30
Miss Ireland, 195
Mister Lincoln, 196
Mme Butterfly, 196
  Climbing, 244
Mme Caroline Testout, 18, 196, 269
  Climbing, 244
Mme de Tartas, 18
Mme Edouard Herriot, Climbing, 244
Mme Ernst Calvat, 253
Mme Falcot, 18
Mme Gregoire Staechelin, 56p, 244
Mme Hardy, 257
Mme Henri Guillot, Climbing, 244
Mme Louis Laperrière, 196
Mme Mélanie Soupert, 17
Mme Pierre Ogier, 253

Mme Plantier, 257
Mojave, 196
Molly McGredy, 177p, 223
Monique, 196
Montezuma, 21, 196
Moonlight, 152, 253
Moonraker, 223
Moulin Rouge, 224
Mrs Herbert Stevens, Climbing, 244
Mrs Pierre S. du Pont, Climbing, 244
Mrs Sam McGredy, 196-7
  Climbing, 27, 79, 244-5
Multiflora ramblers, 116
  rootstocks, 23, 96, 120, 149
Musk, *see Rosa moschata*
Musk hybrids, 116, 117
  pruning, 89p
My Choice, 197
My Girl, 224
Nevada, 224p, 253
New Dawn, 33p, 63, 154, 245
New Penny, 248-9p
New Style, 197
Nuage Parfumé, *see* Rose Fragrant Cloud
Nuits de Young, 257
Numéro Un, 197
Nymphenburg, 253
Ohlala, 224
Old Black, *see* Rose Nuits de Young
Old Velvet Moss, *see* Rose William Lobb
Opera, 197
Ophelia, 151, 197
Orangeade, 224
Orange Sensation, 145p, 224
Orange Silk, 184p, 224
Orange Triumph, 224
Orléans Rose, 18, 31
Overture, 224
Paddy McGredy, 224-5
Papa Meilland, 32p, 151, 197
Paprika, 225
Pâquerette, 17
Parade, 78, 245
Parasol, 197
Paris-Match, 198
Parkdirektor Riggers, 236, 245, 248p
Pascali, 198
Paul Crampel, 31, 77
Paul's Lemon Pillar, 33, 245
Paul's Scarlet Climber, 32, 78, 245
Pax, 253
Peace, 56, 138, 198
  standard, 192p

Rose *cont.:* Peer Gynt, 198
  Penelope, 82, 152, 248-9p, 253-4
  Percy Thrower, 113p, 198
  Perfecta, 138, 198
  Perle d'Or, 18
  Pernetiana, 17, 151
  Pernille Poulsen, 225
  Pharaoh, 198-9
  Phoenician, *see Rosa phoenicia*
  Piccadilly, 3p, 199
  Picture, 199
  Pilar Landecho, 199
  Pink Favourite, 199
  Pink Grootendorst, 249p, 254
  Pink Parfait, 225
  Pink Peace, 199
  Pink Perpetue, 216-17p, 245
  Pink Supreme, 199
  Plentiful, 225
  Polly, 200
  Polyantha compacta, 231
  Portland, 16
  Posy, 225
  Poulsen's Yellow, 18, 30
  Première Ballerina, *see* Rose Prima
    Ballerina
  President Herbert Hoover, 200
  President Pats, 200
  Prima Ballerina, 200
  Prince of Denmark, 200
  Princess, 200
  Princess Michiko, 225
  Prosperity, 82, 118, 254
  Queen Elizabeth, 56p, 225
  Queen of Hearts, *see* Rose Dame de
    Coeur
  Queen of the Violets, *see* Rose Reine des
    Violettes
  Rayon d'Or, 17
  Red, *see Rosa gallica*
  Red Dandy, 225-6
  Red Devil, 200
  Red Dorothy Perkins, *see* Rose Excelsa
  Red Favourite, 226
  Redgold, 226
  Red Star, 18
  Regalia, 201
  Reina Elisenda, *see* Rose Independence
  Reine des Violettes, 254
  Rodeo, 226
  Roger Lambelin, 254
  Rosa Mundi, *see Rosa gallica versicolor*
  Rose Gaujard, 56, 201

Rosemary Rose, 226
Rose of Tralee, 226
Royal Gold, 246
Royal Highness, 201
Rugosa hybrids, 117
  as rootstock, 120-1, 123, 149
  for standards, 96-7
  suckers, 25, 96
Rumba, 226
Ruth Hewitt, 226
Ruth Leuwerik, 227
Sabrina, 201
Safari, 227
Sam McGredy, 201
Sanders' White, 246
Sangria, 227
Santa Fé, 201
Sarabande, 227
Sarah Arnot, 201
Sarah van Fleet, 254
Saratoga, 227
Scandale, 201-2
Scania, 227
Scarlet Fire, 259
Scarlet Queen Elizabeth, 227
Scented Air, 227
Scharlachglut, *see* Rose Scarlet Fire
Schlösser's Brillant, *see* Rose Brilliant
Schneezwerg, 255
Schoolgirl, 240p, 246
Schweizer Gruss, *see* Rose Red Favourite
Sea Pearl, 227
Serenade, 202
Shannon, 202
She, 228
Shepherdess, 152-3p, 228
Shepherd's Delight, 228
Shot Silk, 151
  Climbing, 26, 79, 140, 154, 246
Show Girl, 202
Siesta, 228
Signora, 202
Silva, 64p, 202
Silver lining, 202
Sir Lancelot, 160p, 228
Sissi, *see* Rose Blue Moon
Sleepy, 232
Sneezy, 232
Snow Queen, *see* Rose Frau Karl
  Druschki
Soldier Boy, 238, 246
Soleil d'Eté, *see* Rose Summer Sunshine
Soleil d'Or, 17

Rose *cont.:* Solus, 255
  Sombrero, 228
  Sondermeldung, 17
  Soraya, 202-3
  Souvenir de Jacques Verschuren, 203
  Souvenir de la Malmaison, 255
  Sparrieshoop, 255
  Spartan, 100, 151, 228
  Spek's Yellow, 31, 203
    Climbing, 246
  Staatspräsident Päts, *see* Rose President
    Pats
  Stella, 203
  Sterling Silver, 203
  Sultane, 203
  Summer Song, 228
  Summer Sunshine, 203
  Sundance, 228-9
  Sunset Glory, *see* Rose Flaming Sunset
  Super Star, 56-7p, 203
  Sutter's Gold, 204
    Climbing, 246
  Sweet Repose, 229
  Sympathie, 246
  Symphonie, 204
  Tahiti, 204
  Tally Ho, 204
  Tamango, 229
  Tambourine, 229
  Teenager, 204
  Telstar, 229
  The Doctor, 204
  The Fairy, 232
  The Optimist, *see* Rose Sweet Repose
  Tiffany, 21, 204-5
  Tiki, 229
  Tivoli, 229
  Tombola, 229-30
  Toni Lander, 230
  Tour de Malakoff, 259
  Town Crier, 205
  Tradition, 88-9p, 205
  Travesti, 230
  Traviata, 205
  Tropicana, *see* Rose Super Star
  Tzigane, 151, 205
  Ulster Monarch, 205
  Uncle Walter, 82, 255
  Vagabonde, 230
  Valerie Boughey, 205
  Vanity, 255
  Variegata di Bologna, 255
  Variety Club, 230

  Veilchenblau, 246
  Vera Dalton, 230
  Vesper, 230
  Vienna Charm, 205
  Vilia, 230
  Violet Carson, 230-1
  Violinista Costa, 206
  Virgo, 206
  Vivien Leigh, 206
  Vogue, 231
  Wendy Cussons, 206
  Western Sun, 206
  Westminster, 206
  Westward Ho, 206
  Whisky Mac, 206-7
  White Christmas, 207
  White Knight, *see* Rose Message
  Wichuraiana climbers, 32-3
    pruning, 78
  Wichuraiana ramblers, 24, 32, 146
    autumn tidying, 166
    propagation, 116
    pruning, 77
  Wiener Charme, *see* Rose Vienna Charm
  William Lobb, 259
  Will Scarlet, 255
  Winefred Clarke, 207
  Wisbech Gold, 207
  Woburn Abbey, 231
  Yellowhammer, 231
  York & Lancaster, *see* Rosa damascena
    versicolor
  Youki San, 207
  Yvonne Rabier, 231
  Zambra, 231
  Zéphirine Drouhin, 82, 247, 248p
  Zingaro, 231
Royal National Rose Society, 42
  Display Gardens, 15p, 273-4
  trials and awards, 267-8, 271
rust, 21, 45, 112-3, 153p

sandy soil, 49-50
sawfly, 106-7, 129p, 152p
Saxifraga, 62
scale insects, 107, 144p
screens, 26
  roses used as, 120-1p
seed, roses from, 117-18, 127
seedlings: transplanting, 128
selecting plants, 40-3
selections: for various purposes, 277-82
sewage composts, 88-9

shoots: B.S.I. ruling, 289
shrub roses, 27, 34
  colour chart, 260-1
  descriptive list, 250-9
  general care, 249-50
  pruning, 79
sites: choosing, 44-5, 217p
  unsuitable, 22
soil: acidity caused by liquid feeds, 88
  alkaline: improving, 22
  condition for planting, 55
  dictating pruning methods, 72, 73
  flinty, 50-1
  gravelly, 50-1
  heavy: treatment, 47-9
  light, 49-50
  planting mixture, 55
  requirements, 22-3, 47
  sandy, 49-50
  shallow, over chalk, 22, 50
  testing, 46-7
  treatment in neglected beds, 173
soot: dry, 85
  liquid, 85
south-facing wall, 281
Southport, 274
spacing, 55-6
Spain: display gardens, 275
specialists: importance of buying from,
  36-7
  list, 283-4
species. For names of species,
  see Rosa
  colours, 15
  flowers, 15
  number, 15
  propagation, 116
sports, 16
  climbing, of Floribundas, 33
    pruning, 78-9
  climbing, of H.T.'s 33, 146-7, 237
    pruning, 72-3, 78-9
spraying, 93-5
  autumn treatment 166
  equipment for, 94d
  on sensitive foliage, 95
  under glass, 144
stable manure, 89
staking, 58, 162, 225p
standards: B.S.I. rulings, 289-90
  budding, 122-3, 184-5p
  disadvantages of, 148-9
  fragrant varieties, 154

height, 157d
Hybrid Tea varieties for, 159
neglected: treatment, 173
planting, 57d, 58, 162, 225p
protecting in winter, 167d
pruning, 80d, 80, 81d, 162-3
  in pots, 142d
suckers, 25, 96, 163
supporting, 58, 162, 225p
uses, 156-9
standards, half, 159-60
  budding, 122-3
  Floribunda varieties for, 160
  fragrant varieties, 154
  height, 157d
  planting depth, 57d, 58
  suckers, 25
  supporting, 58, 162
  uses, 158d
standards, weeping, 160-1
  autumn tidying, 166
  pruning, 80-1, 97p
  training, 160, 161d
  uses, 159
  varieties for, 160-1
stocks: deterioration of, 269
suckers, 23-4, 95-7, 163
  on neglected plants, 170-1
  recognising, 24-5, 273p
  removing, 121
  suppliers, 283-4
Switzerland: display gardens, 275

tall roses: Floribundas, 280
  H.T.'s, 207-9
Taunton, 274
Taxus baccata fastigiata, 62-3
Tea roses, 16-17, 24
temperatures, 143-4
thrips, 107-8
thunder flies, 107-8
Tonks' rose fertiliser, 84
tools: pruning, 71d, 71-2
tortrix moths, 108
towns: growing roses in, 20-1
training, 82, 97p, 101d, 100-1, 160, 161d
transplanting, 165
transportation, 136
Trial Ground Certificate, 267, 268
tripod, 238d
turkey manure, 89
tying in shoots, 100-1
types: labour saving, 148

types *cont.*:
  to avoid, for labour saving, 148-9

'umbrella' trainer, 161d
U.S.A.: display gardens, 276
uses of roses in modern gardens, 26-7

varieties. For names of varieties, *see* Rose
  colour charts: Floribundas, 233-4
  H.T.'s 207-9
  ramblers etc, 247-8
  shrub and hedging, 260-1
  descriptive lists: Floribundas, 210-31
  H.T.'s 179-207
  miniatures, 264
  ramblers etc, 239-47
  shrub and hedging, 250-9
  deterioration, 269
  key to list of, 176-8

new: need for, 270
  to avoid, for labour saving, 148-9
  ventilation, 143-4
Viola, 61-2
  cornuta, 61
virus diseases, 113-14

walls: varieties for various aspects, 281
wasps, gall, 105-6
watering, 91-2
  under glass, 143, 144
weedkillers, 149-50
  applying, 150d
weeds, 97-8, 149-50
  in neglected gardens, 173
west-facing wall, 281
winter protection, 166-8
wood, shrivelled: treatment, 54